REDEMPTION AND UTOPIA
Jewish Libertarian Thought in Central Europe

A Study in Elective Affinity

MICHAEL LÖWY

Translated by Hope Heaney

VERSO

London • New York

This edition published by Verso 2017
English-language edition first published by The Athlone Press 1992
First published in French as *Rédemption et Utopie: Le judaïsme libertaire en Europe centrale*

© Presses Universitaires de France 1988
Translation © Hope Heaney 1992, 2017

1 3 5 7 9 10 8 6 4 2

Verso
UK: 6 Meard Street, London W1F 0EG
US: 20 Jay Street, Suite 1010, Brooklyn, NY 11201
versobooks.com

Verso is the imprint of New Left Books

ISBN-13: 978-1-78663-085-8
ISBN-13: 978-1-78663-086-5 (UK EBK)
ISBN-13: 978-1-78663-087-2 (US EBK)

British Library Cataloguing in Publication Data
A catalogue record for this book is available from the British Library

Library of Congress Cataloging-in-Publication Data
A catalog record for this book is available from the Library of Congress

Printed in the US by Maple Press

REDEMPTION AND UTOPIA
Jewish Libertarian Thought
in Central Europe

Contents

Introduction:
The Defeated of History

> Our generation has learnt the hard way that the only image we shall
> leave is that of a vanquished generation. That will be our legacy to
> those who follow.
>
> Walter Benjamin
> Thesis XII, from *On the Philosophy of History*, 1940

The term 'Central Europe' or *Mitteleuropa* refers to a geographi-
cal, cultural and historical area united by German culture –
that of Germany and the Austro-Hungarian Empire. From the
middle of the nineteenth century up to 1933, the culture of the
Central European Jewish community blossomed in the most
extraordinary way, experiencing a *Golden Age* comparable to
that of the Judeo-Arab community in twelfth-century Spain.
It was the product of a spiritual synthesis unique in its kind,
which gave the world Heine and Marx, Freud and Kafka, Ernst
Bloch and Walter Benjamin. Today this German-Jewish culture
seems like a vanished world, a continent erased from history,
an Atlantis engulfed by the ocean, along with its palaces, temples
and monuments. It was destroyed by the Nazi tide, surviving
only in scattered pockets or in exile, and its last representatives – Marcuse, Fromm and Bloch – have now passed away,
like the final embers of a huge spiritual fire. It did, however,
leave its mark on twentieth-century culture, in its richest and
most innovative accomplishments in the sciences, literature and
philosophy.

This book studies a generation as well as a particular current
within the Jewish cultural universe of *Mitteleuropa*: a generation
of intellectuals born during the last quarter of the nineteenth
century, whose writings were inspired by both German (romantic) and Jewish (messianic) sources. Their thinking was profoundly, 'organically' and inseparably *Judeo-Germanic*, whether

1

they accepted this syncretism with pride (Gustav Landauer) or with wrenching pain (Franz Kafka), whether they tried to deny their German sources (Gershom Scholem) or their Jewish identity (Georg Lukács). Their thinking took shape around the Jewish (cabbalistic) idea of *Tikkun*, a polysemic term for *redemption (Erlösung)*, restoration, reparation, reformation and the recovery of lost harmony.

Theirs was a generation of dreamers and utopians: they aspired to a radically other world, to the kingdom of God on earth, to a kingdom of the spirit, a kingdom of freedom, a kingdom of peace. An egalitarian community, libertarian socialism, anti-authoritarian rebellion and a permanent revolution of the spirit were their ideals. Several fell like lonely soldiers in a twentieth-century Thermopylae, victims of a barbarism that was either still budding (Gustav Landauer, Munich 1919) or already triumphant (Walter Benjamin, Port-Bou 1940). For the most part, they were unarmed prophets. One episode from the life of Georg Lukács could apply to many of them. Following the defeat of the Hungarian revolution in November 1956 (in which he had participated as Minister of Culture in the Imre Nagy government), Lukács found himself under arrest. A Soviet officer, brandishing his machine gun, ordered: 'Hand over your weapons immediately!' Not having any choice, the old Jewish-Hungarian philosopher took his pen from his pocket and handed it over to the forces of order.

Their generation were the defeated of history. It is not surprising that so many of them chose suicide: Tucholsky, Toller, Wolfenstein, Carl Einstein, Hasenclever, Benjamin.

In his *Theses on the Philosophy of History*, Walter Benjamin insisted that history be written from the point of view of the defeated. This book tries to apply that method.

Through a paradox that is more apparent than real, it is precisely because they were the defeated, because they were outsiders going against the tide of their era, and because they were obstinate romantics and incurable utopians, that, as we approach the end of the twentieth century, their work is becoming increasingly relevant and meaningful.

It goes without saying that the romantic and messianic generation contained the most diverse and contradictory political and ideological currents. The aim of this book is not to resolve its debates or to take a stand in the controversies, but rather to *understand* the overall movement, its genesis in Central Europe at an historical and social conjuncture of crisis and renewal for both the Jewish tradition and German culture. Written within the framework of the sociology of culture, it analyses the development of a new social category, the Jewish intelligentsia, and the conditions that favoured the dawning within that group of a twofold spiritual configuration of romantic utopia and restorative messianism. The key concept, which may open up new and still largely unexplored possibilities for the sociology of culture, is that of *elective affinity* – a concept which appeared in the works of Goethe and Max Weber, but which I have formulated differently in this analysis. In studying the works of more than a dozen authors, both known and unknown, famous and obscure, revered and forgotten, I do not intend to sketch the history of their ideas, nor to present a short philosophical monograph on each of them; rather, I shall attempt to reconstruct an entire socially-conditioned cultural universe in its multidimensional unity. This approach seeks to throw new light on a broad expanse of modern European culture by identifying a subterranean network of correspondences linking several of the most creative intellects. I shall also try to account for the eruption, within a magnetic field polarized by libertarian romanticism and Jewish messianism, of a new concept of history, including a new perception of temporality at variance with evolutionism and the philosophy of progress.

The author who formulated this heretical concept – this new mode of perceiving history and time – in the deepest, most radical and subversive way was Walter Benjamin. For that reason, and because all the tensions, dilemmas and contradictions of the German-Jewish cultural universe were concentrated in his person, he takes centre stage in this essay. He is, in effect, at the heart of the messianic-romantic generation; and his thinking, though slightly out-of-date and strangely anachronistic, is also the most topical and the most charged with utopian explosiveness. His work clarifies the thinking of the others within the group; and they in turn illuminate his work, in a two-way game not of endlessly reflecting mirrors but of mutually questioning looks.

I would like to end this Introduction on a personal note. Having been a sort of wandering Jew myself, born in Brazil of Viennese parents, variously resident in São Paulo, Ramat-Aviv and Manchester, and now settled (permanently?) in Paris for the last twenty years, I also saw in this book a way of rediscovering my own cultural and historical roots.

My family came from Vienna, but my father's side (Löwy) was originally from the Czechoslovakian province of the Austro-Hungarian Empire. No relation, as far as I know, to Julia Löwy, Franz Kafka's mother: the name was fairly common among Jews of the Empire. On my mother's side of the family, the origin of Löwinger is Hungarian. No relation either, as far as I know, to Joseph Löwinger, the Budapest banker and father of Georg Lukács.

Although I do not have famous ancestors, I nevertheless feel intimately implicated or summoned by my cultural heritage and by the lost spiritual universe of Central European Judaism – that extinguished star whose broken and dispersed light still travels through space and time, continents and generations.

As I read certain of Walter Benjamin's texts, while also exploring the Gustav Landauer Archives at the library of the Hebrew University of Jerusalem, I had the intuitive feeling that I was touching upon a much vaster subterranean whole. I drew up the outline of a research project and submitted it to the late Gershom Scholem at a meeting in December 1979. A first version in article form was completed in 1980 and corrected by Scholem; it was published in 1981 in the *Archives de Sciences sociales des Religions* no. 51 as 'Messianisme juif et utopies libertaires en Europe centrale (1905–1923)' [Jewish Messianism and Libertarian Utopias in Central Europe (1905–1923)]. In October 1983, a first version of the chapter on Walter Benjamin appeared in *Les Temps modernes* as 'Le messianisme anarchiste de Walter Benjamin' [Walter Benjamin's Anarchist Messianism].

I continued my research with the aid of the Buber Archives at the Hebrew University of Jerusalem; the Lukács Archives in Budapest; the Archives of the Institute of Social History in Amsterdam; the Hannah Arendt Archives at the Library of Congress (Washington, D.C.); the unpublished papers of Walter Benjamin, which are preserved at the Bibliothèque Nationale in Paris; the Archives at the Leo Baeck Institute in Jerusalem and New York; and through meetings with Ernst Bloch (1974),

Gershom Scholem (1979), Werner Kraft (1980), Pierre Missac (1982), and Leo Löwenthal (1984).

Finally, I derived great benefit from the assistance, encouragement and criticism I received from my colleagues at the Groupe de Sociologie des Religions [Department of the Sociology of Religion] – notably from Jean Séguy and Danièle Hervieu-Léger – as well as from Rachel Ertel, Rosemarie Ferenczi, Claude Lefort, Sami Nair, Guy Petitdemange, Eleni Varikas, Irving Wohlfarth, Martin Jay, Leo Löwenthal and the late Michel de Certeau.

I would like to thank Miguel Abensour in particular, whose suggestions and critical advice were invaluable to me in editing the final version of this text.

1

On the Concept of Elective Affinity

A century after Auguste Comte, sociology continues to borrow its conceptual terminology from physics or biology. Is it not time to break away from this positivist tradition and to draw upon a spiritual and cultural heritage that is broader, richer in meaning and closer to the very texture of social facts? Why not use the vast semantic field of religions, myths, literature and even esoteric traditions to enrich the language of the social sciences? Did not Max Weber borrow the concept of 'charisma' from Christian theology, and Karl Mannheim that of 'constellation' from classical astrology?

This book is a study in *elective affinity*. The expression has taken an unusual path: it has gone from alchemy to sociology by way of Romantic literature. Its patrons have been Albertus Magnus (in the thirteenth century), Johann Wolfgang Goethe and Max Weber. In my own use of it, I have tried to integrate the various meanings that the term has acquired over the centuries. By 'elective affinity' I mean a very special kind of dialectical relationship that develops between two social or cultural configurations, one that cannot be reduced to direct casuality or to 'influences' in the traditional sense. Starting from a certain structural analogy, the relationship consists of a convergence, a mutual attraction, an active confluence, a combination that can go as far as a fusion. It would be interesting, in my opinion, to try to build on the methodological status of the concept as an interdisciplinary research tool which could enrich, qualify and make more dynamic the analysis of the relationship between economic, political, religious and cultural phenomena.

Let us begin by briefly reconstructing the strange spiritual itinerary of this expression, so as to capture all its accumulated richness of meaning. The idea that a visible or hidden analogy determines the predisposition of bodies to unite dates back to

Greek Antiquity, notably to the Hippocratic formula 'like draws to like' (*omoion erchetai pros to omoion; simile venit ad simile*). However, the term *affinity* as an alchemical metaphor does not appear until the Middle Ages. Its first source is probably Albertus Magnus, according to whom if sulphur combines with metals, it is 'because of its natural affinity' for them (*propter affinitatem naturae metalla adurit*). This idea recurs in the works of Johannes Conradus Barchusen, the famous seventeenth-century German alchemist, who speaks of 'mutual affinity' (*reciprocam affinitatem*);[1] and most notably in the writings of Hermannus Boerhave, the eighteenth-century Dutch alchemist. In *Elementa Chemiae* [Basic Principles of Chemistry] (1724), Boerhave explains that the solvent particles and those that are dissolved gather into homogeneous bodies through the affinity of their own nature (*'particulae solventes et solutae se affinitate suae naturae colligunt in corpora homogenae'*). Noting the relationship between gold and aqua regia in a container he asks:

> Why does not gold, which is eighteen times heavier than aqua regia, collect at the bottom of the vessel containing the aqua regia? Can you not see clearly that, between each particle of gold and aqua regia, there is a *force* by virtue of which they seek out each other, are united and join each other?

Affinity is the force that makes these heterogeneous entities form a union, a kind of marriage or chemical wedding, arising more from love than from hate (*'magis ex amore quam ex odio'*).[2]

The term *'attractionis electivae'* (elective attraction) was first used by the Swedish chemist Torbern Olof Bergman. His work *De attractionibus electivis* (Uppsala, 1775), was translated into French as *Traité des affinités chimiques ou attractions électives* (1788) [Treatise on Chemical Affinities, or Elective Attractions]. Bergman explains his use of the term as follows: 'Several people call *affinity* what we have named *attraction*. I would consequently use these two terms interchangeably, even though the former, being more metaphorical, seems less appropriate in a work on physics.' In discussion with Bergman, Baron Guyton de Morveau, a contemporary French chemist, emphasized that affinity is a particular kind of attraction, distinguished by a specific intensity of attractive power, through which two or more entities 'form a being whose properties are new and distinct from those that belonged to each prior to combining'.[3] In the German translation of Bergman's book (Frankfurt-am-Main, Verlag Tabor, 1782–90), the expression 'elective attraction' is rendered as *Wahlverwandtschaft*, elective affinity.

It was probably from this German version that Goethe drew the title of his novel *Die Wahlverwandtschaften* (1809), in which one of the characters mentions a work on chemistry 'that dates back ten years'. Several passages describing the chemical phenomenon seem to be taken directly from Bergman – particularly the analysis of the reaction between AB and CD, which re-combine as AD and BC. Goethe's transposition of a chemical concept onto the social terrain of human spirituality and feelings was all the easier because, for several alchemists (such as Boerhave), the expression was already heavily laden with social and erotic metaphors. For Goethe there was elective affinity when two beings or elements 'seek each other out, attract each other and seize . . . each other, and then suddenly reappear again out of this intimate union, and come forward in fresh, unexpected form (*Gestalt*)'.[4] The resemblance between this and Boerhave's formula (two elements that 'seek each other out, are united and join each other') is striking, and the possibility that Goethe was also familiar with, and inspired by, the Dutch alchemist's work cannot be ruled out.

Through Goethe's novel, the expression established itself within German culture to designate a special kind of bond between souls. Thus, it was in Germany that 'elective affinity' underwent its third metamorphosis: through the work of Max Weber, that great alchemist of the social sciences, it became a sociological concept. The connotation of mutual choice, attraction and combination is retained from its former meaning, but the aspect of newness seems to disappear. In Weber's writings, the concept of *Wahlverwandtschaft* – as well as that of *Sinnaffinitäten* (affinities of meaning), which denotes something very similar – appears in three specific contexts.

First, it characterizes a precise mode of relationship between different religious forms; for example, between the mission of prophecy (in which the chosen feel like an instrument of God) and the concept of a personal, extra-worldly, irascible and powerful God there is *'eine tiefe Wahlverwandtschaft'*.[5]

Next, it defines the link between class interests and world-views. According to Weber, *Weltanschauungen* have their own autonomy, but an individual's adherence to one world-view or another depends to a large extent on its *Wahlverwandtschaft* with his class interests.[6]

Finally – and this is the most important case – it serves to analyse the relationship between religious doctrines and forms of economic ethos. The *locus classicus* of this use of the concept is the following passage from *The Protestant Ethic and the Spirit of Capitalism*:

> In view of the tremendous confusion of interdependent influences between the material basis, the forms of social and political organization, and the ideas current in the time of the Reformation, we can only proceed by investigating whether and at what points certain correlations [i.e., elective affinities – *Wahlverwandtschaften*] between forms of religious belief and practical ethics can be worked out. At the same time we shall as far as possible clarify the manner and the general *direction* in which, by virtue of those relationships [*Wahlverwandtschaften*], the religious movements have influenced the development of material culture.[7]

We should note that the expression first appeared between quotation marks, as if Weber had wanted to apologize for the intrusion ⌐f a romantic and literary metaphor in a scientific analysis. But he subsequently dropped the quotation marks; the expression had become a concept.

It is not surprising that this expression was not understood in the positivist Anglo-American reception of Max Weber. One example bordering on caricature is Talcott Parsons' English translation in 1930 of *The Protestant Ethic* from which we have just quoted. Here, *Wahlverwandtschaft* is rendered first as 'certain correlations', and then as 'those relationships'.[8] Whereas the Weberian concept refers to a rich and meaningful internal relationship between two configurations, Parsons' distorting translation replaces this with a banal, external and meaningless relation (or 'correlation'). There could be no better illustration of the inseparability of the concept from its cultural context, from a tradition that gives it all its expressive and analytical force.

In these three Weberian modalities, then, elective affinity

unites socio-cultural, economic and/or religious structures without forming a new substance or significantly modifying the initial components – even though the interaction has the effect of reinforcing the characteristic logic of each structure.

Max Weber never tried to examine the meaning of the concept closely, nor did he discuss its methodological implications or define its field of application. It appears here and there in German sociology, but no consideration is given to the conceptual implications of the term. Karl Mannheim, for example, in his remarkable study of conservative thought, writes:

> In the confluence (*Zusammenfliessen*) of two streams of thought, the task of the sociology of knowledge is to find the moments within the two movements which, even *before* the synthesis, reveal an internal affinity (*innere Verwandtschaft*), and which, as a result, make unification possible.[9]

In the course of my study of the links between Jewish messianism and social utopia, the concept of elective affinity appeared to be the most appropriate and fertile tool with which to examine this relationship. Moreover, it seems to me that the concept could be applied to many other aspects of social reality. It enables us to understand (in the strong sense of *verstehen*) a certain kind of connection between seemingly disparate phenomena within the same cultural field (religion, philosophy, literature), or between distinct social spheres: religion and economy, mysticism and politics, among others. For example, the concept of *Wahlverwandtschaft* might throw considerable light upon the type of relationship that developed during the Middle Ages between the ethic of chivalry and Church doctrine;[10] or, starting in the sixteenth century, between the cabbala and alchemy (see Gershom Scholem's fine study 'Alchemie und Kabbala', *Eranos Jahrbuch*, no. 45, 1977); in the nineteenth century, between traditionalist conservatism and Romantic aesthetics (see the previously mentioned article by Mannheim), German Idealism and Judaism (cf. Habermas's study), or Darwinism and Malthusianism; at the turn of the century, between Kantian moral philosophy and the positivist epistemology of the social sciences; and in the twentieth century, between psychoanalysis and Marxism, Surrealism and anarchism, etc. If we are to make systematic use of the concept, however, we need to be rather more precise in its definition. First of all, we must take into consideration that elective affinity has several levels or degrees:

(1) The first level is that of simple affinity: a spiritual relationship, a structural homology (a concept used in Lucien Goldmann's sociology of literature), a correspondence (in the Baudelairean sense).

The first systematic formulation of the theory of correspondences was Swedenborg's mystical doctrine which postulated a one-to-one correspondence between heaven and earth and between spiritual and natural things. Baudelaire referred several times to Swedenborg as the person who had taught him 'that everything, form, movement, number, colour, scent, *spiritually* as well as *naturally*, is meaningful, reciprocal, converse, *correspondent*'. In Baudelaire, however, the concept loses its original mystical connotations and designates the system of mutual analogies in the universe, 'the intimate and secret relations of things'.[11]

It is important to emphasize that correspondence (or affinity) is an analogy that remains static; it creates the possibility, but not the necessity, of active convergence or *attractio electiva*. (I am here taking into account Danièle Hervieu-Léger's criticism that I used the term too imprecisely in my 1981 article on messianism and utopia.)[12] Transforming potentiality into activity, making the analogy dynamic, having it evolve towards active interaction – this depends upon concrete historical circumstances such as economic transformation, the reactions of classes and social categories, cultural movements or political events.

(2) The *election*, reciprocal attraction and active mutual choice of the two socio-cultural configurations lead to certain forms of interaction, mutual stimulation and convergence. Here the analogies and correspondences start to become dynamic, but the two structures remain separate.

It is at this level (or at the transition between it and the next) that Weber's *Wahlverwandtschaft* occurs between the Protestant ethic and the spirit of capitalism.

(3) The articulation, combination or 'alloying' of partners can result in various modalities of union: (a) what might be called 'cultural symbiosis', in which the two figures remain distinct but are organically associated; (b) partial fusion; and (c) total fusion (Boerhave's 'chemical wedding').

(4) A *new figure* may be created through the fusion of the component elements. This possibility, suggested by the 'Goethian' meaning of the term, is absent from Weber's analyses. It is not easy to distinguish between levels three and four: for example, is Freudo-Marxism the articulation of two component parts or a new mode of thought, as distinct from psychoanalysis as it is from historical materialism?

In order to grasp the specificity, and possible interest, of the concept, it is useful to compare it with other categories or expressions that are commonly employed in analysing the relationship between meaningful structures. Elective affinity, as I have defined it here, is not the ideological affinity inherent in different variants of the same social and cultural current (for example, between economic and political liberalism, or between socialism and egalitarianism). The election, the mutual choice, implies a prior distance, a spiritual gap that must be filled, a certain ideological heterogeneity. On the other hand, *Wahlverwandtschaft* is not at all the same as 'correlation', a vague term that merely denotes a link between two distinct phenomena. *Wahlverwandtschaft* implies a specific type of significant relationship, which has nothing in common with (for example) the statistical correlation between economic growth and demographic decline. Nor is elective affinity synonymous with 'influence', for it entails a much more active relationship and a mutual articulation (that can even go as far as fusion). The concept allows us to understand processes of interaction which arise neither from direct causality nor from the 'expressive' relationship between form and content (where, for example, the religious form is the 'expression' of a political or social content). Without claiming to be a substitute for other paradigms of analysis, explanation and comprehension, the concept may provide a new angle of approach, little explored until now, in the field of the sociology of culture. It is surprising that, since Max Weber, so few attempts have been made to re-examine it and to use it in real research.

Of course, elective affinity occurs neither in a vacuum nor in the azure of pure spirituality; it is encouraged (or discouraged) by historical and social conditions. Whereas the analogy or likeness as such derives only from the spiritual content of the relevant structures of meaning, their contact and active interaction depend on specific socio-economic, political and cultural circumstances. In this sense, an analysis in terms of elective affinity is perfectly compatible with a recognition of the determining role of economic and social conditions. Contrary to a common belief, this also applies to the classic Weberian analysis of the relationship between the Protestant ethic and the spirit of capitalism – an analysis which, apart from a few polemical digressions, seeks less to define a 'spiritualistic' causal relationship than to grasp the *Wahlverwandtschaft* between religious doctrine and economic ethos. Let it be said in passing that, in a passage from the *Grundrisse* – a work unknown to Max Weber, as it was first published in 1939 – Marx himself refers to the relationship (*Zusammenhang*) between English or Dutch Protestantism and the accumulation of money-capital.[13]

2

Jewish Messianism and Libertarian Utopia: From 'Correspondences' to 'Attractio Electiva'

What could there be in common between Jewish messianism and twentieth-century libertarian utopias: between a religious tradition indifferent to the realm of politics, turned towards the supernatural and the sacred, and a revolutionary social imaginary that has generally been atheist and materialist? It seems evident that the messianic religiosity of rabbis and Talmudists, so deeply rooted in tradition and ritual, had no common ground with the subversive anarchist ideology of a Bakunin or a Kropotkin – especially since the cultural ethno-centrism of the Jewish religion was poles apart from the militant universalism of revolutionary utopias.

Yet the increasingly active role of Jewish intellectuals (from the middle of the nineteenth century onwards) in generating radically anti-establishment ideas inspired attempts to find Jewish religious roots within socialist utopias. Max Weber was probably one of the first among the sociologists of religion to suggest that the religious tradition of ancient Judaism had a potentially revolutionary nature. In the Bible, he argued, the world was perceived not as eternal or unchanging, but as an historical product destined to be replaced by a divine order. The whole attitude to life was determined by this conception of a future God-guided political and social revolution.[1] Weber's hypothesis, though extremely fertile, is still too general. For it does not allow us to identify, within the heterogeneous group of modern revolutionary doctrines, those that might have had a real affinity with the Jewish tradition. In the opinion of many authors, such as Max Scheler, Karl Löwith and Nikolai Berdyaev – some of whom were Weber's disciples – Marx's thinking was typically a secularized version of biblical messianism. However, this is a questionable and rather reductionist interpretation of the Marxist philosophy of history.

Karl Mannheim would seem to have stood on firmer and more accurate ground when, in *Ideology and Utopia* (1929), he put forward the idea that 'radical anarchism' was the modern figure *par excellence* of the chiliastic principle, the purest and most genuine form of the modern utopian/millennial consciousness. Mannheim did not differentiate between Christian millenarianism and Jewish messianism; but in his opinion, the twentieth-century thinker who most completely personified that 'demoniacally deep' spiritual attitude was Gustav Landauer, the Jewish anarchist writer.[2] It is a well-known fact that Landauer was one of the leaders of the Munich Commune in 1919; and it is interesting to note that, according to the German sociologist Paul Honigsheim (a former member of the Max Weber circle in Heidelberg and a friend of Lukács and Bloch), some of the participants in the Republics of Workers' Councils in Munich and Budapest were instilled with the sense of a mission to achieve world redemption and with the belief that they belonged to a collective Messiah.[3] In fact, apart from Gustav Landauer, other Jewish intellectuals such as Kurt Eisner, Eugen Leviné, Ernst Toller and Erich Mühsam played an important role in the Councils Republic in Bavaria; and in 1919, Georg Lukács and other members of the Jewish intelligentsia of Budapest were among the leaders of the Hungarian Councils.

Are there aspects of Jewish messianism, then, which can be linked to a revolutionary (and particularly anarchist) world-view? Gershom Scholem's remarkable analyses may serve as a starting-point for closer examination of this question. In his essay 'Toward an Understanding of the Messianic Idea in Judaism', Scholem was not afraid to state that 'for popular apocalypticism . . . there is an anarchic element in the very nature of Messianic utopianism: the dissolution of old ties which lose their meaning in the new context of Messianic freedom'.[4] This is a very profound remark, but it seems to me that the analogy (or 'correspondence') between messianic and libertarian utopia stretches much further and emerges in several other decisive 'moments' of the two cultural configurations. Let us consider this correspondence by referring to the theoretical paradigm – the ideal type, one might say – of Jewish messianism, as

constructed by Gershom Scholem, and to several remarks made
by Karl Mannheim on radical anarchism.

(1) Jewish messianism embodies two tendencies that are at
once intimately linked and contradictory: a *restorative* current
focusing on the re-establishment of a past ideal state, a lost
Golden Age, a shattered Edenic harmony; and a *utopian* current
which aspires to a radically new future, to a state of things
that has never existed before. The proportion between the two
tendencies may vary, but the messianic idea crystallizes only
on the basis of their combination. They are inseparable within
a dialectical relationship that Scholem draws out so admirably:

> Even the restorative force has a utopian factor, and in
> utopianism restorative factors are at work. . . . The completely
> new order has elements of the completely old, but even this
> old order does not consist of the actual past; rather, it is a
> past transformed and transfigured in a dream brightened by
> the rays of utopianism.[5]

According to the felicitous expression of the great historian of
Messianism, Sigmund Mowinckel, in the Jewish tradition 'eschatology is a reinterpretation of the mythology of primordial time'.[6]

The Hebraic concept of *Tikkun* is the supreme expression of
this duality in Jewish messianism. For the cabbalists – notably
Isaac Luria and the Safed school – the *Tikkun* re-establishes the
great harmony that was disturbed by the Breaking of the Vessels
(*'Shevirat Ha-Kelim'*) and later by the fall of Adam. As Scholem
notes, 'the *Tikkun*, the path to the end of all things, is also the path
to the beginning'. The *Tikkun* implies 'restoration of the original
harmony'; in other words, 'the re-institution, the re-integration of
every original thing'. The coming of the Messiah is the accomplishment of *Tikkun*, the Redemption is the 'return of all things
to their original contact with God'. This 'World of *Tikkun*' (*'Olam
Ha-Tikkun'*) is, therefore, the utopian world of messianic reform,
of the removal of the blemish, the disappearance of evil.[7]

In libertarian thought, there is clearly an analogous duality
between restoration and utopia, which was noted by Mannheim.[8]
For Mikhail Bakunin, Georges Sorel, Pierre-Joseph Proudhon and
Gustav Landauer, revolutionary utopia was always accompanied
by a deep nostalgia for aspects of the pre-capitalist past, the traditional peasant community, or the artisan economy. Landauer went

so far as to offer an explicit apology for the Middle Ages. In reality, the majority of the great anarchist thinkers integrated a romantic attitude towards the past into the core of their thinking.

The parallel can be drawn even further. In an article written in 1904, the anti-militarist writer Georges Darien complained about the 'religious nature of Anarchism', whose doctrine he defined in the following terms: (i) There was once a Golden Age, which disappeared with the birth of authority. (ii) We must return to that Golden Age, and for that a revolution is desirable. (iii) Once the revolution has been carried out, there will be a general interruption in life on earth. (iv) After that, the Golden Age will return.[9] This is, of course, a caricature, yet it does relate to an aspect of anarchist prophecy. For his part, in *Economy and Society*, Max Weber argued that anarcho-syndicalism was the sole form of socialism in Western Europe that could claim to be 'the real equivalent to a religious faith'.[10]

Contrary to what is generally thought, a romantic-nostalgic dimension has been present in all anti-capitalist revolutionary thought – including Marxism. In the case of Marx and his disciples, this dimension was tempered by their admiration for industry and for the economic progress that capital brings. But in the anarchists, who in no way shared that industrialism, the same dimension manifested itself with a particular, even unique, intensity and fire. Of all the modern revolutionary movements, anarchism (along with Russian populism) was undoubtedly the one in which utopia had the most powerful romantic and restorative charge. In this respect, Gustav Landauer's work was the supreme expression of the romantic spirit of libertarian utopia.

It is perhaps here that the analogy between Jewish messianism and anarchism is the most significant, fundamental and decisive; it alone would suffice to create the possibility of a privileged spiritual link between the two. We shall return to this idea later in the text.

(2) According to Gershom Scholem, for Jewish (as opposed to Christian) messianism, redemption is an event which necessarily takes place on the historical stage, 'publicly' so to speak, in the visible world; redemption is not conceivable as a purely spiritual process, within the soul of each individual, which results in an essentially inward transformation. What type of 'visible' event is

it? In the Jewish religious tradition, the arrival of the Messiah is a catastrophic eruption: 'Jewish messianism is in its origins and by its nature – this cannot be sufficiently emphasized – a theory of catastrophe. This theory stresses the revolutionary, cataclysmic element in the transition from every historical present to the Messianic future.'[11]

There is an abyss between the present and the future, between current decline and redemption: moreover, in many talmudic texts there appears the idea that the Messiah will come only in an era of total corruption and guilt. This abyss cannot be overcome by just any 'progress' or 'development': only revolutionary catastrophe, with colossal uprooting and total destruction of the existing order, opens the way to messianic redemption. The secularized messianism of nineteenth-century liberal Jewish thought (the neo-Kantian philosopher Hermann Cohen, for example), with its idea of uninterrupted progress and gradual perfection of humanity, has nothing to do with the tradition of the prophets and the Haggadists, for whom the advent of the Messiah always implies a general upheaval and a universal revolutionary tempest. As Scholem so aptly puts it: 'The Bible and the apocalyptic writers know of no progress in history leading to redemption . . . it is rather transcendence breaking in upon history, [. . .] struck by a beam of light shining into it from an outside source.'[12] Along the same line, Max Weber had already noted in *Economy and Society* that the Jewish people always lived in 'mute, faithful and questioning expectation' for the Great Day on which Yahveh 'by an act that might come suddenly at any time but that no one could accelerate . . . would transform the social structure of the world, creating a messianic realm'.[13]

Scholem himself suggested the analogy between that structure of meaning and modern revolutionary doctrines: 'Messianism in our age proves its immense force precisely in this form of the revolutionary apocalypse, and no longer in that of the rational utopia (if one may call it that) of eternal progress as the Enlightenment's surrogate for Redemption.' In Scholem's eyes, the inheritors of that Jewish tradition are those he calls 'the most important ideologists of revolutionary messianism' of our century: Ernst Bloch, Walter Benjamin, Theodor Adorno and Herbert Marcuse.[14]

None the less, without denying the more general scope of that comparison, it seems to me that the most striking parallel is with libertarian thought (including that of Walter Benjamin and the young Ernst Bloch). Indeed, the revolutionary/ catastrophic aspect of emancipation is most obvious in the anarchists: 'Destructive passion is a creative passion', wrote Bakunin. On the other hand, as Mannheim again noted with reference to Gustav Landauer, the abyss between every existing order (*'Topie'*) and Utopia was most sharply defined in the anarchists. A *qualitative* differentiation of time contrasted epochs pregnant with meaning and epochs devoid of meaning: any possibility of progress or evolution was denied, and revolution was conceived as an eruption into the world.[15]

(3) In the Jewish (notably biblical) tradition, the *Et Ketz*, the Time of the End, brings general, universal and radical change. *Et Ketz* does not mean an improvement of everything hitherto experienced on earth, but rather the creation of a wholly *other* world.[16] The advent of the Messiah, *ba'akharit hayyamim*, at the end of days, will establish (or *re-establish*) an age of harmony between man and God, between man and nature, and among men. These are the well-known images of Isaiah 11:8, which show the child playing with the asp, or of Isaiah 2:4, which proclaim eternal peace: nation shall not lift up sword against nation, neither shall they learn war any more (*'lo essa goy el goy cherev ve lo ilmedu od milchama'*).[17]

Here the correspondence with revolutionary utopias relates both to the absolute, radical nature of the transformation and to the actual content of the new (or restored) world. However, of all the socialist movements, the one that most sharply rejects any idea of improvement in the established order is, in fact, anarchism.

(4) One of the main aspects of generalized eschatological subversion is the overthrow of the powers of this world. To restate the famous words of the prophet Isaiah (13:11, 14:5–6), when the day of the Lord comes, the Everlasting will overthrow the pride of the arrogant (*'geut aritzim'*) and will break the rulers' sceptre (*'shevet moshlim'*) that smote the peoples in wrath with an incessant stroke, that ruled the nations in anger with a persecution that none restrained.[18]

However, certain biblical and apocalyptic texts go further still.

They suggest the abolition of all power or human authority – to the benefit of theocracy, in the strictest sense of rule by God himself, directly, without intermediaries or 'vicars'. As Mowinckel noted, Yahweh himself was the king of the future messianic kingdom:[19] God was both King of Israel *'Melekh Israel'* and its redeemer *'ve-Goalo'* (Isaiah 44:6). Jakob Taubes, an eminent historian of eschatological systems, wrote the following on this aspect of Jewish messianism: 'Theocracy is built on the anarchist spiritual foundation (*Seelengrund*) of Israel. Mankind's tendency to free itself from all earthly constraints and to establish a pact (*Bund*) with God is found in theocracy.'[20]

That is, of course, very far from modern anarchism, whose motto, 'Neither God nor master', demonstrates its rejection of all authority, divine as well as secular. Yet the negation of all human power 'in flesh and blood' is a significant analogy-correspondence, which by itself makes it possible to understand why certain twentieth-century Jewish intellectuals (Benjamin and Scholem, among others) display this astonishing spiritual combination: theocratic anarchism.

(5) Finally, there is the aspect of Jewish messianism that Scholem referred to as intrinsically 'anarchist': namely, the idea to be found in several talmudic or cabbalistic texts that the advent of the Messiah implies an abolition of the restrictions that the *Torah* has until then imposed on the Jews. In the messianic age, the former *Torah* will lose its validity and be replaced by a new law, the *'Torah* of the Redemption', in which bans and prohibitions will disappear. In this new, paradisiacal world, dominated by the light of the Tree of Life, the force of evil will be broken and the restrictions imposed by the Tree of the Knowledge of Good and Evil will lose their significance. As Scholem aptly demonstrates, this 'anarchist' element is also present in certain interpretations of Psalms 146:7 which offer a new reading of the Hebrew text: in place of the traditional version, according to which in the messianic age, 'The Lord releases the prisoners' (*mattir asurim*), we should read, 'The Lord allows the forbidden' (*mattir isurim*).[21] Scholem is not wrong to qualify this as an 'anarchist' theme. We need think only of Bakunin's famous expression, which Mannheim quotes as a characteristic example of the chiliastic stance of radical anarchy: 'I do not believe in constitutions or in laws. . . We need something

different: storm and vitality and a new lawless and consequently free world.'[22]

The above analysis, which treats the five aspects in turn, must nevertheless be considered as a single whole. It then reveals a remarkable structural homology, an undeniable spiritual iso-morphism, between two cultural universes, apparently set in completely distinct spheres: namely, the Jewish messianic tra-dition and modern revolutionary, especially libertarian, utopias. By 'libertarian utopia', I mean not only anarchist (or anarcho-syndicalist) doctrines in the strictest sense, but also the revolu-tionary trends of socialist thought – including some that claim allegiance to Marxism – which have been characterized by a strongly anti-authoritarian and anti-statist orientation.

So far, we have only defined the field of correspondences (in the Baudelairean sense): that is, a subterranean network of analogies, similitudes or equivalences among several elements of the two cultural configurations. These correspondences in themselves do not constitute an effectual link: the anarchism of a Proudhon or a Bakunin (both anti-Semites, incidentally) bears no relation to the Jewish religious tradition. It was only during a given historical era – the first half of the twentieth century – and in the precise social and cultural arena of the Central European Jewish intelligentsia that the homology or connection became dynamic and, in the works of some thinkers, took the form of a true *elective affinity*. In other words, to use a concept that Mannheim very successfully transplanted from astrology to the sociology of knowledge, there had to appear a certain *constellation* of historical, social and cultural factors. Only then could a process of *attractio electiva* or 'cultural symbiosis' develop between messianism and revolutionary utopia within the *Weltanschauung* of a large group of German-speaking Jewish intellectuals, involving mutual stimulation and nourishment and, in certain cases, even combination or fusion of the two spiritual figures. The concrete form of the articulation or alloy and of its component elements – one or several of the correspondences we have discussed – varied according to the authors in question.

The simplest explanation for this relationship, appearing to the mind as immediately self-evident, is to consider the messianic

tradition as the more or less direct source for the development
of libertarian utopianism in Jewish writers and thinkers. Without
rejecting that hypothesis completely, as it probably holds some
element of truth, one must recognize that it creates more problems than it solves:

(a) Influence alone is not a sufficient explanatory factor. The
influence itself needs to be explained. Why does a particular
doctrine and not another influence a particular author? This is all
the more pertinent in that nearly all the authors in question, like
the great majority of Jewish intellectuals of German cultural background, were far removed through their upbringing from Jewish
religious traditions (which remained much more alive in Eastern
Europe). The milieu of their origins was largely assimilated: the
Jewish intelligentsia of Central Europe drew its cultural references from German literature and philosophy. Goethe, Schiller,
Kant and Hegel were the recognized and respected sources, and
not the Talmud or the cabbala, which, for the most part, were
considered atavistic and obscurantist vestiges of the past.

(b) The Jewish messianic tradition lends itself to multiple
interpretations: purely conservative, as in some rabbinical texts,
or purely rationalist (Maimonides), or even influenced by the
liberal-progressive spirit of the *Aufklärung* (Enlightenment) and
its Jewish equivalent, the *Haskala*, as in Hermann Cohen. Why
was it precisely the apocalyptic interpretation, at once restorative
and utopian, which was 'selected' by a certain group of thinkers?
The opposite explanation, according to which the utopian tendency of these authors accounts for their interest in the messianic
tradition, is as limited and narrow as the first. One of the great
merits of the concept of *Wahlverwandtschaft* is precisely that it
allows us to go beyond these two unilateral approaches, and to
move towards a dialectical understanding of the relationship.

Another explanatory model that seems unsatisfactory centres
on the concept of secularization, which is frequently used to
account for the link between religion and social or political
ideologies. Its significance for the phenomenon under study
here is limited, because the religious messianic dimension is
never absent from the writings of the majority of these authors;
it remains (explicitly) a central aspect of their world-view. In
fact, in this German-Jewish thought, there is as much 'making
sacred' of the profane as there is secularization of the religious:

the relationship between religion and utopia is not here, as in the case of secularization, a one-way movement, an absorption of the sacred by the profane, but rather a mutual relationship that links the two spheres without suppressing either one.

It seems more useful to start from the larger socio-cultural context, the general framework common to the two tendencies which grew organically, so to speak, out of the Central European societies in crisis. I am referring to the development of neo-romanticism from the late nineteenth century until the beginning of the 1930s. In this context, the term *romanticism* denotes not a literary or artistic style but a much broader and deeper current that emerged both in the field of art and literature and in economic, sociological and political thought. Essentially it involved nostalgia for pre-capitalist cultures and cultural critique of industrial/bourgeois society.

Anti-capitalist romanticism – to use Lukács's expression – is a specific political and cultural phenomenon which, in eluding all the usual classifications, has not so far received the attention it deserves. It is not captured within the traditional division of the political field into left/centre/right – or conservatives/liberals/revolutionaries or even regression/*status quo*/progress; it slips between the cracks of that classical grid and appears not to fall within the categories that have defined the major political options since the French Revolution. This problem is even more acute when applied to that tendency within romanticism which might be described as *romantic revolutionary*, and to which thinkers such as Hölderlin, Fourier, William Morris and Landauer belong. In this tendency, restoration and utopia, nostalgia for the pre-capitalist past (real or imaginary, near or remote) and revolutionary hope in a new future, are intimately and inseparably bound up with each other.[23]

Thus, the concept of neo-romanticism helps us to understand more clearly the resurgence, the *rapprochement* through elective affinity, and the occasional convergence and fusion of Jewish messianism (in its restorative/utopian interpretation) and libertarian utopia. The two had their roots in the same ethico-cultural and 'ideological' ground and grew in the same spiritual climate, that of the anti-capitalist romanticism of the German intelligentsia. Indeed, that cultural movement, particularly in its revolutionary romantic version, could not but favour the discovery, the revitalization or the development of both a restorative/utopian interpretation of messianism and a restorative/utopian interpretation of revolution (anarchism).

This dual process characterized a number of Jewish intellectuals from Central Europe, who made up an extremely heterogeneous group but were united by a common problematic. Among them were several of the greatest minds of the century: poets and philosophers, revolutionary leaders and religious guides, people's commissars and theologians, writers and cabbalists, and even writers-cum-philosophers-cum-theologians-cum-revolutionaries: for example, Franz Rosenzweig, Martin Buber, Gershom Scholem, Gustav Landauer, Franz Kafka, Walter Benjamin, Ernst Bloch, Ernst Toller, Erich Fromm, Manes Sperber, Georg Lukács (to name but a few).

These authors have all been studied in sufficient detail, but until now no one has ever suggested that their thinking could have had a fundamental dimension in common. It seems paradoxical and even arbitrary to group under the same roof personalities so diverse and remote from each other. But let us note, first of all, that although they did not form a group in the concrete and immediate sense of the word, they were linked together by a complex and subtle social network: relationships based on deep friendship and/or intellectual and political affinity united Gustav Landauer and Martin Buber, Gershom Scholem and Walter Benjamin, Ernst Bloch and Georg Lukács, Martin Buber and Franz Rosenzweig, Gustav Landauer and Ernst Toller; Scholem was attracted by Buber and Landauer; Buber corresponded with Kafka, Bloch and Lukács; Erich Fromm was a student of Scholem. At the heart of this network, at the intersection of all the threads of this cultural fabric, embodying opposite poles, was Walter Benjamin. On very close terms with Scholem, he was also a friend of Bloch, was profoundly influenced by Lukács, Rosenzweig and Kafka, and was a critical reader of Landauer, Buber and Fromm.

This is not, however, the most important reason why these personalities (and others lesser known, whom I will also discuss, such as Hans Kohn, Rudolf Kayser, Eugen Leviné and Erich Unger) can be thought of as a group. The key point is that their work, resting upon a neo-romantic cultural basis and a relationship of elective affinity, contained a Jewish messianic and a libertarian-utopian dimension. For some, this relationship is but a brief episode in their intellectual journey (Lukács); for others, it is the central axis of their entire work (Benjamin). Of course, the relative weight of the two dimensions is not the same: for some the religious component is decisive (Rosenzweig), while for others the utopian/revolutionary project is predominant (Bloch); yet, both aspects are found in every one of these personalities.

It would be pointless to look in these writers for a systematic and explicit presence of the two configurations in their entirety. Both Jewish messianism and libertarian utopia are powerful currents in their work, sometimes running beneath the surface, at other times more clearly visible. Now one theme and now another is manifest, depending on the author or the period in his life. Sometimes the themes are separate, sometimes combined (or merged), sometimes explicit, sometimes implicit or 'deep set'. At one point they may dominate the thinker's entire work, while at others they may do no more than flash here and there in his writings.

According to whether one dimension or the other plays the dominant role, it seems possible to divide this network into two distinct poles. First, the *religious Jews with anarchist tendencies*: Franz Rosenzweig, Rudolf Kayser, Martin Buber, Gershom Scholem and Hans Kohn, among others. The latter were Zionists, the former rather hostile or reticent toward Zionism. Despite their refusal to assimilate and despite their return to Judaism as a religion and a national culture, universal political and social concerns (utopian and libertarian) were present in their work and removed them from narrow or chauvinistic nationalism. Thus, Scholem and Buber led organizations in Palestine (*Brit Shalom* for Scholem, *Ihud* for Buber) which preached fraternization with the Arab population and opposed the establishment of an exclusively Jewish nation-state. To a certain extent, Kafka could be added to this current, but his relationship with the Jewish religion was much more problematic, and his attitude towards assimilation was less negative.

At the other pole are the assimilated (religious-atheist) libertarian Jews – that is to say, anarchists, anarcho-bolsheviks and anti-authoritarian Marxists: Landauer, Bloch, Fromm, Toller and Lukács, among others. Unlike those in the first category, they more or less distanced themselves from their Jewish identity, all the while maintaining a (more or less explicit) link with Judaism.

Their religious atheism (a phrase coined by Lukács) drew on both Jewish and Christian references, and several of them developed their anarchist ideas in the direction of Marxism or Bolshevism.

Outside all currents (as Adorno put it), at the crossing of the ways, and linked to both the above groups at the same time was the person who, more than any other, personified the German-Jewish messianic/libertarian culture: Walter Benjamin.

That a distinction can be made between the two groups shows that, within the elective affinity between Jewish messianism and libertarian utopia, there is also a tension, if not a contradiction, between the Jewish (national-cultural) particularism of messianism and the universal (humanist/internationalist) nature of the emancipatory utopia. In the first group, the predominance of Jewish particularism tends to limit the universal revolutionary aspect of utopia, without causing it to disappear altogether; in the second group, the universality of utopia is the preponderant dimension, and messianism tends to be stripped of its Jewish specificity – without being entirely erased.

Why did this political and cultural phenomenon arise in Central Europe and not in another European Jewish community? And why at that precise moment in history? To answer these questions, and to understand the specific reception of anti-capitalist romanticism by Jewish intellectuals of German cultural origin, we need to examine from a sociological point of view their peculiarly contradictory situation within the social and cultural life of Central Europe.

3

Pariahs, Rebels and Romantics: A Sociological Analysis of the Central European Jewish Intelligentsia

As we noted at the outset, the term *Mitteleuropa* designates an area united by German culture: the area of Germany and the Austro-Hungarian Empire. The specific situation of the Jewish community of the region (and of its intellectuals) cannot be understood without first examining the historical changes that took place in *Mitteleuropa* from the late nineteenth century onward. And the changes in the cultural and religious forms of life cannot be comprehended without relating them to changes in the economic and social structure. Rather than speak of 'determination' by the economy, we should speak, as did Mannheim, of *Seinsgebundenheit*, the culture's attachment to (or dependence on) socio-economic reality.

In other words, the starting-point for analysing the figures of the German and Jewish intellectual world during this period has to be a basic social fact: the dizzying growth of capitalism and the rapid industrialization that took place in Germany, Austria and Hungary during the last quarter of the nineteenth century. Between 1870 and 1914, Germany was transformed from a semi-feudal and backward country into one of the world's principal industrial powers. Only one example is needed to illustrate this change: in 1860 Germany was behind France, and far behind England, in steel production (a typical sector of modern industry); in 1910 Germany produced more steel than France and England combined! Banking and industrial capital were concentrated, and powerful cartels were formed in the textile, coal, steel, chemical and electrical industries, among others.[1] A similar process took place in Austria, Hungary and Czechoslovakia, although to a lesser degree. The speed, brutality, intensity and overwhelming power of this industrialization drastically changed Central European societies, their class structures (flourishing bourgeoisies and ongoing formation of the proletariat), their political systems and their hierarchy of values.

In the face of the irresistible rise of capitalism and the invasive development of scientific and technical civilization, of large industrial production and the universe of commodities and market values, there was a cultural reaction – now desperate and tragic, now resigned – in various social milieux, but particularly in the traditional intelligentsia. This reaction could be described as romantic anti-capitalist.

Anti-capitalist romanticism – which, we repeat, must not be confused with Romanticism as a literary style – is a *world-view* characterized by a (more or less) radical critique of industrial/bourgeois civilization in the name of pre-capitalist social, cultural, ethical or religious values.[2] In Central Europe, and especially in Germany, this *Weltanschauung* was, at the turn of the century, the dominant sensibility in cultural and academic life. The academic mandarinate, a traditionally influential and privileged social category, was one of its primary social foundations. Threatened by the new system that tended to reduce it to a marginal and powerless position, it reacted with horror to what it considered a soulless, standardized, superficial and materialistic society.[3] One of the principal themes of this critique, recurring like an obsession among writers, poets, philosophers and historians, was the conflict between *Kultur*, a spiritual universe of ethical, religious or aesthetic values, and *Zivilisation*, the materialistic and vulgar world of economic and technical progress. If, to use Max Weber's implacably lucid expression, capitalism is disenchantment of the world (*Entzauberung der Welt*), anti-capitalist romanticism must be considered first and foremost as a nostalgic and desperate attempt at re-enchantment of the world, one of whose main aspects was a return to religion, a rebirth of various forms of religious spirituality.

The romantic anti-capitalist world-view was present in an astonishing variety of cultural works and social movements of this period: novels by Thomas Mann and Theodor Storm; poems by Stefan George and Richard Beer-Hoffmann; the sociology of Tönnies, Simmel or Mannheim; the historical school of economics; the *Kathedersozialismus* of Gustav Schmoller, Adolph Wagner or Lujo Brentano; the philosophy of Heidegger and

Spengler, the Youth Movement and the *Wandervogel*, Symbolism and Expressionism. United in its rejection of capitalism in the name of nostalgia for the past, this cultural configuration was totally heterogeneous from a political point of view: reactionary ideologues (Moeller Van der Bruck, Julius Langbehn, Ludwig Klages) as well as revolutionary utopians (Bloch, Landauer) could be characterized as anti-capitalist romantics. It might be said that the main part of literary, artistic and social-scientific (in the sense of *Geisteswissenschaften*) production in Germany and Central Europe occurred in the magnetic field of this movement.

What consequences did these economic, social and cultural developments have for the Jewish communities of *Mitteleuropa*? The flourishing of capitalism created a favourable environment in which the Jewish bourgeoisie could blossom. The Jewish population left the ghettos and villages and quickly became urbanized: in 1867, seventy per cent of Prussian Jews lived in small villages; by 1927, the figure had dropped to fifteen per cent.[4] The same phenomenon occurred in the Austro-Hungarian Empire, where the Jewish population was concentrated in Budapest, Prague and, above all, Vienna. (I can even cite my own family as an example: towards the end of the nineteenth century, my grandparents left their respective villages in Czechoslovakia and Hungary and settled in the capital of the Empire.) An upper and middle bourgeoisie formed in the cities and took a larger share of business, trade, industry and banking. As this 'Jewish middle class' grew richer, and as civil and political restrictions on it were lifted (between 1869 and 1871 in Germany), it set itself only one goal: to be socially and culturally assimilated into the German nation. A letter written in 1916 by the Jewish industrialist Walther Rathenau (who was to become a minister in the Weimar Republic) typified this mentality:

> I have – and I know – nothing but German blood, German ethnicity, and German people. If I were to be driven from my German land, I would continue to be German, and nothing would change that. . . My ancestors and I have been nourished of German soil and of the German mind . . . and we have had no thoughts that were not German or for Germany.[5]

This example, of course, represents virtually the outer line, but even for those who continued to think of themselves as Jewish, German culture was the only valid culture. All that remained from Judaism were some ritualistic hangovers (such as a trip to the synagogue on *Yom Kippur*) and biblical monotheism. The examplars of wisdom were no longer Moses or Solomon, but rather Lessing and Goethe, Schiller and Kant. Schiller in particular was truly venerated: his *Complete Works* were required in the library of every self-respecting German or Austrian Jew (when my parents left Vienna in 1935, they took their copy with them). In Germany, the most resolute assimilationist current was the Central-Verein deutscher Staatsbürger jüdischen Glaubens [Central Association of German Citizens of Jewish Denomination]. Describing this social milieu (to which his own family belonged), Gershom Scholem noted:

> Education and readings were oriented exclusively to Germany, and in the majority of cases, any dissidence, notably in the direction of a return to Judaism, was met with decided opposition. Assimilation ran very deep. Each time, they emphasized over and over, albeit with slight differences, that we belonged to the German nation, at the center of which we formed a religious group, like the others. What was even more paradoxical was that in the majority of the cases, the religious element – which was the only difference – did not exist nor did it exert any influence over how they conducted their lives.[6]

None the less, it would be wrong to regard this thirst for cultural integration as mere opportunism: it could also express sincere and authentic convictions. Even as profoundly religious a Jew as Franz Rosenzweig wrote in 1923, shortly after the publication of his great theological work, *Der Stern der Erlösung* (*The Star of Redemption*):

> I believe that my return to Judaism (*Verjüdung*) made me a better and not a worse German. . . And I believe that *Der Stern* will one day be duly recognized and appreciated as a gift that the German mind owes to its Jewish enclave.[7]

Assimilation was successful to a certain degree, but it came up against an insurmountable social barrier. According to Moritz Goldstein's famous lament of unfulfilled love, which he wrote in 1912 ('Deutsch-Jüdischer Parnass'), in vain we think of ourselves as Germans; others think of us as completely *un-German [undeutsch]*. . . But were we not raised on German legends? Does not the Germanic forest live within us, can we too not see its elves and its gnomes?[8]

Assimilation also came up against *de facto* exclusion from a series of areas: State administration, the armed forces, the magistrature, education – and after 1890 in particular, against growing anti-Semitism, which had its ideologues, activists and press. For all of these reasons, the Jewish communities in Central Europe did not truly integrate into the surrounding society. To use Max Weber's classic definition, they shared several of the hallmarks of a *pariah* people: 'a distinctive hereditary social group lacking autonomous political organization', and characterized by endogamy on the one hand and by *negative privileges*, both political and social, on the other.[9] Of course, their condition could not be compared to that of the castes in India, or of the Jewish ghettoes in the Middle Ages: economic security and (formal) equality of civic rights had been won through emancipation. But socially, the Jew continued to be a pariah and realized, as Hannah Arendt put it, 'how treacherous was the promise of equality which assimilation held out'.[10]

In Germany and in Central Europe, the university was the royal road to respectability and honour. As Friedrich Paulsen, the neo-Kantian philosopher, wrote, in Germany citizens with a higher education made up a type of intellectual and spiritual aristocracy; not to hold a university degree was a 'shortcoming' that neither wealth nor prestigious birth could fully make up for.[11] The logic of cultural assimilation and the desire to climb the ladder of prestige led the Jewish bourgeoisie to send its sons to the University, especially towards the end of the nineteenth century:

> Just like the majority of German businessmen, Jews wanted to climb socially. . . They wanted their sons and sons-in-law to be more valued than they were. A career as an officer or as a high-ranking government official, which were the goals of a young Christian man, was closed to Jews . . . only university studies were open to him.[12]

As a result, in 1895 Jews comprised 10% of the student body

in German universities, which was ten times the percentage of Jews in the overall population (1.05%).[13] This massive presence of bourgeois Jewish youth in higher education quickly led to the formation of a new social category: the Jewish intelligentsia. Jewish intellectuals of German culture had, of course, existed since the late eighteenth century (Moses Mendelssohn), but it was only at the end of the nineteenth century that the phenomenon became so widespread as to constitute a new social fact. These Jewish intellectuals, *déclassé*, unstable and free of any precise social attachment, were a typical example of the *sozialfreischwebende Intelligenz* that Mannheim spoke of. Their condition was eminently contradictory: deeply assimilated yet largely marginalized; linked to German culture yet cosmopolitan; uprooted and at odds with their business and bourgeois milieu of origin; rejected by the traditional rural aristocracy yet excluded in career terms within their natural sphere of acceptance (the university). In a state of ideological availability, they were soon attracted to the two principal poles of German cultural life, which could be named after the famous characters from Thomas Mann's *Magic Mountain*: 'Settembrini', the liberal, democratic and republican philanthropist, and 'Naphta', the conservative/revolutionary romantic.

For many young Jewish intellectuals, rationalism, progressive evolutionism, *Aufklärung* and neo-Kantian philosophy became the primary reference, in some cases combined with a Judaism that was diluted or reduced to monotheist ethics (Hermann Cohen). From this world-view several political options were available, ranging from moderate liberalism (the ideology of the Jewish bourgeoisie itself), to social democracy (Eduard Bernstein), Marxism (Max Adler, Otto Bauer and the Austrian Marxists) and even Communism (Paul Levi, Ruth Fischer, Paul Frölich, August Thalheimer).

Nevertheless, at the turn of the century, anti-capitalist romanticism was the dominant movement within the culture of *Mitteleuropa*. Sociologically speaking, it was inevitable that a significant portion of the new university-trained Jewish intelligentsia would be attracted by the romantic critique of industrial civilization: 'Naphta!' The intelligentsia eagerly discovered the nostalgic and anti-bourgeois *Weltanschauung* predominant in academia – notably in the *Geisteswissenschaften* (Humanities), where the majority of Jewish students enrolled. These students subsequently rejected their fathers' business careers, revolted against their bourgeois family milieu and aspired intensely to an 'intellectual life style'.[14] This generational break, which many Jewish intellectuals speak of in their autobiographies, opposed the anti-bourgeois youth – passionately interested in *Kultur*, spirituality, religion and art – to their entrepreneurial parents – merchants or bankers, moderate liberals and good German patriots, indifferent to religious matters.[15] In a recent autobiographical interview, Leo Löwenthal, the Frankfurt School sociologist of literature, summarized the feeling that was common among many intellectuals of his generation: 'My family household, as it were, was the symbol of everything I did not want – shoddy liberalism, shoddy *Aufklärung*, and double standards.'[16]

Mannheim used the term *Generationszusammenhang* (generational bonding) to designate the concrete link deriving from participation in a common historical-social destiny.[17] In fact, the generational break is not a biological fact: it is only under particular social conditions that a gap or even an abyss develops between generations. And it was a specific type of *Generationszusammenhang* that was found in the new Jewish intelligentsia, born during the last quarter of the nineteenth century. The group of intellectuals whom I shall examine in this work belonged to that generation, as their dates of birth fell during the last twenty years of the century: Martin Buber (1878), Franz Kafka (1883), Ernst Bloch (1885), Georg Lukács (1885), Franz Rosenzweig (1886), Walter Benjamin (1892), Ernst Toller (1893), Gershom Scholem (1897), Erich Fromm (1900), Leo Löwenthal (1900). It should be stressed, however, that the sociological analysis sketched in the preceding paragraphs can only delineate the chances that a certain number of Jewish intellectuals would be attracted to the anti-capitalist romantic pole of German culture; it does not enable us to explain each individual's personal choice, which also involved psychologic and other variables. I need only mention the example of Scholem's family: one of the sons (Reinhold) became a German Nationalist and remained so even after 1945; another (Werner) became a Communist deputy; and a third (Gershom) became a Zionist and historian of the cabbala. Obviously the social milieu could not possibly account for such diversity.

For the Jewish intellectual who belonged to the 'romantic generation' of the 1880s, who sometimes attended the informal German
circles at which romantic anti-capitalist culture was being developed – such as the Max Weber Circle in Heidelberg, frequented
by Lukács and Bloch – one problem arose immediately. A
return to the past, which was at the heart of the romantic
orientation, drew upon German ancestry, medieval aristocracy
or Protestant or Catholic Christianity – that is to say, upon
national, social or cultural references from which he, as a Jew,
was completely excluded. True, some Jewish thinkers (especially
in the Stefan George Circle) were able to make the leap and to
be transformed into German nationalists (Rudolf Borchardt), conservative German scholars (Friedrich Gundolf, Karl Wolfskehl) or
Protestant theologians (Hans Ehrenberg). But these were fairly
rare cases which involved a total and rather artificial negation
of Jewish identity – the supreme example being the works of
the Jewish anti-Semites (Otto Weininger, Theodor Lessing). As
for the others, the majority of Jewish intellectuals of German
cultural background, only two solutions were possible within
the framework of neo-romanticism: either a return to their own
historical roots, to their own culture, nationality or ancestral religion; or adherence to a universal romantic-revolutionary utopia.
Not surprisingly, given the structural homology between these
two paths, a number of Jewish thinkers close to anti-capitalist
romanticism chose both simultaneously: on the one hand, a (re-
)discovery of the Jewish religion – most notably, the restorative/
utopian dimension of messianism; on the other hand, sympathy
for, or identification with, revolutionary (especially libertarian)
utopias loaded with nostalgia for the past.

Let us examine these two paths more closely. In the atmosphere permeated with neo-romantic religiosity, many Jewish
intellectuals revolted against their parents' assimilation and
sought to save the Jewish religious culture of the past from
oblivion. As a result, there was a process of de-secularization,
partial dis-assimilation, cultural and religious anamnesis, and 're-
culturalization',[18] which certain circles or literary groups actively
promoted: the Bar-Kochba Club in Prague (Hugo Bergmann, Hans
Kohn, Max Brod); the circle around Rabbi Nobel in Frankfurt
(Siegfried Krakauer, Erich Fromm, Leo Löwenthal, Ernst Simon);

the *Freies Jüdisches Lehrhaus* (Franz Rosenzweig, Gershom Scholem, Nahum Glatzer, Margarete Süssmann); Martin Buber's magazine, *Der Jude*, among other examples. But 're-culturalization' spread even further to embrace, in varying degrees, a large number of Jewish intellectuals influenced by neo-romanticism. It sometimes took on a national character (especially through Zionism), but the religious aspect predominated. Assimilation ran so deep in *Mitteleuropa* that it was extremely difficult to break with the German national-cultural identity. As religion was the sole legitimate specific for 'German citizens of Israelite denomination', it understandably became the primary means of expression for the movement of cultural anamnesis.

This was, however, a new type of religiosity, charged with German romantic spirituality, which was very different from the traditionalism ritualistically preserved within certain non-assimilated orthodox Jewish milieux. The paradox was that, through German neo-romanticism, these young Jewish intellectuals rediscovered their own religion: their path to the prophet Isaiah went by way of Novalis, Hölderlin or Schelling. In other words, assimilation and cultural integration were the preconditions and the points of departure for their dis-assimilation and re-culturalization. It was not by chance that Buber wrote on Jakob Böhme *before* he wrote his works on Hasidism;[19] that Franz Rosenzweig almost converted to Protestantism before becoming the reformer of Jewish theology; that Gustav Landauer translated the mystical writings of Meister Eckhart before turning towards the Jewish tradition; and that Gershom Scholem rediscovered the cabbala through the writings of the German Romantic Franz Joseph Molitor. Consequently, the Jewish religious heritage was seen through a grid of romantic interpretation which favoured its non-rational and non-institutional dimension, its mystical, explosive, apocalyptic, 'anti-bourgeois' aspects (to use Scholem's phrase from the first article he wrote on the cabbala in 1919). Messianism is the theme which, as in a pool of radiant light, concentrates all of the *Sturm und Drang* aspects of the Jewish religion – provided, of course, that it is stripped of the liberal, neo-Kantian and *Aufklärer* interpretation (in which messianism equals the gradual perfection of mankind) and that the original tradition is re-established in all its eschatological force, from the prophets to the cabbala, from the Bible to Sabbatai Sevi. It is therefore not surprising that the messianic reference, in its double restorative and utopian meaning, became the *Shibboleth* of the religious anamnesis of the Jewish-romantic generation of the 1880s. On the other hand, it goes without saying that this sort of Jewish messianism, charged with romantic explosiveness, was far more susceptible to political activation than the rabbinical (quietist or abstentionist) messianism of the orthodox milieux.

How did this activation work? Or rather, how can we explain that a large fringe of this generation adhered to the path of revolutionary utopias?

This question must be placed in a broader context: that of the attraction of Jewish intellectuals in general to left-wing movements and socialist ideas. For, as historians have noted, the majority of left-wing Jews in Central Europe (the situation was different in Eastern Europe, with its Jewish proletariat) were intellectuals.[20]

Anti-Semites had their own 'explanation': the stateless and cosmopolitan Jews tended instinctively towards red internationalism. This platitude is obviously false – the majority of Jews were good-and-proper German or Austrian patriots – but probably the situation of national assimilation/rejection/marginalization of the Jewish intellectuals made them potentially more sensitive than their non-Jewish counterparts to the internationalist themes of socialism. The intelligentsia felt more directly than did the bourgeoisie and the business class the pariah condition of the Jew in Central Europe, the pervading anti-Semitism, the professional and social discrimination. As Hannah Arendt wrote, this new stratum of intellectuals, which had to find both their daily bread and their self-respect outside of Jewish society, was particularly exposed ('without shelter and defence') to the new wave of Jew-hatred at the turn of the century, and it was within the intelligentsia that a rebel 'pariah consciousness' developed in opposition to the conformist posture of the *parvenu*.[21] There were only two possibilities for the pariah: either radical self-negation (Otto Weininger!) or radical questioning of the societal values that devalued his otherness. The pariah consciousness, by definition marginal or outside, tended to be critical and could become, in the words of Elisabeth Lenk, 'the quintessential mirror of society'.[22]

The 'negative privileges' (to use Max Weber's phrase) of

Jewish pariah intellectuals in Central European societies took various forms. At the socio-professional level, civil-service and (to a large extent) academic positions were closed to Jews – a situation which condemned them to marginal intellectual occupations such as 'freelance' journalist or writer, independent artist or researcher, 'private' educator, and so on. According to the German sociologist Robert Michels, it was this discrimination and marginalization which explained 'the Jews' predisposition to joining revolutionary parties'.[23] Analysing this same phenomenon in Hungary, Karady and Kameny underscored that

> the formation of a hard revolutionary core within the liberal *intelligentsia* seemed directly indebted to the rigidities within the marketplace of intellectual occupations, in which institutionalized anti-Semitism within certain professional bodies (such as higher education) was but one aspect . . . that could only reinforce the conviction held by the excluded that 'normal' integration into the intellectual marketplace required subversion of its ground-rules.[24]

Now, the importance of this point should not be underestimated. But it seems to me that the revolutionary radicalization of a large number of Jewish intellectuals – be it in Hungary or Germany – cannot not be reduced to a problem of the job market or career opportunities. Other factors must be taken into consideration in order to explain why the son of a Jewish banker (Georg Lukács) became a People's Commissar in the Budapest Commune, or why the son of a rich Jewish merchant (Eugen Leviné) led the Bavarian Soviet Republic.

In an attempt to understand why Jews turned to Socialism, Walter Laqueur wrote, in his book on the Weimar Republic:

> They gravitated towards the left because it was the party of reason, progress and freedom which had helped them to attain equal rights. The right on the other hand, was to varying degrees anti-semitic because it regarded the Jew as an alien element in the body politic. This attitude had been a basic fact of political life throughout the nineteenth century and it did not change during the first third of the twentieth.[25]

Such an analysis certainly helps to clarify why many Jewish

intellectuals in Germany and especially in Austria joined social democracy. However, it does not explain the radicalization of the romantic Jewish generation of the 1880s, which was distrustful of rationalism, industrial progress and political liberalism – and none of whose members was attracted by social democracy.

What was the spiritual road that led a part of this current to socialist ideas – or, more precisely, to the revolutionary socialist version of anti-capitalism? Why was it, for example, that in one of the main discussion centres of the neo-romantic world-view, the Max Weber circle of Heidelberg, it was precisely the Jews (Lukács, Bloch, Toller) who opted for revolution?

As noted earlier, their social condition as pariahs, their marginalization and uprooting clearly made Jewish intellectuals receptive to ideologies that radically contested the established order. But other motivations entered into play, which were specific to the anti-capitalist romantic milieu. Jewish national/cultural romanticism (i.e. Zionism) did not gain the support of the majority. Assimilation was too deep for Jewish intellectuals to be able to identify with a rather abstract Jewish nation in Central Europe (unlike in Eastern Europe). It is, there-fore, understandable that most of them refused all nationalism and opted instead for an internationalist, anti-capitalist roman-tic utopia, in which social and national inequalities would be completely abolished: in other words, anarchism, anarcho-syndicalism, or a romantic and libertarian interpretation of Marxism. The attractive power of this ideal was so great that it even influenced Zionists such as Buber, Hans Kohn or Gershom Scholem.

There are various reasons why, above all before 1917, libertar-ian utopia held a particular attraction: first, as we have already seen, of all socialist doctrines, libertarian utopia was the one most charged with anti-capitalist romanticism – while orthodox Marxism, then identified with social democracy, appeared as a more left-wing version of liberal/rationalist philosophy and worship of industrial civilization (Gustav Landauer's criticism of Marxism as the 'son of the steam-engine' typifies this attitude). On the other hand, the authoritarian and militarist character of the German imperial state also stimulated the libertarian anti-authoritarianism of the rebel intelligentsia, especially after 1914, when it appeared to the intelligentsia like a Moloch avid for human sacrifices. Finally, anarchism corresponded better to the intellectual's posture of being 'without social attachments', uprooted and marginal, especially in Germany where (unlike in France, Italy or Spain) the libertarian current was not an organized mass social movement.

It was the combination of all these economic, social, political and cultural conditions which made it possible – at a specific moment in history, and within a specific generation of Central European Jewish intellectuals – for the correspondence between Jewish messianism and libertarian utopia to become dynamic and to turn into a relationship of *elective affinity*. It is hard to know which of the two was the primordial or determining element: what is important is that they sustained, reinforced and stimulated each other. This was the context, then, in which a complex network of links took shape, between anti-capitalist romanticism, Jewish religious rebirth, messianism, anti-bourgeois and anti-statist cultural revolt, revolutionary utopia, anarchism and Socialism. To this socio-historical process, which began to unfold in the last quarter of the nineteenth century, must now be added the concrete political conjuncture of a revolutionary upsurge without precedent in modern European history, stretching from the Russian Revolution in 1905 to the final defeat of the German Revolution in 1923. It was not by chance that the main works displaying the *Wahlverwandtschaft* between messianism and utopia were written in this period, from Landauer's 'Die Revolution' (1907) to Lukács' *History and Class Consciousness* and the second edition of Bloch's *Geist der Utopia* [Spirit of Utopia], both published in 1923. It was not by chance, either, that the writings in which this affinity was the most intense and profound, and in which both messianism and libertarian utopia were expressed most completely and explosively, dated from the crest of the revolutionary wave: 1917–21. These were the years that saw the publication of: Buber's 'Der heilige Weg' ('The Holy Way'), the Preface to the re-issue of Landauer's *Aufruf zum Sozialismus* [Summons to Socialism], Benjamin's 'Zur Kritik der Gewalt' ('Critique of Violence'), Bloch's *Geist der Utopie* [Spirit of Utopia, first edition 1918], Lukács' 'Bolshevism as a Moral Problem', and Toller's two great plays, *Die Wandlung* [The Transfiguration] and *Masse Mensch* (*Man and the Masses*). This does not mean, of course, that the problematic did not survive after 1923, although it changed in form, character and intensity. It reappeared most notably during certain periods of catastrophe – for example, between 1940 and 1945, when Walter Benjamin wrote the *Theses on the Philosophy of History*, Martin Buber his *Pfade in Utopia* (Paths in Utopia), and Ernst Bloch the main portion of *Das Prinzip Hoffnung* [The Principle of Hope].

What remains to be explained is why this phenomenon – the emergence of a 'metaphysical-anarchist' or revolutionary-messianic movement inspired by romanticism – should have been confined almost exclusively to Central Europe.

The figure of the Jewish revolutionary had been virtually non-existent in the political and cultural arena of Western Europe. In England and the United States towards the end of the nineteenth century, Jews originating from Eastern Europe came to form a super-exploited proletariat, a breeding ground for anarchist and socialist militants. But Jews with their origins in the West were completely assimilated, both nationally and culturally, and quite conformist in social and political terms. Intellectuals stemming from this milieu identified in their whole being with the prevailing bourgeois liberalism. The roots of this were to be found in the bourgeois revolutions of sixteenth-century Holland, seventeenth-century England and post-1789 France, which had emancipated the Jews and made possible their economic, social and political integration into capitalist society. If the revolutionary Jew appeared in Central and Eastern Europe, this was principally due to the delay or failure of bourgeois revolutions – and the lagging development of capitalism – in that part of the continent, which restricted the emancipation/assimilation of Jews and maintained their pariah condition.

Romantic/revolutionary messianism never attracted the West European and American Jewish intelligentsia: on the contrary, the most important liberal rationalist polemics against utopias of religious inspiration were written by Jewish intellectuals of Anglo-Saxon cultural origins – for example, the well-known book by Norman Cohn (born in London in 1915), *The Pursuit of the Millennium. Revolutionary Millenarians and Mystical Anarchists of the Middle Ages* (London: Secker & Warburg, 1957); or that of

Jacob Talmon (former Foreign Office official), *Political Messianism. The Romantic Phase* (London: Secker & Warburg, 1960).

The Dreyfus Affair was (prior to the Second World War) the only rift in the Western system of assimilation/integration, but even this traumatic event could not shake the patriotic, bourgeois-republican faith of French Jews. However, it did make possible the emergence of an exceptional messianic/libertarian revolutionary figure: Bernard Lazare. He may be the only Western Jewish thinker who can be compared to Buber or Landauer. But he was doomed to remain isolated, rejected and misunderstood by the great majority of the French Jewish community.[26]

The situation was completely different in Eastern Europe, notably in the Russian Empire, which, prior to 1918, included Poland and the Baltic countries. Here the Jews' participation in revolutionary movements was far greater than in Central Europe, and unlike in Germany, not limited to intellectuals: an entire Jewish proletariat organized itself within the *Bund* or joined the Bolshevik or Menshevik faction of the RSDLP (Russian Social/Democratic Labour Party). This can easily be explained by the qualitatively higher degree of oppression, the different social composition of the Jewish population (with its working-class and/or impoverished mass) and the strength and violence of anti-Semitism; in short, by the much more directly pariah condition of the Jews living in the tsarist Empire. As a result, a huge and varied mass of Jewish intellectuals was present in all East European revolutionary movements, be they socialist, Marxist or anarchist, including in leadership positions as organizers, ideologists and theoreticians. As Leopold H. Haimson noted, the major role of Jews within the Russian revolutionary intelligentsia was out of all proportion to their numerical weight in the population.[27]

The most well-known were but the tip of the iceberg: Leon D. Trotsky (Bronstein); Rosa Luxemburg; Leo Jogiches; Julius Martov (Tsederbaum); Raphael Abramovich; Lev Deutsch; Pavel Axelrod; Mark Liber (Goldman); Fyodor Dan (Gurvytch); Lev Kamenev (Rosenfeld); Karl Radek (Sobelsohn); Grigory Zinoviev (Radomylsky); Yakov Sverdlov; David Ryazanov (Goldendach); Maxim Litvinov (Wallach); Adolf Joffe; Mikhail Borodin (Grusenberg); Adolf Warski; Isaac Deutscher, and so on. In addition,

of course, there were the leading figures of specifically Jew-
ish socialist organizations, such as the *Bund* and the left-wing
Zionists, and the numerous Jews originally from the East who
participated in the revolutionary workers' movement abroad;
in Germany, Rosa Luxemburg and Leo Jogiches, Parvus (Israel
Helphand), Arkadi Maslow (Isaac Chereminsky), August Kleine
(Samuel Haifiz), among others; in England (Aron Lieberman,
Lazar Goldenberg); or in the United States (Emma Goldmann,
Alexander Berkman, S. Yanofsky).

Yet all of these Jewish revolutionary ideologues, militants and
leaders, who had widely different if not conflicting political ori-
entations, and whose relationship to Judaism went from complete
and deliberate assimilation in the name of internationalism to
proud affirmation of a national/cultural Jewish identity, still had
one element in common: rejection of the Jewish religion. Their
world-view was always rationalist, atheist, secular, *Aufklärer*,
materialist. The Jewish religious tradition, the mysticism of the
cabbala, Hasidism and messianism were of no interest to them.
In their eyes, these were but obscurantist relics of the past, reactionary medieval ideologies which they had to be rid of as quickly
as possible in favour of science, Enlightenment and progress.
When a revolutionary Yiddish writer such as Moishe Kulback
wrote on messianism (with a mixture of attraction, repulsion and
nostalgia), it was mainly to show the sad role of false messiahs
like Jakob Frank, who had led their followers to catastrophe.[28]
An anarchist of Russian origins, such as Emma Goldmann, had
nothing in common with the mystical spiritualism of someone
like Landauer: in her libertarian universalism, there was no
room for Jewish particularity, and religion (Jewish or Christian)
belonged to the realm of superstition. In the best cases, as with
the *Bundist* Medem, the first visit to a synagogue 'made a deep
impression' because of the 'great beauty present in the passion
of mass feeling': the actual religious content of worship was alien
to him.[29] The passion of revolutionary Jewish intellectuals for
atheism and science is marvellously illustrated by the story
that Leo Jogiches, organizer of the first Jewish workers' circles
in Vilna, began his activities as a political educator by bringing
along a real skeleton and lecturing on anatomy.[30]

Many historians believe that, in the socialist and revolutionary
convictions of Russian Jewish intellectuals, they can discern

a secularized expression of messianism, a manifestation, in atheist and materialist form, of mental attitudes inherited from millennia of religious tradition. This hypothesis may prove to be applicable in certain cases. But for most of the Marxist or anarchist leaders mentioned above, it is implausible because their education and their familial and social milieux were so assimilated, so unreligious, that a real cultural link with the messianic heritage would be sought in vain. In any case, the writings of radical Russian-Jewish intellectuals, unlike those of many Central European Jewish revolutionaries, did not make the least reference to religion, nor did they display the least trace of a messianic/religious dimension.

How can this marked difference in world-view between the Jewish intelligentsia of German cultural origins and the Jewish intelligentsia of the tsarist Empire be explained?

Let us first note that the great majority of Jewish revolutionary intellectuals from the East came from 'enlightened', assimilated and religiously indifferent families; several were born or grew up in three cities that were the bastions of the *Haskala* in Russia: Odessa (Martov, Trotsky, Parvus); Vilna (Jogiches); Zamosc (Rosa Luxemburg). This was the movement that advocated opening the Jewish world to rationalist culture and the Enlightenment, which Moses Mendelssohn, the Jewish philosopher from Berlin, had inaugurated in the late eighteenth century. But the difference between the *Haskala* in Germany and Russia needs to be considered. As Rachel Ertel showed so well in her study on the *Shtetl*, the *Haskala* and the emancipation of the Jews 'in a Western Europe made up of nation-states, required a "denominationalization" of the Jewish religion stripped of all its national characteristics'. On the other hand, 'the East European *Haskala* had deeply national characteristics. If, in the West, the movement aspired to denominationalization, in the East it aimed at secularization.'[31]

The national content of emancipation was an outcome both of the nature of the tsarist State – a multinational, authoritarian and anti-Semitic Empire – and of the situation of the Jewish communities: a pariah condition characterized by segregation, discrimination, persecutions and pogroms; territorial concentration in ghettos and in the *Shtetl*; cultural and linguistic unity (Yiddish).

Of course, many Marxist Jewish intellectuals (unlike the *Bund* and socialist Zionists) rejected any and all national or Jewish cultural references. One need only recall Trotsky's famous response to questioning by the *Bundist* Medem at the 1903 Congress of the Russian Social Democratic Labour Party: 'I assume that you consider yourself to be either a Russian or a Jew?' 'No', replied Trotsky, 'you are wrong. I am nothing but a Social Democrat.' In any event, whether the Jewish identity was accepted or rejected, it was – at least after the terrible pogroms of 1881 – a national/cultural and not merely a religious identity. Unlike in Germany, there were very few Jews in the tsarist Empire who thought of themselves merely as 'Russian citizens of Jewish denomination'.

The atheist and secular orientation of the Eastern European revolutionary intelligentsia will be better understood if we look more closely at the religious aspect proper of the *Haskala* movement. In Germany, the *Haskala* actually did succeed in 'enlightening', modernizing, rationalizing and 'Germanizing' the Jewish religion. The movement of religious reform led by Rabbi Abraham Geiger (1810–74) and the more prudent reformist current ('the historical school') of Rabbi Zacharias Frankel (1801–75) gained hegemony in the religious institutions of the Jewish community. Even the minority neo-orthodox movement founded by Rabbi Samson Raphael Hirsch (1808–88) accepted certain reforms and values of the German secular culture.

Such was not the case in Russia where reform synagogues had few followers except in a small layer of the Jewish *haute bourgeoisie*. The iconoclastic attack of the *maskilim* ('enlightened') on the dogmas of orthodoxy only caused traditionalists to burrow into the most dogged immobility: 'Before *Haskala* . . . rabbinic Judaism had been more worldly, more tolerant, and more responsive to social change. After the *Haskala*, rabbinic Judaism became conservative, inflexible, and repressive; Hasidism, too, followed suit.'[32] While in Germany (and to a certain extent, in all of Central Europe) the Jewish religion was reformed and became more flexible and receptive to outside influences – neo-Kantian (Hermann Cohen) or neo-romantic (Buber) – in Eastern Europe, the traditional religious cultural universe remained largely intact, rigid, closed, impervious to any outside cultural input. The quietist and politically indifferentist messianism of orthodox circles (rabbinical or Hasidic) could not combine or link up with a secular utopia, which these circles rejected as a foreign body. One first had to be freed of religion, to become atheist or 'enlightened', in order to accede to the 'outside' world of revolutionary ideas. It was not surprising, therefore, that such ideas chiefly developed in Jewish concentrations furthest from all religious practices, as in Odessa, for example, which the orthodox considered a true den of sinners.

Another aspect to be taken into consideration is the immense authoritarian power of the orthodox Rabbis and Hasidic *Zadikkim* in the traditionalist communities, for which there was no equivalent in Central Europe. As a result, there was open conflict between the rebellious youth, be it *Bundist*, socialist or anarchist, and the religious establishment:

> Feeling threatened, the traditional circles often responded with open or insidious violence, trying to maintain their hold by all means, including moral pressure and intellectual terrorism. . . . The youth was completely moulded by the traditional heritage . . . but it no longer wanted to be subjected to its law, and did not accept its restrictions. Therefore, the youth violently rejected this heritage and built its own culture against it: it was its inner enemy.[33]

This was the context in which a virulent 'anti-clericalism' developed among progressive Jewish intellectuals, leaving countless evidence in the shape of polemical articles, autobiographical works and imaginative literature.

Directly confronted with the most conservative and authoritarian traditionalism, the young Jewish rebel from Russia (or Poland) could not 'romanticize' it in the way his German or Austrian counterpart could. There was not the distance that favours what Benjamin called an *auratic* perception of religion.

Isaac Deutscher was educated in a *heder* (religious school for children) in the Polish *Shtetl* Kranow. But although his family intended him to become a rabbi in the Hasidic sect of the *Zaddik* of Gere, he broke with religion as a teenager and became a leader of Polish Communism (and later the biographer of Leon Trotsky). Contrasting his attitude to religion with that of the German Jews, he described it as follows:

We knew the Talmud, we had been steeped in Hasidism. All its idealizations were for us nothing but dust thrown into our eyes. We had grown up in that Jewish past. We had the eleventh, and thirteenth and sixteenth centuries of Jewish history living next door to us and under our very roof; and we wanted to escape it to live in the twentieth century. Through all the thick gilt and varnish of romanticists like Martin Buber, we could see, and smell, the obscurantism of our archaic religion and a way of life unchanged since the middle ages. To someone of my background the fashionable longing of the Western Jew for a return to the sixteenth century, a return which is supposed to help him in recovering, or re-discovering, his Jewish cultural identity, seems unreal and Kafkaesque.[34]

This striking passage reveals in the clearest and most concise way what motivated the Eastern European revolutionary intelligentsia; it shows why a spiritualist movement, like the one spreading throughout *Mitteleuropa*, could not emerge from within its ranks.

It is a striking fact that the only Jewish socialist intellectual within the Russian Empire who was attracted by the powerful movement of religious/revolutionary rebirth that developed in Petrograd at the turn of the century around D. S. Merezhkovsky and Zinaida Gippius, Nikolai Berdyaev and S. N. Bulgakov (not to mention the 'God-builders' within the Bolshevik Party, Bogdanov and Lunacharsky) was someone who converted to orthodox Christianity: Nikolai Maksimovich Minsky (N.M. Vilenkin). A member of the Philosophical-Religious Association of Petrograd and of Gorky's socialist journal *Novaya Zhizn* [New Life], Minsky was inspired by Russian-Orthodox spirituality and seemed not to have any ties to Judaism.[35]

Were there no revolutionary Jews in Eastern Europe who were an exception to the rule – such as Bernard Lazare in Western Europe? Probably yes, but in all my research to date, I have yet to find one.[36]

4

Religious Jews Tending to Anarchism: Martin Buber, Franz Rosenzweig, Gershom Scholem, Leo Löwenthal

Within the turn-of-the-century generation of Jewish rebel romantics, the trend of religious semi-anarchism was one whose works
were dominated by the Jewish dimension, both national-cultural
and religious. This current had no common attitude to Zionism:
Rosenzweig never accepted it, Löwenthal gave it up quite soon,
and Buber and Scholem joined the movement but found themselves marginalized because of their hostility to the principle of
the State. Their religious feeling ran deep and was charged with
messianism, but it had little in common with orthodox ritual and
traditional rules. Their aim of Jewish national revival did not lead
them into political nationalism, and their conception of Judaism
was still marked by German culture. In varying degrees, they
all supported libertarian socialism as their utopian goal – a goal
close to anarchism which they linked (directly or indirectly,
explicitly or implicitly) with their messianic religious faith. With
the exception of Leo Löwenthal, they criticized Marxism as being
too centralist or too closely identified with industrial civilization.
They were sympathetic to the revolutionary movements that
shook Europe between 1917 and 1923, but they did not take an
active part in them. Their primary centre of cultural influence was
the magazine *Der Jude*, which Martin Buber edited between 1916
and 1924.

In addition to these four authors, many other intellectuals can
be considered as belonging to this current: Hans Kohn, Rudolf
Kayser, Erich Unger, to name but a few. The young Erich Fromm
of the years 1921–26 could also be added, but his published work
after 1927 falls into the opposite pole of religious atheism and
libertarian Marxism. This example demonstrates that within the
messianic/revolutionary domain it was quite possible to move

from one category to another: there were frontiers, but they were
far from being hermetically sealed.

Martin Buber was probably the most important and representative author of religious socialism within German-Jewish culture.
His rediscovery of the Hasidic legends (1906-8), and his famous
lectures on Judaism at the *Bar-Kochba* Club of Prague (1909-11),
brought about a profound renewal of modern Jewish spirituality.
His political and religious ideas left their mark on an entire
generation of Jewish intellectuals, from Prague to Vienna and
from Budapest to Berlin. Buber's image of Judaism was as
different from assimilationist liberalism (and the *Wissenschaft
des Judentums*) as it was from rabbinical orthodoxy: his was a
romantic and mystical religiosity, permeated with social critique
and a longing for community. Buber was a close friend of both
Franz Rosenzweig (with whom he collaborated on a German
translation of the Bible) and of the libertarian philosopher Gustav
Landauer (who made him the executor of his will); Buber
also played a role in the spiritual development of Gershom
Scholem and of many other young Zionists associated with the
Hapoel Hatzair movement. Few indeed were the German-speaking
Jewish thinkers of that era who were not touched, at some point
in their life, by Buber's writings.

Raised by a grandfather who spoke Hebrew and was a follower
of the *Haskala*, Buber moved away from the Jewish religion in
his youth. As a student in Vienna, Leipzig and Berlin (where he
studied under Simmel and Dilthey), he was attracted by neo-
romantic movements and by the rebirth of religious spirituality.
His first works were not on Jewish themes; they focused instead
on Viennese writers (Peter Altenberg, Hugo von Hoffmanstahl);
on Jakob Böhme (*Wiener Rundschau*, vol. v, no. 12, 1901); on
'Kultur und Zivilisation' (*Kunstwart*, vol. xiv, 1901). Buber
soon became involved in the Zionist movement, but his ideas
rapidly came into conflict with Theodor Herzl's State-centred
diplomacy and, around 1902, he withdrew from political activity
and devoted himself to the study of religion. Typically for this
entire generation, Buber was at first interested in Christian
mysticism: his doctoral thesis, which he presented in 1904,
was written on 'The History of the Problem of Individuation:
Nicholas of Cusa and Jakob Böhme'. It was not until later

that Buber took an interest in Jewish mysticism: he wrote his first book on Hasidism (*Die Geschichte des Rabbi Nachmann*) in 1906.

Buber's writings (until 1920 in particular) were permeated with references to German Romantic thought (Görres, Novalis, Hölderlin, Franz von Baader, among others). But he established particularly close ties to neo-romantic philosophy (Nietzsche) and sociology; not only because in his *Die Gesellschaft* collection he published the writings of Tönnies, Simmel and Sombart (from 1906 to 1912), but also because Buber's concept of the *interhuman* (*Zwischenmenschliche*) was directly influenced by their concerns, most notably by their longing for a *Gemeinschaft*.

In 1900, Martin Buber joined *Die neue Gemeinschaft* [The New Community], a neo-romantic circle in Berlin where he met Gustav Landauer. He gave a lecture before the circle entitled 'Alte und neue Gemeinschaft' [The New and the Old Community], which, though unpublished until ten years after his death, contained the seeds of several of the key ideas that guided him throughout his life. Right from this first lecture, Buber's originality is evident as one of the great renewers of communitarian thought in the twentieth century. In Buber's opinion, it was neither possible nor desirable to return to the traditional community. Rather, he spoke of the struggle for a new community, not *pre-social* (like the one described by Tönnies) but *post-social*. The most crucial difference between the old and the new community organization was that the former was based upon blood relations (*Blutverwandtschaft*), while the latter was the outcome of *elective affinities* (*Wahlverwandtschaft*) – in other words, it expressed a free choice. This community was not to be bound by religious, regional or national borders: to use Gustav Landauer's cosmopolitan and mystical formulation, which Buber quoted, the community leaned towards 'the oldest and most universal community: that of the human species and the cosmos'. In spite of the fact that he rejected all 'retrogressive' utopias, neo-romantic references to the traditional community remained alive in Buber's mind: first, in his dream of deserting 'the swarming of the cities' in order to build the new world on the 'powerful and virginal soil' of the countryside, closer to nature and the land; and second, in the idea that the new community meant the return (*Wiederkehren*), albeit in a different form and on a higher level, of 'the vital unity

of primeval man' (*Lebenseinheit des Urmenschen*) – shattered and
torn by the serfdom of modern 'society' (*Gesellschaft*).[1]

Buber took up and developed these themes again in 'Gemeinschaft', an article published in 1919. Like Tönnies, to whom he
directly referred, Buber contrasted the organic, natural community of the past with the modern, artificial and mechanical
Gesellschaft. However, he did not advocate a restoration of the
past: 'Certainly we cannot turn back the clock on our mechanized
society, but we can go beyond, towards a new organicity (*einer
neuen Organik*).' By that he meant a community that resulted not
from primal growth but rather from conscious action (*bewussten
Wirkens*) to establish the principle of community; the goal of
such action would be to construct a socialist society through
an alliance of autonomous communes (*Gemeinden*).[2] Buber no
longer believed that a return to the land was an alternative to
modern industrial cities; in a lecture he gave in Zurich in 1923,
he said:

> We cannot leave the city to take refuge in the village. The
> village is still close to the primitive community. The city is
> the form that corresponds to differentiation. We can no longer
> turn back the clock on the city, we must overcome (*überwinden*)
> the city itself.

The solution would be a third form of communal life, as distinct
from the rural village as it was from the big city, which could
arise from a new organization of labour.[3]

It was in this context that Buber rediscovered the tradition of
Hasidism as a Jewish mystical current equivalent to a Böhme
or a Meister Eckhart, and as the religious manifestation of an
organic community, united and welded by its spirituality and
culture. As he wrote several years later, what gave Hasidism
its particularity and its grandeur was not a doctrine but an
attitude of life (*Lebenshaltung*), a mode of behaviour, that was
'community-forming' (*gemeindebildend*) in its very essence.[4]

According to Gershom Scholem, Buber's interpretation of
Hasidism was inspired by his 'religious anarchism' – that is,
by his refusal to grant a place to restrictive commandments
in the world of the living relationship between the I and the
Thou.[5] In fact, in his famous *Ich und Du* (1923), Buber used the
paradigm of dialogue and encounter (*Begegnung*) to define the

true relationship between man and man, and between man and God – a model as deeply subversive of the rigid and ritualistic forms of institutional religion (which Hasidism questioned) as it was of political and state institutions.

The success of Buber's books on the masters of Hasidism (Baal Schem and Rabbi Nachmann) was due to the fact that they expressed the subterranean current of religious rebirth flowing within the Jewish intelligentsia of romantic cultural origins. Like himself, the members of that intelligentsia re-discovered, in the eighteenth-century Jewish-Polish legends, something ancient (*Uraltes*) and original (*Urkünftiges*), a lost past (*Verlorenes*), an object of longing (*Ersehntes*).[6] The interpretation of Judaism as an essentially rationalist religion was common to the *Wissenschaft des Judentums*, Jewish liberalism and academic sociology (Max Weber, Sombart). For example, according to Sombart, 'Jewish mysticism along the lines of Jakob Böhme is very hard for us to imagine'; as for the cabbala, there was

> nothing more foreign to romanticism than that purely dis-
> cursive way of conceiving and understanding the world;
> romanticism assumes, in fact, the fusion of man with the
> world, with nature, and with his fellow man, all things
> that the Jew, the extreme intellectual, is totally incapable of
> doing.[7]

By presenting a mystical romantic reading of the Jewish religion in his works, Buber broke this consensus and created a new image of Judaism, with which the rebellious generation at odds with bourgeois liberalism could identify.

One of the most significant aspects of Buber's neo-romantic interpretation was the importance he attached to messianism. In the lectures he gave in Prague, Buber proclaimed that messianism was 'Judaism's most profoundly original idea'. It meant the yearning for 'an absolute future that transcends all reality of past and present as the true and perfect life', and the coming of the 'world of unity', in which the separation between good and evil would be overcome, as sin would forever be destroyed.[8] As Gershom Scholem had showed so well, the theme of the messianic era as a world delivered from evil was potentially one of the religious foundations of anarchist utopia: the absence of evil makes restriction, coercion and sanctions superfluous. In

Buber's mind, the coming of the Messiah would take place not in the other world but in the world here below: it would not be a historical event, but it was 'being prepared in history'. Seen from a utopian-restorative perspective, the arrival of the Messiah was a mystery 'in which the past and future, the end of time and history are linked. . . . It takes the form of the absolute past and carries the seed of the absolute future.'[9]

It was from a romantic/messianic vision of history that Buber (like Rosenzweig, Landauer and Benjamin) questioned the concept of evolution, progress or improvement (*Verbesserung*): 'For by "renewal", I do not in any way mean something gradual, a sum total of minor changes. I mean something sudden and immense (*Ungeheures*) by no means a continuation or an improvement, but a return and transformation.' Rather than hope for ordinary progress (*Fortschritt*), one should 'desire the impossible' (*das Unmögliche*). Buber found the paradigm for this complete renewal in the Jewish messianic tradition: 'The last part of Isaiah has God say: "I create new heavens and a new earth." (Isaiah 65:17). . . This was not a metaphor but a direct experience.'[10]

Martin Buber, more than any other modern religious Jewish thinker, placed the active participation of men in redemption – as God's partners – at the heart of his idea of messianism: 'The central Jewish *Theologumenon*, which remains unformulated and undogmatic, but which forms the background and cohesion of all doctrine and prophecy, is the belief that human action will actively participate in the task of world redemption.'[11] The message of Hasidism, according to Buber, was that man was not condemned to waiting and contemplation: redemption was his to act upon, by collecting and releasing the sparks of holy light dispersed throughout the world.[12] Does this mean that God is not omnipotent – that He *cannot* save the world without man's help? No, Buber responds, it means only that He does not *will* redemption without the participation of man: generations of men had been granted a 'collaborative force' (*mitwirkende Kraft*), an active messianic force (*messianische Kraft*).[13]

It was for this reason that Buber contrasted more and more categorically, messianic prophetism (Jewish eschatology proper) and Apocalyptics (an eschatological conception that originated in Iran): the former accorded the preparation of redemption to

humanity, to the decision-making power of each human being
so called upon; while the latter conceived redemption as an
immutable future, predetermined in the smallest detail, which
used human beings only as instruments.[14] For Buber this active
messianic hope, turned towards an open eschatological future,
set Jewish religious thought apart from Christianity. In a letter
he wrote in 1926, Buber formulated the thesis in terms that are
not too dissimilar from Ernst Bloch's utopia of Not-yet Being:

> According to my belief, the Messiah did not come at a determi-
> nate point in history: his arrival can only be the end of history.
> According to my belief, world redemption did not take place
> nineteen centuries ago; we are living in an unsaved (*unerlösten*)
> world, and we are waiting for redemption, in which we have
> been called upon to participate in a most unfathomable way.
> Israel is the human community that bears this purely messi-
> anic expectation . . . this belief in the still-to-be-accomplished
> and must-be-accomplished Being (*Noch-nicht-geschehn-sein und
> Geschehn-sollen*) of world redemption.[15]

How did Buber articulate his messianic faith with his socialist/lib-
ertarian utopia? In 1914 he, like many German-Jewish intellectuals, was carried away by the 'patriotic' drive to war; but little
by little, under the influence of events and the harsh criticisms of
his friend, Gustav Landauer, he changed his position.

It was through a polemic in 1916–1917 with Hermann Cohen
– the champion of 'state consciousness' (*Staatsbewusstsein*) – that
Buber crystallized his own political-religious views. After having
supported imperialist Germany at the beginning of the First
World War (as Cohen himself had done), Buber now rejected the
cult of German nation-statehood advocated by the neo-Kantian
philosopher from Marburg: 'Humanity – and to say that, Profes-
sor Cohen, is now more than ever the duty of every man living in
God – is greater than the state.' Buber summed up his differences
in a biting sentence: 'Cohen, . . . whether he is aware of it or not,
wants the State to subjugate the Spirit; as for me, I want the Spirit
to subjugate the State.' This subjugation would be completed in
the messianic era, which would ultimately make it possible for
a higher form of society to supersede the state dialectically: the
separation between the people (principle of creativity) and the
state (principle of order) would be maintained only 'until the

Kingdom, the *Malkhut Shamayim*, is established on earth; until, through a messianic form of the human world, creativity and order, people and State, merge in a new unity, in the *Gemeinschaft* of salvation'.[16]

As the European revolution gathered momentum between 1917 and 1920, Buber clarified, radicalized and developed his vision. In 'Die Revolution und Wir', an article published in 1919 in his magazine *Der Jude*, he insisted on the necessity for Jews to contribute to the revolution of Mankind – that is, to the rebirth of society through a spirit of community. He voiced his solidarity with the revolutionary tide that was rising in Central Europe: 'Situated in its camp . . . not as profiteers but as comrades in the struggle, we salute the revolution.'[17] More than ever, there was an anti-State dimension in Buber's writings: in the previously mentioned article 'Gemeinschaft', written in 1919, he appealed to Kropotkin, Tolstoy and Landauer in condemning State tyranny, that 'homonculus which drinks blood from the veins of communities', that clockwork puppet which seeks to replace organic life.[18] In a homage to Gustav Landauer, published shortly after his assassination in April 1919, Buber wrote: 'He rejected mechanical, centralist pseudo-socialism, because he longed for a communitarian, organic and federalist socialism.'[19] From this perspective, Buber criticized Bolshevism and instead showed a sympathy for the neo-romantic 'guild socialism' developing in England at that time, and for the *kibbutzim* that were starting to be formed in Palestine.[20]

In a major essay published in 1919, 'Der heilige Weg' ('The Holy Way'), which he dedicated to the memory of Landauer, the central axis was the unity between messianism and communitarian utopia. In Buber's mind, community with God and community among human beings were inseparable from each other, so that 'its [Judaism's] waiting for the Messiah is a wait in expectation of the true community'. Their achievement would depend upon men:

> So long as the Kingdom of God has not come, Judaism will not recognize any man as the true Messiah, yet it will never cease to expect redemption to come from man, for it is man's task to lay the foundation for (*begründen*) God's power on earth.

He called this task active messianism, which did not wait passively for the arrival of the Messiah but sought to 'prepare the world to be God's kingdom'. Buber did not recognize Jesus as the Messiah, but regarded him as a true Jewish prophet for whom the future Kingdom of God was identical to 'the perfection of men's life together'; in other words, 'the true community, and as such, God's immediate realm, His *basileia*, His earthly kingdom. . . . The Kingdom of God is the community to come in which all those who hunger and thirst for righteousness will be satisfied.'[21] In a lecture that he gave in Frankfurt in 1924 (minutes of which can be found at the Buber Archives in Jerusalem), Buber set out in a particularly striking way this relationship between community and messianism: '*Gemeinschaft* is a messianic, non-historical category. To the extent that it is historical, its messianic character shows through.' Analysing the Russian Revolution, he argued that the soviets were true communes (*Gemeinden*) on which 'revolutionary community-being' should have been constructed; but the course of events had led to their weakening, with the centralizing tendency of the state gaining as a result. State action, even if revolutionary, cannot bring messianic redemption (*Erlösung*); only the community is the genuine precursor and annunciator of the Kingdom of God, whose essence is 'the fulfilment of creation in a *Gemeinschaft*'.[22]

Buber's concept of the Kingdom of God is also charged with libertarian meaning. In the major work he wrote in 1932, *Königtum Gottes* [The Kingdom of God], he spoke like Scholem and Benjamin of anarchist theocracy: biblical theocracy, as the direct power of God, rejected all human domination and found its spiritual foundation in anarchism.[23] Thus, Buber's political philosophy can be defined (in the words of a recent essay by Avraham Yassour) as 'a communitarian religious socialism tinged with anarchism'.[24] His ideas were very close to those of Gustav Landauer, although, unlike his friend, he was not actively involved in revolutionary politics. He outlined his goal of libertarian socialism in various articles between 1917 and 1923, and later, more systematically, in *Paths in Utopia* (1945).

In this latter work, Buber presented a highly original formulation of the communitarian paradigm, reinterpreting the whole of the socialist tradition – utopian (Fourier, Saint-Simon, Owen) as well as anarchist (Proudhon, Kropotkin, Landauer) and Marxist

(Marx, Engels, Lenin) – and assessing the various attempts to put it into practice, from isolated commune experiments through the Russian Revolution and the soviets to the 'exemplary non-failure' of the *kibbutzim*.

Buber's point of departure was a radical critique of the modern capitalist State, which had 'broken the structure of society'. The new, advanced capitalist centralism succeeded in what the former despotic state had failed to accomplish: the atomization of society. Capital wanted to have nothing but individuals facing it, and the modern state was placing itself in the service of capital by gradually stripping group life of its autonomy. Medieval society had been richly structured, with an interlocking network of local and work communities. But the essence of the community was 'gradually emptied by the constraints of the capitalist economy and state', which disintegrated organic forms and atomized individuals. However, 'we cannot, nor do we want to, return to primitive agrarian communism or to the corporate state of the Christian Middle Ages'. Our task is to build the communitarian socialism of the future 'with the materials we have today, whatever their resistance'.[25]

According to Buber, socialist utopia seeks above all to replace the state with society. But this requires that society should no longer be, as it is today, an aggregate of individuals without any internal cohesion between them, 'because such an aggregate could be maintained again only through a "political" principle, a principle of domination and coercion'. The true society capable of replacing the state must be rich – that is, it must be structured by the free association of communities. The advent of such a society implies not only 'external' change – the elimination of capital and the State as the economic and political obstacles to the realization of socialism – but also an 'internal' transformation of social life through the communitarian restructuring of human relations. The new organic whole, based on regeneration of the 'cells' of the social fabric, will be the rebirth (not the return) of the organic commune, under the form of a decentralized federation of small communities.[26] This concept of socialism presents obvious affinities with anarchist thinking, but Buber also discovered it in certain writings of Marx – on the Paris Commune and on the Russian rural communes – and even of Lenin (on the soviets).

As Emmanuel Levinas correctly notes in his introduction to

the French edition of *Paths in Utopia*, Buber's utopian socialism is, in the final analysis, based upon his philosophical anthropology: man's future relationship with his fellow human beings is defined according to the model of the 'I and Thou', which makes it possible to conceive a collectivity without 'powers'.[27]

In spite of its secular and realistic form, Buber's libertarian utopia is no less charged with messianic energy. His introduction to the book draws a distinction between two forms of nostalgia for justice: messianic eschatology, as the image of a perfect time, the culmination of creation; and utopia, as the image of a perfect space, a living-together based on justice. For utopia, everything is subject to man's conscious will; for eschatology – insofar as it is prophetic and not apocalyptic – man plays an active role in redemption: a convergence between the two is, therefore, possible. The age of the Enlightenment and modern culture gradually stripped religious eschatology of its influence, but it did not disappear altogether: 'The whole force of discarded messianism is now making its way into the "utopian" social system.' Imbued with a hidden eschatological spirit, true utopia could gain a prophetic dimension, a 'character of proclamation and appeal'.[28]

As a religious Jew, Buber was radically opposed to the orthodox rabbinical establishment and invoked Jesus or Spinoza as much as he did Jeremiah. His source of inspiration was what he called subterranean Judaism (to set it apart from official Judaism): the prophetic, the Essenic-early Christian, and the cabbalist-Hasidic.[29] As a Zionist, Buber was from the beginning critical of the politics of the movement's leadership, and after his arrival in Palestine in 1938 he became one of the main organizers of *Ihud* (Union), a Jewish-Arab fraternization movement which advocated the establishment of a bi-national state in Palestine. As a cultural nationalist, Buber always maintained a humanistic-universal utopian goal. In an (unpublished) lecture from April 1925, he said of the messianic prophecy of the Old Testament: 'Its aim is not emancipation of a people, but the redemption of the world; the emancipation of a people is but a sign and a pathway to the emancipation of the world.'[30] Finally, while being inspired by mysticism and messianism, Buber still sought to implement his spiritual ideal on earth, within the concrete life of society.

Franz Rosenzweig, founder of the Frankfurt-based *Freies Jüdisches Lehrhaus* (Free House for Jewish Studies) – where Martin Buber, Gershom Scholem, Erich Fromm, Ernst Simon and Leo Löwenthal all taught during the 1920s – was the author of one of the most important modern attempts at a philosophical renewal of Jewish theology: *Der Stern der Erlösung* (*The Star of Redemption*), which was first published in 1921. The roots of this book are undeniably romantic, as Günther Henning so accurately perceived: 'Rosenzweig, more than any other, translated the objectives of romanticism into a systematic philosophy of religion.'[31] Paul Honigsheim mentioned Rosenzweig and his cousin Hans Ehrenberg (a Jew who converted to Protestantism) – together with Lukács and Bloch – as typical examples of the neo-romantic, anti-bourgeois German intelligentsia craving for religion.[32] Born into a culturally assimilated milieu, Rosenzweig began by questioning the world-view of the *Aufklärung*. At first, his religious aspirations made him consider following the example of his cousin and converting to Christianity (1909–13); ultimately, he turned to Judaism, but his hesitation between the Synagogue and the Church gives clear testimony to the fact that his spiritual itinerary was linked to the more general movement of religious restoration within the German culture of the time.

Before the war, Rosenzweig had written a work on Hegel and the state, under the direction of Friedrich Meinecke. The First World War brought on a deep crisis in Rosenzweig, and he broke completely with rationalist philosophy, historicism and Hegelianism.[33] It was in the trenches of the Balkan front that he began to write *Der Stern der Erlösung* (*The Star of Redemption*), which was completed in 1919.

In this work, which drew its inspiration as much from Schelling's theory of world ages as from the mysticism of the cabbala, Rosenzweig contrasted the temporality of nations and states with the messianic temporality of Judaism. Rejecting 'the specifically modern concept of "progress" in history' – that is, the idea of 'eternal' progress – he sought to replace it with the Jewish idea that 'each moment must be ready to inherit the fullness of eternity'. (This phrase calls almost literally to mind Benjamin's notion that, for Jews, 'each second was the narrow door through which the Messiah could enter' (the 1940 *Theses on the Philosophy of History*). For messianic temporality, the ideal goal 'could and should be reached, perhaps in the next moment, or even this very moment'. According to Rosenzweig's view of the religious concept of time,

> the believer in the Kingdom [of God] uses the term "progress" only in order to employ the language of his time; in reality he means the Kingdom. This is the veritable *shibboleth* that distinguishes him from the authentic devotee of progress: does he or does he not resist the prospect and duty of anticipating the "goal" at the very next moment? . . . Without this anticipation and the inner compulsion for it, without this "wish to bring about the Messiah before his time" and the temptation to "coerce the Kingdom of God into being", . . . the future is no future . . . but only a past distended endlessly and projected forward. For without such anticipation, the moment is not eternal; it is something that drags itself everlastingly along the long, long trail of time.[34]

It was over this issue that Rosenzweig clashed with his teacher, the Jewish neo-Kantian Hermann Cohen, questioning his Enlightenment belief in uninterrupted ('eternal') progress and his adherence to German nationalism. In a violent altercation, Rosenzweig accused Cohen of having 'betrayed the messianic idea'.[35] In a text that he wrote in 1927 on Jehuda Halevi, Rosenzweig emphasized that 'the hope in the coming of the Messiah' was the aspiration 'through which and for which Judaism lives'; he viewed the coming of the messianic era as a break in historical continuity, 'a complete change, the complete change . . . that would put an end to the hell of world history'.[36] His correspondence at the time gives us some further clues about his vision of the messianic future: it was to be not a celestial but an earthly (*irdischen*) coming of the New Jerusalem, which would bring eternal peace between peoples through its complete – and from today's perspective, even miraculous – recasting (*Umschaffung*) of human nature.[37]

The few strictly political works that Rosenzweig wrote reveal a passionately romantic, anti-capitalist world-view. For example, in an article from 1919, he sees in capitalism 'as cursed a system as slavery', which had to be done away with in order to return to 'the artisan and his golden land'. The path to freedom was therefore a 'relinquishing of the free and unrestricted market and a return to a production linked to and ordered in advance by a client'.[38] His anti-capitalism went hand in hand with a profound hostility to the State. In *The Star of Redemption*, he wrote that coercion and not law constituted the true face of the State; moreover, he insisted on the essential opposition between the Jewish people, which is in itself eternal, and the false eternity of the State; it followed that 'the true eternity of the eternal people must always be alien and vexing to the state'.[39] Commenting on these and similar reflections, some researchers speak of Franz Rosenzweig's 'anarchism'.[40]

What is most interesting is that the author of *Der Stern der Erlösung explicitly* links the emancipatory revolution to the coming of the Messiah, in terms that are surprisingly reminiscent of Walter Benjamin's 'theology of the revolution':

> After all, it is no coincidence that the demands of the Kingdom of God begin only now to be genuinely transformed into temporal demands. The great deeds of liberation, as little as they constitute in themselves the Kingdom of God, nevertheless are the indispensable preconditions of its advent. Liberty, equality, and fraternity, the canons of faith, now become the slogans of the age; in blood and tears, in hatred and zeal they fight their way into the apathetic world in unending battles.[41]

According to Günther Henning, this passage, entitled 'Revolution', refers to the Revolution of 1917:

> Rosenzweig interpreted the Bolshevik revolution in Russia, in the light of Dostoevsky's hopes, as an upheaval realizing the ultimate teachings of Christianity; consequently, he attributed to this revolution a redemptive meaning that was linked to the coming of the messianic kingdom.[42]

This hypothesis remains to be proven. Rosenzweig did write that 'a renewal of the forces of faith and love accrued to . . . the Russia of Alyosha Karamazov',[43] but it is not clear that he is referring to the Russian Revolution. In any event, revolutionary concerns were very marginal in Rosenzweig's work, which was primarily devoted to philosophy and religion. His writings are significant mainly for their probable influence on Walter Benjamin, and because of their analogy with the works of other contemporary Jewish thinkers.

Unlike Rosenzweig, Gershom (Gerhard) Scholem was not a theologian but a historian. His works were not only an unrivalled monument of modern historiography; they also shed new light on the Jewish religious tradition by restoring that messianic and apocalyptic dimension which had been conjured away by the narrow rationalist interpretation characteristic of the *Wissenschaft des Judentums* (Graetz, Zunz, Steinschneider) and of German sociology. Max Weber and Werner Sombart saw only rationalist calculation in Jewish spirituality: Scholem brought to the fore the subterranean mystical, heretical, eschatological and anarchist religious movements in the history of Judaism.

Born into an assimilated Jewish middle-class family in Berlin, Scholem was initially brought up on German culture. In his youth, Romantic or neo-romantic writers were among his favourites: Jean Paul, Novalis, Eduard Mörike, Stefan George, Paul Scheerbart. According to David Biale (author of the first work on Scholem's thought),

> like many other Germans in the 1920s, Scholem and Buber found in a certain strain in German Romanticism a unique *Weltanschauung* which inspired their own thinking. . . . In philosophy as in historiography, Scholem's sympathy for a particular strand of German Romanticism played a crucial role in his intellectual makeup.[44]

It is in fact quite significant that the first book on the cabbala that Scholem studied – and it had a major impact on him – was the work by the German Christian and Romantic theosophist, Franz Joseph Molitor, *Philosophie der Geschichte oder über die Tradition* [Philosophy of History, or On Tradition].[45] In an interview that he granted me, Scholem remembered having read with much interest Novalis's *Fragmente* in 1915, one of the most characteristic works of the Romantic world-view at its peak. Nevertheless, he thought that the role of German sources in his thinking should not be exaggerated, for his main inspiration as a young man came from Hebrew texts, beginning with the Bible, the Talmud and the Midrash, which were the first books he read. In fact, he soon revolted against his family's assimilationist ideology (his father expelled him from home during the First World War because of his 'anti-patriotic' attitude!); and he resolutely turned to the sources of Judaism, to the search for the 'lost tradition of my social circle, which attracted me with a great magic'.[46]

This search led him – initially under the influence of Martin Buber – to study Jewish mysticism, and then to join Zionism.[47] Scholem's (non-orthodox) religious attitude was close to Buber's, but his Zionism was more radical: he passionately rejected the Judeo-Germanic cultural synthesis, and this made him drift away both from Buber (notably because of the latter's support for Germany in 1914) and from Franz Rosenzweig, with whom he had a stormy discussion in 1922 over this issue.[48] However, jealous affirmation of his Jewish identity did not lead him to nationalism in the political sense: after his departure for Palestine, he joined (as Buber did later) the *Brit Shalom* (Alliance for Peace), a Zionist-pacifist movement for Jewish-Arab fraternization that was opposed to 'political', State-centred Zionism. During the 1920s, he came out several times for Jewish recognition of the national aspirations of the Arab population in Palestine and its right to self-determination. In an article published in 1931 in *Sheifotenu* [Our Aspirations], the magazine of the *Brit Shalom*, he wrote: 'The Zionist movement has not yet freed itself from the reactionary imperialist image given to it not only by the Revisionists but also by all those who refuse to consider the real situation of our movement in the awakening East.'[49]

Scholem's great originality probably lay in his discovery, or rather re-discovery, of an almost completely forgotten realm within the Jewish religious tradition. This realm, which was dismissed as obscurantist by the nineteenth-century *Wissenschaft des Judentums* [Science of Judaism], was the one of mystical doctrines, from the cabbala to the heretical messianism of Sabbatai Sevi. Scholem, like Buber, was initially attracted by the magical, irrational and 'anti-bourgeois' aspect of Jewish mysticism. In the first piece he wrote on the cabbala in 1921, he referred to the Jewish tradition as 'a giant . . . an un-bourgeois (*unbürgerlich*) and explosive being'.[50] However, in a second phase that superseded the first without cancelling it, Scholem parted with Buber and became resolutely historicist in his thinking. Now it was in history that he, like a number of German romantics, found the appropriate cultural response to the cold, abstract rationalism of the bourgeois world.[51] It was typical of this new position that he defined history as *religio*, in the etymological sense of *link* (to the past).[52]

Scholem's studies of cabbalistic sources began around 1915, and on his first contact with the Hebrew texts, he was deeply attracted by the eschatological vision that permeated them. At that time, he wrote numerous speculative texts on messianism – of which he would later say that he was very glad they were never published![53] In his article from 1921 on the cabbala, Scholem expressed an interest in the prophetic conception that 'messianic humanity will speak in hymns' (a theme that will be found also in Benjamin's writings on language). Scholem, at least implicitly, drew a contrast between messianic and historical temporality when he argued that the verdict on the positive or negative value of tradition 'does not rest with world history but with the World Tribunal' – in other words, the Last Judgement – a phrase that directly targeted Hegelian historicism and its conflation of the two.[54]

In 1923, shortly before he left for Palestine, Scholem gave a series of lectures in Frankfurt on the Book of Daniel, the first apocalypse of Jewish religious literature; among those in his audience were Erich Fromm, Ernst Simon (religious socialist, philosopher, and friend of Martin Buber) and Nahum Glatzer (the future biographer of Franz Rosenzweig).[55]

The centre of gravity for most of Scholem's works on the cabbala in the 1920s and early 1930s was its messianic/apocalyptic dimension. One of his first writings in Hebrew (in 1925), dedicated to the fifteenth- to sixteenth-century cabbalist Abraham Ben Eliezer Halevi, is quite rare in that it openly displays the intensity of his personal rapport with the ethos of his research topic. He refers to the *Mashre Kitrin*, the book of apocalyptic prophecies that Halevi wrote in 1508, as a work without equal in cabbalistic literature

> because of the force of its language and the way it stirs feelings. Its long introduction, written in the tongue of the *Zohar*, truly touched the soul of this reader; neither before nor after have I seen pages as beautiful in this language. It announced the coming of the Just Redeemer (*Ha-Goël Tzedek*): after the fall of Constantinople and the expulsion of the Jews in Spain came the arrival of The Time of the End (*Et Ketz*).[56]

Three years later, in the *Encyclopaedia Judaica* of Berlin, Scholem
wrote a shorter article showing how, after the tragedy of the
Spanish Jews, Halevi interpreted the Bible, the Talmud, the *Zohar*
and the Book of Daniel from a new perspective; foreseeing the
coming of the Messiah during the year 1530–1, Halevi contributed
to the rapid development of the messianic movement around
Solomon Molcho.

Other articles in the *Encyclopaedia Judaica* testify to Scholem's
interest in cabbalistic messianism – for example, the piece on
Abraham Ben Samuel Abulafia, the eighteenth-century Spanish
cabbalist who tried to convert Pope Nicholas III to Judaism and
was condemned to burn at the stake; he owed the sparing of
his life only to the pontiff's sudden death. After that incident,
Abulafia announced that the messianic era was imminent and
stirred considerable emotion among the Jews of Sicily.[57]

Around the same time (1928), Scholem published his first article on seventeenth-century heretical messianism, dealing with the
theology of Sabbatianism in the writings of Abraham Cardozo.[58]
The first comprehensive summary of Scholem's interpretation of
cabbalistic messianism is also found in the *Encyclopaedia* (vol.
9, 1932): namely, his remarkable article, 'Kabbala'. According
to Scholem, original sin and the means for restitution of the
fallen creature were at the centre of cabbalist anthropology.
This restitution – *Tikkun* in Hebrew – implies the collapse of
the forces of evil and a catastrophic end to historical order, which
are nothing but the reverse side of messianic redemption. The
re-establishment of cosmic order foreseen by divine providence
is at the same time the Redemption, and the 'World of the *Tikkun*'
is also the messianic Kingdom. Adam's original sin can be erased
only through messianic Redemption, in which things will return
to their initial place – *apokatastasis* is the Church's equivalent
theological concept, literally taken from the cabbala (*Ha-Shavat
Kol ha-Dvarim le-Havaiatam*). Thus, the *Tikkun* is both restitution of
an original state and the establishment of an entirely new world
(*Olam ha-Tikkun*).[59]

It was much later, during the 1950s, that Scholem systematized
his theory of Jewish messianism as a restorative/utopian doctrine
(notably in his famous essay from 1959, 'Toward an Understanding of the Messianic Idea in Judaism'), but the roots of his analysis
go back to his writings of the 1920s and 1930s. In fact, this theme

runs through all of Scholem's writings, and his position was not
merely that of an erudite historian: one need but read his works
to perceive the researcher's *sym-pathy* (in the Greek etymology of
the word) with his subject.

In Scholem's opinion, the messianic utopia *par excellence* was
not Zionism, but rather anarchism. An ardent Zionist, Scholem
nevertheless categorically rejected all links between messianism
and Zionism. Thus in 1929, in a polemical article defending
Brit Shalom, he wrote: 'The Zionist ideal is one thing, and the
messianic ideal is another; the two do not come into contact
with one another except in the pompous phraseology of mass
meetings.'[60] Scholem's interest in anarchist ideas dated back to
his youth: starting in 1914–15, he read Nettlau's biography of
Bakunin, and the writings of Kropotkin, Proudhon and Elisée
Reclus. However, Gustav Landauer's works – *Die Revolution* and
Aufruf zum Sozialismus [Summons to Socialism] – were especially
fascinating to him, and he tried to communicate this feeling to his
friend Walter Benjamin.[61] Scholem met with Landauer between
1915 and 1916, when the anarchist philosopher was lecturing to
Zionist circles in Berlin; the subject of their conversations was
their common opposition to the war and their criticism of Martin
Buber's positions on it.[62]

In January 1918, Scholem's hostility to the war earned him a
letter from Ernst Toller, inviting him to join an association of
pacifist students that Toller was trying to organize at the time.[63]
Scholem, however, did not want to become involved in German
political life; his eyes were turned toward Palestine, where certain
movements linked to the *kibbutzim* espoused a doctrine with 'an
anarchist element'. In this connection, Scholem sympathetically
mentioned an article published in Austria in 1921 by Meir Yaari,
leader of the Zionist youth movement, *Hashomer Hatzair* (the
Young Guard) – influenced by Buber and Landauer at the time
– which defined its social ideal as 'a free association of anarchist
communities'.[64]

In an interview granted in 1975, Scholem remembered that
at that time he was 'on the crest of a wave of moral-religious
awakening. . . . My sympathy for anarchism was also moral.
I believed that organizing society in absolute freedom was
a divine mandate.'[65] But, beyond this youthful enthusiasm,
libertarian anti-state ideas remained a permanent part of his

66 Redemption and Utopia

thought, always in intimate rapport with religion. Even in 1971, he scandalized Israeli teachers by saying in conversation with them: 'I am a religious anarchist'. He went so far as to suggest that in the State of Israel, the prophet Jeremiah 'would end up in prison', both because prophetism tended to conflict with patriotic conformity and, on a still more fundamental level, because '"state" and "prophecy" do not mix'.[66] And in the 1975 interview, he maintained that 'the only social theory that makes sense – religious sense, too – is anarchism'. Scholem also thought that it was an impossible utopia, practically speaking at least: 'It doesn't stand a chance because it doesn't take the human being into consideration: it is based on an extremely optimistic assessment of the human spirit; it has a messianic dimension.'[67] Thus, the purely historical impossibility of achieving libertarian utopia appeared as one of the foundations of its spiritual affinity with messianism.

Of course, Gershom Scholem was neither a theologian nor a political philosopher; it was as a historian that he wove the web of his reflections. And as a historian, he discovered both the anarchist dimension of Jewish (religious) messianism and the messianic (secularized or 'theological') dimension in the revolutionary libertarian utopias of our time.[68] A typical example of the first dimension – evidently the more important in his work – is his study of the evolution of eighteenth-century Sabbatian heretical messianism, led by the new Messiah, Jakob Frank. Analysing the strange religious doctrine of 'Frankism', Scholem wrote:

> The elimination of all laws and standards was the vision of nihilist redemption . . . which finds no other expression than in rituals that bring out the force of the negative and the destructive. Bakunin, the father of anarchism, coined the phrase: The force of destruction is a creative force. One hundred years earlier, Frank had placed the redemptive power of destruction at the centre of his Utopia.[69]

It was probably as a comment on this and other no less striking passages in Scholem's historical writings that his biographer, David Biale, felt he could define his way of thinking as 'demonic anarchism' – in the Goethian sense of the word *dämonisch* – which 'conceives demonic irrationalism as a creative force: destruction is required for future construction'.[70]

The significance of this theme cannot be limited to the history of religions: in the last analysis, it was also Scholem's own vision of the world. True, the anarchist tendency remained underground in Scholem's works; it rarely appeared as a social philosophy that he embraced as such (except in the autobiographical writings and interviews of his final years). But anarchism was probably one of the spiritual sources for his entire approach to religious phenomena and, in particular, for his interest in 'anarchist' heretical-messianic movements of the seventeenth and eighteenth centuries (Sabbatai Sevi, Jakob Frank). Anarchism was also one of the roots of his deep, life-long affinity with Walter Benjamin, whose *oeuvre* was similarly permeated by anarchist and messianic currents, above all in the theological and linguistic writings of his youth and in the 1940 *Theses on the Philosophy of History*.

In other words: Scholem the historian cannot be separated from Scholem the religious anarchist. This does not mean, as some of his critics claim, that his historical writing was not objective. According to David Biale, 'it is hard to avoid the impression that Scholem has tried to find a precursor to his own anarchistic theology in Sabbatian antinomianism'.[71] But in my view, it would be more accurate to say that Scholem's anarchist conceptions attracted him to the Sabbatian phenomenon, and to certain of its 'libertarian' aspects, in particular.

Leo Löwenthal is somewhat of an exception in this set of authors: he is the only one who, from an early age, was attracted to Marxism and had ties with the German workers' movement. What linked him to the other intellectuals in this group during the period from 1919 to 1926 was the deeply and explicitly religious (messianic) dimension of his Jewish identity. As a young man, he was friendly with Siegfried Kracauer, Ernst Simon and Erich Fromm, and like them he participated in the circle centred around the charismatic personality of Rabbi Nobel in Frankfurt, as well as in Rosenzweig's *Freies Jüdisches Lehrhaus*.

In rebellion against his family, which was dominated by an assimilated bourgeois, *aufklärerisch*, anti-religious, materialist and scientistic atmosphere, he turned towards mysticism, socialism and, for a short period, Zionism.[72] His doctoral thesis, presented in 1923, was devoted to the social philosophy of Franz von

Baader. Commenting on that work in a recent autobiographical interview, Löwenthal explained that what attracted him to this philosopher – 'the most conservative thinker imaginable at the beginning of the nineteenth century', who had advocated an alliance between the proletariat and the Church, against the secularized bourgeoisie – was Baader's radical critique of liberal society as a 'one-dimensional' universe, excluding everything truly human.[73] It should be noted in passing that Walter Benjamin, Gershom Scholem and Ernst Bloch were also attracted – fascinated even – by Baader's Romantic/mystical philosophy.

In his thesis, Löwenthal delighted in revealing Baader's diatribes against capitalist 'democracy', the power of money 'as heir to the tribe of Cain', and 'rationalist-bourgeois (*spiessbürgerlich*), myopic/egoistic industry' – which should be replaced by the 'true and grandiose culture' of a mankind reconciled with God and nature. Löwenthal was attracted, as was Benjamin later, by the cosmopolitan dimension of a Romantic philosophy which saw in a reunited Christian Church (regrouping Catholicism and Orthodoxy) the 'world corporation' that would shatter 'national limitations'. In Baader, Löwenthal also discovered an aspect of anarchist theocracy, the nostalgia for a 'natural society' subject only to divine authority ('theocratic in the strictest sense'), in which no one dominates or is dominated, because all men are both priests and kings. Such a theocracy existed in all its purity only before the Fall; the human community that came closest to it was that of the Jews under Moses. For Baader, historical temporality was a punishment inflicted upon men after Adam's sin: redemption meant 'the reintegration of time in eternity', the return of men to God, the advent of the Kingdom of God – a messianic/restorative concept of time that coincides with the Jewish tradition (which Baader was very familiar with).[74]

Löwenthal's revolt against his atheist/assimilated father, and the search for his Jewish identity, led him not only to follow Rabbi Nobel but also, for a brief period (1923), to try to live according to the rules of traditional religious orthodoxy. Another endeavour – equally short-lived – was that of joining up with Zionism. In 1924, along with Ernst Simon (a close friend of Martin Buber), he founded a Jewish magazine with a Zionist slant: *Jüdisches Wochenblatt*. As he would later attest, what attracted him to Zionism was not so much its strictly national dimension as its utopian/messianic goal of establishing an exemplary socialist society in the Land of Israel. However, he became disenchanted very quickly; and in his magazine, he published an article (signed 'Hereticus') that radically challenged Zionist practices in Palestine, which he described as 'a colonial European policy toward the Arabs'. This essay, entitled 'The Lessons of China' (1925), called on the Zionists to change not their tactics but their attitude, because in Palestine, as in China, 'a national majority is crying out for justice'. But although it concluded his brief incursion into the Zionist movement, it did not end his interest in Jewish culture and religion.[75]

The young Löwenthal also expressed his anti-bourgeois rebellion in a directly political way. Hailing the Russian Revolution as 'an act liberating mankind', he joined an association of socialist students in 1918 and then, between 1919 and 1920, the Independent Socialist Party (USPD). When that Party split in 1920, Löwenthal remained with the left-wing majority that fused with the Communist Party, because he had always regarded social democracy as a *'petit bourgeois* or bourgeois' force, 'a traitor to the revolution'. From the mid-twenties on, however, Löwenthal distanced himself from the Soviet Union, which seemed to him to have abandoned the German revolution to its fate. At the time, his general attitude was one of radical, revolutionary opposition to everything that constituted 'the infamy of existing reality' (*die Infamie des Bestehenden*) – to use Lukács' expression in *The Theory of the Novel* from which Löwenthal drew his inspiration. Convinced that world revolution was imminent, Löwenthal advocated a Marxist/messianic philosophy which he described (sixty years later) as 'a mixture of revolutionary radicalism, Jewish messianism . . . and a hymnic philosophy akin to Bloch's'.[76]

Löwenthal's attraction to Marxism did not keep him from admiring Gustav Landauer, one of the great heroes of his youth whose portrait adorned his workroom for quite some time. It is characteristic of his political evolution that, in a text written in 1930, he mentioned among the 'great Jewish names' of our century (next to Einstein and Freud) those of Landauer and Trotsky.[77]

Löwenthal's principal work of this period was an essay entitled 'Das Dämonische' [The Demonic], published in 1921 in a collection in honour of Rabbi Nobel (to which Martin Buber,

Franz Rosenzweig, Siegfried Kracauer and Ernst Simon also contributed). A strange alloy of Jewish mysticism and Marxism, this rather esoteric text was received enthusiastically by Bloch – and with reservations by Rosenzweig. It sketched the foundations of a negative theology which drew upon Marx, Lukács and Bloch to argue that we are living in a world without God and without redemption, a cold world handed over to despair, a space between paradise and the Messiah which seeks God without finding him. The key formula of this religious philosophy was found in a quotation from *The Theory of the Novel*: 'The irony of the writer is the negative mysticism of godless eras.' However, Löwenthal could not rest content with such a diagnosis: he ardently aspired to an ending of this condition of the world and to the advent of that 'shining messianic light' (*strahlendes messianisches Licht*) which would do away with everything crepuscular and demonic.[78]

After 1926, Löwenthal became increasingly involved in scientific work at the Institute of Social Research in Frankfurt, and he abandoned his mystical and messianic concerns to become the School's primary sociologist of literature.

5
'Theologia negativa' *and* 'Utopia negativa': *Franz Kafka*

During a conversation with Gustav Janouch about Plato's exclusion of the poet from the Republic, Kafka said: 'Poets . . . are politically dangerous for the State because they want to change it. The State, and all its devoted servants, want only one thing, to persist.' It is not by chance that Kafka's works have also been labelled 'dangerous' by every twentieth-century authoritarian state.

Kafka occupied a quite special place in the German-Jewish cultural firmament. Like Benjamin, he did not belong to any of the identifiable constellations: he was neither truly religious nor completely assimilated, neither a Zionist nor a committed revolutionary. But whereas Walter Benjamin stood at the crossroads, torn by contradictory movements, Kafka actually seemed to be on the outside. His position was completely marginal *vis-à-vis* all the authors mentioned in this work: Martin Buber was the only one with whom he maintained a personal relationship (although he did have a considerable influence on Scholem, Benjamin and Bloch). What set Kafka apart was the strictly negative form which Jewish messianism and libertarian utopia both took in his works. These two dimensions, linked by a readily discernible elective affinity, played a crucial role in his writings but were oriented towards a radical negativity.

As was the case with the other Jewish intellectuals from Central Europe, Kafka's relationship with Judaism developed late and was preceded by a deep immersion in German culture. His link with German Romanticism was not as direct as Landauer's, Benjamin's or Bloch's had been: Novalis, Schlegel and Hölderlin did not inspire his works. Kleist was the only 'classical' Romantic author who had an important formative impact on Kafka – so much so that Kurt Tucholsky spoke of him as 'Kleist's grandson'.[1] All the same, the majority of Kafka's favourite

71

authors belonged to the European 'anti-bourgeois' romantic current: Schopenhauer, Nietzsche, Kierkegaard, Flaubert, Tolstoy,
Dostoesvky, Strindberg, among others.

To a large extent, Kafka shared the neo-romantic critique of
modern (capitalist) *Zivilisation* which his friends developed at
Bar Kochba, the Zionist-cultural circle, – for example, in their
Vom Judentum collection of essays from 1913 (a copy of which can
be found in Kafka's library).[2] This critique is strikingly present
in *America* – notably in the description of mechanized labour.
The employees of the Uncle – who owns a huge commercial
enterprise – spend their day enclosed in telephone booths,
oblivious to everything, heads bound in a steel band: only their
fingers move, in a mechanical gesture of 'inhuman regularity
and speed'. Similarly, the work of the lift boys at the Hotel
Occidental is exhausting, stressful and monotonous (*einförmig*);
they do nothing but press the buttons, and they know nothing
about the inner mechanism of the lifts. In the offices and streets,
the noise is invasive, the ringing deafens, cars honk their horns
'as if caught up in a whirlwind and roaring like some strange
element quite unconnected with humanity'.[3] Examples abound:
the entire atmosphere of the book depicts the anxiety and distress
felt by human beings who have been handed over to a pitiless
world and a technical civilization that eludes them. As Wilhelm
Emrich acutely observed, *America* is 'one of the most lucid
critiques of modern industrial society in modern literature. The
secret economic and psychological mechanism of this society and
its satanic consequences are unveiled without any concessions'.
It is a world dominated by the monotonous and circular return
of the Ever-the-same, by the purely quantitative temporality of
the clock.[4] The America depicted in the novel is also perceived
as a *Zivilisation* without *Kultur*: the mind and art seem to play no
role, and the only book mentioned is, characteristically, a work on
business correspondence.[5]

One of the principal sources for the novel is known to have
been *Amerika heute und morgen*, a book published in 1912 by
the Jewish socialist Arthur Holitscher. This provided a detailed
description of 'the Hell' of modern American civilization as well
as a biting critique of Taylorism: 'Job specialization, a result of
mass production, reduces the worker more and more to the
level of a dead piece of machinery, a cog or lever functioning

precisely and automatically.'[6] The letters that Kafka wrote during this period revealed his own anxiety feelings in the face of world mechanization. Thus, a letter to Felice from 1913 refers to a dictaphone as an example of a machine 'exercising a greater, more repugnant (*grausamer*) compulsion on one's capacities than any human being'.[7] During a conversation with Janouch several years later, Kafka gave free rein to this 'repugnance' in a near-biblical description of Taylorism:

> Such a violent outrage (*Frevel*) can only end in enslavement to evil (*das Böse*). It is inevitable. Time, the noblest and most essential element in all creative work, is conscripted into the net of corrupt business interests. Thereby not only creative work, but man himself, who is its essential part, is polluted and humiliated. A Taylorized life is a terrible curse which will give rise only to hunger and misery instead of the intended wealth and profit.[8]

Along with Kafka's moral and religious hostility towards industrial/capitalist 'progress', there was a longing for the traditional community, the organic *Gemeinschaft*, which attracted him to the Yiddish culture (and language) of the Eastern Jews, to his sister Ottla's projects for rural living in Palestine, and (in a more ambivalent way) to the romantic/cultural Zionism of his friends in Prague. The Czech peasant community, living in peace and harmony with nature, also aroused his wonder and admiration:

> General impressions of the farmers: noblemen, who have found salvation in their farming, where they have arranged their work so cleverly and humbly that it fits without omission into the whole, and will keep them safe from every wavering sea-sickness until their happy death. Real citizens of the earth.[9]

It is striking to compare this idyllic portrait with the description, in the first chapter of *America*, of the morbid feverishness of New York harbour: 'A movement without end, a restlessness transmitted from the restless element to helpless human beings and their works!'[10]

Kafka, like Scholem and Benjamin, revolted against the assimilationist atmosphere in his family. In 'Letter to His Father', written in 1919, Kafka bitterly reproached his father for the inconsistency and superficiality of his relationship to the Jewish tradition:

> But what sort of Judaism was it I got from you? ! . . . It was also impossible to make a child, over-acutely observant from sheer nervousness, understand that the few flimsy gestures you performed in the name of Judaism, and with an indifference in keeping with their flimsiness, could have any higher meaning.[11]

Throughout his life, Kafka's attitude to Jewish culture and religion and to Zionism remained ambiguous, as did Benjamin's.

It was only after the Yiddish theatre passed through Prague in 1910 that Kafka began to take a more active interest in Judaism. He studied Yiddish literature, Heinrich Graetz's *History of the Jews* and the Hasidic tales, describing the latter in a letter to Max Brod as 'the only Jewish elements I always feel at home with, irrespective of my state of mind'.[12] Prior to that date, Kafka had not used the word 'Judaism' in his writings or letters. In 1913 he went to Berlin to visit Martin Buber and kept up a correspondence with him for several years. In later accounts, Buber remembered having spoken with Kafka about the meaning of Psalm 82, which they both interpreted as a promise by the divine power to punish the unjust judges who were reigning on earth.[13] Finally, around this time, Kafka began to attend some meetings of the Zionist *Bar Kochba* club and to take an interest in the *kibbutzim*; under the influence of his friend Max Brod, he even studied Hebrew and made some rather vague plans to travel to Palestine. None the less, Kafka maintained his reserved and contradictory attitude toward the Jewish religion and Zionism. As he stated ironically in a note written between 1917 and 1919: 'I have not succeeded in catching the tail-end of the Jewish prayer coat, which was taking off, as are the Zionists.'[14] Nevertheless – a point on which most interpreters and exegetes agree – the Jewish religion was one of the principal spiritual sources for Kafka's work.

Was Kafka a believer? In his notes and aphorisms, he seems constantly to hover between doubt and faith. At times, he affirms his confidence in 'something indestructible' in man; one of the ways in which he felt it could be expressed was 'faith in a personal god'. Yet in the following paragraph, Kafka notes drily, 'Heaven is mute, spreading only to the mute'. Kafka's dual stance, which subtly interlaces hope and despair, is sometimes expressed in one and the same passage, as in the enigmatic parable on light.

> Seen from the tarnished eye we have on this world, we are like rail travellers on a train, stuck in a long tunnel after an accident; and we are stuck right at the point where the light from the beginning of the tunnel is no longer visible, and the light at the end of the tunnel is so small that we must constantly strain our eyes to see it. We always lose sight of it, while beginning and end are not even certainties.[15]

However, a strange atmosphere of religiosity undeniably pervades Kafka's great unfinished works. Does it stem from Jewish messianism? Just how can Kafka's mysterious, diffuse and ambivalent spirituality be characterized? Leaving aside the controversial question of his sources – Kierkegaard, Gnosticism, the cabbala, the Bible or Hasidism – what is the structure of meaning in Kafka's religious view of the world? Is it a positive messianism, charged with hope and faith, as Max Brod seemed to believe? Despite Brod's attempt to build a 'positive' image of his friend at any cost, he himself was forced to recognize that negativity dominated Kafka's great novels and sketches; and yet, he tried to sidestep this fact by attributing it to Kafka's 'genius for fantasizing' and 'his highly terrifying imagination'.[16]

In the whole body of Kafka's novels, the only passage that can be seen as a positive allegory of messianic redemption is the well-known final chapter of *America*. Here Kafka describes 'The Nature Theatre of Oklahoma', where there is 'a place for everyone' – including the young Karl Rossmann, the hero/victim of the novel. The messianic interpretation seems to be reinforced by Brod's report of a conversation in which Kafka apparently let it be known 'smilingly, in enigmatic language', that the novel should end with the young Karl regaining his happiness, in an atmosphere of 'celestial magic' (*paradiesischen Zaubers*). But unfortunately, an entry Kafka made in 1915 in his *Diary* envisaged that the book would end on a completely different note: 'Rossmann and K., the innocent and the guilty, finally without distinction destroyed by legal sentence [*strafweise umgebracht*: literally, "killed in a punitive manner"], the innocent with a lighter hand, more pushed to the side than hurled to the ground.'[17] According to Alfred Wirkner, the Theatre of Oklahoma was nothing but a huge deceit to exploit the naivety of immigrants. In this interpretation, the chapter would be in keeping with the rest of the book, and it would show Karl Rossmann falling into his final and worst servitude from which only his murder would deliver him. Wirkner also holds the theory that the pseudonym – 'Negro' – which Karl chose when he signed up with the Theatre, corresponded to a photograph labelled 'Idyll aus Oklahama' in Holitscher's book, which showed a negro being lynched. We know that Kafka must have paid attention to that picture, because in his manuscript for *America* he repeated Holitscher's typographical error in the word '*Oklahama*'. It is possible, therefore, that Karl Rossmann was destined to end up like the black man of that image.[18] Considering the more lenient formulation in Kafka's *Diary* – that Karl would be executed, but that he would be 'more pushed to the side than hurled to the ground' – one could also imagine an ending that would serve as the counterpart to the first chapter: driven by his sense of justice to defend a black man threatened by lynch laws (as he had tried to defend the stoker), Karl Rossmann would be 'pushed to the side' by the lynchers.

What are we to make, then, of *The Trial*? One of the key clues to the religious significance of Kafka's second novel (and even of his entire work) is the fascinating parable 'The Problem of our Laws', which was published during Kafka's lifetime and included in the manuscript for *The Trial*. There are, of course, any number of possible interpretations of this enigmatic text, but the most persuasive for me sees the doorkeeper (the one who prevents the man from the country from gaining access to the Law) as representing a 'world order' based on 'lies' – to repeat the expression used by Joseph K. The man from the country lets himself be intimidated: force does not keep him from entering, but rather fear, lack of confidence in himself, false obedience to authority, and submissive passivity.[19] As for the priest who 'explains' the parable to K. in the cathedral – justifying the position of the doorkeeper as 'not true, but necessary' – in Hannah Arendt's opinion, his argument shows 'the secret theology and the most intimate belief of the bureaucrats as a belief in necessity *per se*, and the bureaucrats are in the final analysis the functionaries of necessity'.[20] Thus, the 'necessity' invoked by the priest is not that

of Law, but that of the laws of a corrupt and fallen world, which
bars access to truth. In conclusion, to quote Marthe Robert: 'The
countryman is lost, because he does not dare put his individual
law above the collective taboos, whose tyranny is personified by
the doorkeeper.'[21] An analogous example would be that of Joseph
K.'s behaviour at the beginning of *The Trial*, when his intuition
told him that 'the simplest solution of the whole business' would
be to forget about the wardens, 'to open the door of the next room
or even the door of the hall' – but he did not dare do it.[22]

The doorkeeper, like the trial judges, the castle officials or the
penal colony commandants, do not in any way represent divinity
(or its servants, angels, messengers, etc.). To ascribe a divine
character to them would be the epitome of social, religious and
moral conformity. Clearly, they stand for a world of non-freedom
and non-redemption, a suffocating world from which God has
withdrawn. In the face of arbitrary, mean and unjust authority,
the only path to salvation is to follow one's own individual law,
by refusing to submit, by rejecting the shameful debasement to
the level of a 'dog'. That is the only way to come within reach of
divine Law, whose light is hidden by the door.

In Kafka's eyes, the coming of the Messiah was closely bound
up with this individualist view of faith. In one of the aphorisms,
dated 30 November 1917, he wrote: 'The Messiah will come just at
the time when the most unbridled individualism is allowable in
faith (*der zügelloseste Individualismus des Glaubens*) – a time when
no one will be there to destroy that possibility, or to tolerate its
destruction: in other words, when the tombs will be opened.'
This astonishing religious anarchism also pervades another note
on messianism dated 4 December 1917: 'The Messiah will come
only when he is no longer needed; he will come only on the
day after his arrival, he will not come on the last day, but
on the very last day.'[23] Comparing these two aphorisms, I
would suggest the following hypothesis. For Kafka, messianic
redemption will be the work of human beings themselves, at the
moment when, following their own inner law, they bring about
the collapse of outside constraints and authorities; the coming
of the Messiah will be nothing but the religious sanctioning of
human self-redemption – or at least, human self-redemption will
be the preparation and the precondition for a messianic era of
absolute freedom.[24] This position brings to mind certain ideas

held by Buber, Benjamin or Rosenzweig on the dialectic of human emancipation and messianic redemption, but it is, of course, quite far removed from the traditional rabbinical/orthodox vision of the coming of the Messiah.

In the parable 'Jackals and Arabs', written in 1917, Kafka indulged in merciless criticism of certain aspects of the Jewish religious tradition – passive expectation of a Supreme Saviour, the dream of bloody vengeance on the nations (*goyim*) – which contradicted his active and universalist view of messianism. It is hard not to see here an ironic metaphor for the Jewish condition in the Diaspora. And the jackals' appeal to the traveller to fulfil their 'old teaching' – by taking the scissors and slitting Arabs' throats (which the traveller refuses to do) – is a fairly transparent reference to a certain way of conceiving the role of the Messiah.[25]

How then can the messianic dimension of *The Trial* be interpreted? In 1934, Gershom Scholem wrote a very beautiful poem, 'Mit einem Exemplar von Kafkas "Prozess"', in which the following verse contains the religious quintessence of Kafka's work:[26]

> So allein strahlt Offenbarung
> in die Zeit, die dich verwarf.
> Nur dein Nichts ist die Erfahrung,
> die sie von dir haben darf.

> [Only so does Revelation shine
> In times that have rejected You.
> The only experience they may have of You
> Is of your Nothingness.]

In response to that poem, Benjamin wrote a letter to his friend Scholem, dated 20 July 1934, in which he stated: 'When you write that "the only experience they may have of you is of your Nothingness", that is the very point at which I try my hand at an interpretation: I try to show how it was on the reverse side (*Kehrseite*) of this "Nothingness", in its lining (*Futter*), if I may say so, that Kafka sought to brush redemption with his finger.' According to Benjamin, the agonizing questions raised by Kafka's work could find an answer (or rather the suppression of the questions themselves) only in another state of the world, a different world, which Kafka did not find but glimpsed 'in flight, or in a dream'.[27] The strange image of the 'lining' – the German word *Futter* refers, in fact, to the lining of a coat – evokes something hidden, invisible, which is the reverse side, the symmetrical opposite of the visible, of the given. Later, in an essay on Benjamin, Scholem had this to say about his letter:

> In Kafka's world, Benjamin perceived the negative inversion (*negativen Umschlag*) to which the Jewish categories are subjected in Kafka's world; there the teaching no longer conveys a positive message, but offers only an absolutely Utopian promise . . . as yet undefinable . . . Benjamin knew that in Kafka we possess the *theologia negativa* of a Judaism not a whit less intense for having lost the Revelation as a positive message.[28]

In a letter to Benjamin written in 1934, Theodor Adorno used an image which also suggested a type of inversion: Kafka's work was 'a photograph of life on earth, from the perspective of life saved by redemption'.[29] So Scholem, Benjamin and Adorno all perceived messianic redemption – in its negative or inverted form – as an essential dimension of Kafka's writings.[30]

It seems to me that the concept of *theologia negativa* is, in fact, the only one that can adequately account for the very particular type of religious problematic that is present in Kafka's novels. Messianic redemption (and, as we shall see, libertarian utopia, too) appears in his works only in the 'lining' of reality, or as if drawn in contrast against the dark contours of the present world. This is especially true of his last major work, *The Castle*.

The most influential attempt at a 'positive' reading of the religious universe in this novel was made by Max Brod. In his famous preface to the first edition (1934), he did not hesitate to write that

> this Castle, in which Kafka was not granted the right to enter and which he could not even approach, was clearly Grace in theological terms, God's rule which steers human destinies (the Village) . . . *The Trial* and *The Castle*, then, apparently show us the two forms – Justice and Grace – in which, according to the Kabbala, Divinity presents itself to us.

Brod even interpreted those episodes which cast high-ranking

figures of the 'Castle' in a truly sordid light (Sortini's obscene
letter to Amalia) as proof that 'the categories of morals and
religion do not coincide'.[31] There is no need to dwell on the gross
inadequacy of such an interpretation: Benjamin already qualified
it as untenable, and it has been increasingly rejected by literary
critics.[32] As Hannah Arendt aptly put it: 'The evil of the world
in which Kafka's heroes are caught up, is its very deification, its
presumption of representing a divine necessity.'[33]

Far from being the symbol of Grace, the Castle seems in the
grip of an infernal logic. Erich Heller rightly noted that, in Kafka's
work, there is both a dream of absolute freedom and the knowledge of terrible bondage: from this irresolvable contradiction is
born 'the certitude of damnation', which is 'all that is left of faith'.
Heller was wrong, however, to believe that a gnostic Manicheism
could be detected in Kafka's works, or even that the Castle
of Kafka's novel was something akin to 'the heavily fortified
garrison of a company of Gnostic demons'.[34] Nothing indicates
that Kafka knew much about gnostic doctrines, and this type
of interpretation (like those that refer to the cabbala) involves an
allegorical, mystical and esoteric reading which has little support
in the text, and which bears no relation to the author's concerns in
his letters, his dairy, and so forth. After the avalanche of symbolic
and allegorical interpretations, we should, perhaps, return to a
more cautious approach. What if the Castle were not a symbol
for something else but quite simply a *castle* – in other words, the
headquarters of an earthly human power?[35] Kafka's religiousness
asserts itself less in an elaborate and hidden system of symbolic
figures than in a certain *Stimmung*, a spiritual atmosphere, a sense
of the world and of the modern human condition.

Martin Buber, too, spoke of 'gnostic demons', but he drew
closer to the deep meaning of *The Castle*'s religious universe
when he defined it as an infernal world suffering from the
lack of redemption (*Unerlöstheit der Welt*).[36] In fact, Kafka seems
to have shared Strindberg's conviction (found also in Benjamin's
works) that 'Hell is the life we are living'. In one of the aphorisms
written in Zürau, Kafka stated: 'There is nothing more diabolical
than what we have here.'[37] It is precisely this desolate look at the
world that points to messianic aspiration. Adorno, better than
anyone, perceived this paradoxical dialectic in *The Castle* (and *The
Trial*): human existence, he wrote, is presented as 'Hell seen from

the perspective of salvation'; our existence is illuminated by a light that 'shows the world's crevices to be infernal'.[38]

In this fallen world, any isolated attempt, like that of K. the surveyor, to set truth against lies is doomed to failure. According to Kafka, 'in a world of lies, a lie is not even eliminated by its opposite; it is eliminated only in a world of truth';[39] in other words, through redemption, which alone can annul the existing world and replace it with a new one.

Nevertheless, the spiritual climate of *The Castle* is not at all that of a pathetic descent into the fifth circle; rather, it is sober and ironic. One could apply to it that phrase from Lukács' *Theory of the Novel* which we have already had occasion to quote: 'The irony of the writer is the negative mysticism of godless eras.'

In conclusion: *The Trial* and *The Castle* depict a despairing world given over to the absurd, to authoritarian injustice and to lies, a world without freedom in which redemption asserts itself only negatively, by its total absence. Not only is there no positive message, but the messianic promise of the future is only implicit in the religious form of conceiving (and rejecting) the contemporary world as infernal. Criticism of the existing state of things is social and political, but it also has a transcendental, metaphysical and theological dimension which sets Kafka's work completely apart from any 'realist' novel.

Kafka's 'theology' – if we can use that word – is therefore negative, in the precise sense that its content is God's non-presence in the world and the lack of redemption for mankind. Kafka's way of expressing the positive only through its opposite, its negative *Gegenstück*, appears in his novels as well as in the paradoxes that make up his aphorisms. As Maurice Blanchot put it: 'Every one of Kafka's works is a search for an affirmation that it wants to reach through negation. . . Transcendence is precisely this affirmation that can be affirmed only through negation.'[40]

Corresponding politically to the *theologia negativa*, to Kafka's negative messianism, is a *utopia negativa*, a negative anarchism. Heinz Politzer speaks of Kafka as a 'metaphysical anarchist'.[41] But it seems to me that his principal works – in particular, *The Trial* and *The Castle* – contain a dimension critical of bureaucratic reification and hierarchical state authority (legal or administrative), which clearly draws its inspiration from anarchism. This 'political' interpretation is, obviously, only a partial one: Kafka's universe is too rich and multifaceted to be reduced to a unilateral formula. However, there is no contradiction between a political and a religious or theological reading of his work: quite the contrary, there is a striking structural analogy between them. Lack of freedom in the stifling universe of bureaucratic arbitrariness corresponds to the lack of redemption which is the religious mark of a damned era. Messianic and utopian hope emerges only in contrast, as the Other. Anarchism is thus charged with religious spirituality and gains a 'metaphysical' projection.

Biographical data shed some light on the young Kafka's interest in anarchist politics and ideas. Around the time that he began to work at the 'Workman's Accident Insurance Institution', he also started to attend meetings of various anarchist organizations in Prague. According to information provided by Michal Kacha, one of the founders of the anarchist movement in Prague, and by Michal Mares, at that time a young Czech anarchist, Kafka went to meetings of the *Klub Mladych* (Youth Club); of *Vilem Körber*, a workers' political association; and of the Czech Anarchist Movement, which had anarcho-syndicalist leanings. The recollections of the two men coincide in telling that Kafka observed and listened with the greatest interest, but that he neither spoke nor participated in the discussions. Kacha, who took a liking to Kafka, called him *Klidas*, 'the silent giant'.[42]

Mares recalls that, at his invitation, Kafka attended several anarchist lectures and rallies. The first, in 1909, was a demonstration against the execution of the Spanish anarchist scholar and thinker, Francisco Ferrer, which was broken up by the police. Others included ones on free love (1910), the anniversary of the Paris Commune (1911), and the struggle against war (also in 1911). Finally, in 1912, Kafka participated in a demonstration against the execution in Paris of the anarchist Liabeuf: the police violently suppressed it and arrested several demonstrators, including Franz Kafka. At the police station, Kafka was given the choice between a fine of one gulden and twenty-four hours in prison. He chose to pay the fine.[43]

According to Mares again, Kafka read with great interest and sympathy the works of a number of anarchist writers and publicists, such as the Reclus brothers, Domela Nieuwenhuis, Vera

Figner, Bakunin, Jean Grave, Kropotkin, and Emma Goldmann. Bakunin and Kropotkin are actually mentioned in Kafka's *Diary*. Moreover, Janouch reports a conversation in which Kafka expressed his interest in Ravachol and the works and lives of anarchists such as Godwin, Proudhon, Stirner, Bakunin, Kropotkin, Tolstoy, Erich Mühsam and Rudolf Grossmann (who went by the name 'Pierre Ramus').[44]

It is a well-known fact that Kafka detested his work at the Workman's Accident Insurance Institution – which he called a 'sombre nest of bureaucrats'[45] – and that he was indignant at the lot of the mutilated workers and impoverished widows who found themselves caught up in the judicial and administrative labyrinths of the Institution. The following short sentence, quoted by Max Brod, is an ironic, succinct and violent expression of Kafka's 'anarchist' feelings towards this type of institution: 'These people are so humble. . . They come here to plead. Instead of attacking the Institution and ransacking it, they come to plead.'[46] Kafka's rebellion against his bureaucratic job was probably one of the sources of the libertarian component in his writings.

Was Kafka's libertarian tendency only a 'youthful episode' in his life, restricted to the years 1909–12? It is true that after 1912, he stopped participating in the activities of the Czech anarchists and drew closer to the Jewish and Zionist circles in Prague. But his conversations with Gustav Janouch, around 1920, show that his initial inclinations still persisted. Not only did he qualify the Prague anarchists as 'very nice and lively' people, 'so nice and friendly, that one has to believe every word they say', but the political and social ideas he expressed remained very close to anarchism.

For example, Kafka's definition of capitalism as 'a system of dependent relationships', in which 'everything is a hierarchy, everything is in chains', lays a typically anarchist stress on the oppressive and authoritarian nature of the existing regime (and not on economic exploitation, as does Marxism). Even Kafka's skeptical attitude toward the organized labour movement seemed to be inspired by a libertarian distrust of political parties and institutions. Referring to a large group of workers who were marching with flags and banners, Kafka observed:

> These people are so self-possessed, so self-confident and good
> humoured. They rule the streets, and therefore think they rule
> the world. In fact, they are mistaken. Behind them already are
> the secretaries, officials, professional politicians, all the mod-
> ern satraps for whom they are preparing the way to power. . .
> The revolution evaporates, and leaves behind only the slime
> of a new bureaucracy. The chains of tormented mankind are
> made out of red tape.[47]

Janouch's account suggests, therefore, that Kafka remained close
to anarchist ideas for the rest of his life. Of course, his was not a
fully-formed doctrinal and activist conviction, but rather a spiritual affinity, a deep sympathy for the anti-authoritarian ideas of
Bakunin, Kropotkin and their Czech followers. Libertarian utopia
was never 'demonstrative' in Kafka's novels.[48] It was perceptible
only in the profoundly critical way in which he presented the
obsessive and ubiquitous face of non-freedom: authority.

Anti-authoritarianism (of libertarian origins) permeates all
of Kafka's novels, its focus becoming increasingly universal
and abstract as it moves from paternal and personal authority
towards administrative and impersonal authority.

First of all, Kafka perceived a connection between the despotic
authority of the father and political and social authority. In 'Letter
to His Father', he remembered: 'For me you took on the enigmatic
quality that all tyrants have whose rights are based on their
person and not on reason.' Commenting on the brutal, unjust and
arbitrary manner in which his father treated his employees, Kafka
wrote: 'It made the business insufferable to me, reminding me
far too much of my relations with you. . . That was why I could
not but side with the staff.'[49] Here we find one of the intimate
personal roots of Kafka's sympathy for the Prague anarchists
– and also, more directly, of his interest in Otto Gross. This
Freudian anarchist, who had been imprisoned in a psychiatric
hospital (1913) on his father's orders, owed his freedom to a press
campaign led by Expressionist writers. Inspired by Nietzsche,
Freud and Max Stirner, his writings attacked patriarchal power
and the principle of authority both in the family and in society.
Kafka came to know Otto Gross on a train trip in July 1917; and
shortly afterwards, when they met in Prague, Gross proposd to
Werfel and Kafka the publication of a magazine entitled *Blätter*

zur Bekämpfung des Machtwillens [Struggle Against the Will for Power]. Writing to Brod in November 1917, Kafka expressed his enthusiastic support for the project. In Kafka's eyes, no doubt, Gross personified the convergence of revolt against paternal tyranny and (anarchist) resistance to all institutional authority.[50]

In his first major work, 'The Judgement' (1912), Kafka only brought paternal authority into the picture; it was also one of the few writings in which the hero (Georg Bendemann) seemed to submit completely and without resistance to the authoritarian verdict (by drowning himself in the river). Comparing 'The Judgement' to *The Trial*, Milan Kundera noted: 'The similarity between the two charges, the two guilty verdicts and the two executions, reveals the continuity which links the intimate "totalitarianism" of the family with that of Kafka's great visions.'[51] This continuity is indeed essential for an understanding of the atmosphere of Kafka's three novels, but these later works differ from 'The Judgement' in the increasingly anonymous, hierarchical, opaque and remote character of power.

In this respect, *America* (1913–14) marks a transition. Here the bearers of power are paternal figures (Karl Rossmann's father and Uncle Jakob), marginal characters (Delamarche) and high-ranking administrators (the Head Waiter and the Head Porter). All have in common that unbearable authoritarianism whose features will reappear in Kafka's later novels and short-stories: (1) an entirely arbitrary attitude, without any moral, rational or human justification; (2) inordinate and absurd demands on the hero/victim; (3) injustice: guilt is wrongly considered to be self-evident, beyond any doubt; (4) punishment out of all proportion to the (non-existent or trivial) 'fault'. He who unresistingly obeys every command ends up becoming 'a dog'; 'If you're always treated like a dog', says Robinson, 'you begin to think you actually are one.' Yet the young Karl Rossmann thinks that this holds only for 'those who let themselves be talked into it': he obeys only the sentences of paternal figures and tries to resist the others even by physical means. Without question, the most odious are the heads of the administrative hierarchy at the Hotel Occidental, who embody the Principle of Authority. Rejecting the Manageress's conciliatory moves, the Head Waiter cries out: 'It's a matter of authority, there's too much at stake, a boy like this might corrupt the whole lot of them.'[52] However, their authority retains a dimension of personal tyranny; it combines bureaucratic coldness with individual despotism to the point of sadism – particularly in the case of the Head Porter, who gets sinister pleasure out of brutalizing the young Rossmann.

The symbol of this punitive authoritarianism looms on the very first page of the book. In a twist fraught with meaning, Kafka presents the Statue of Liberty at the entrance to New York harbour as carrying, in place of the traditional torch, a sword. In a world without justice or freedom, naked force and arbitrary power reign supreme. The hero's sympathy goes out to the victims of that society: for example, the stoker in the first chapter – an example of the 'suffering of the poor man confronting the great' – or Theresa's mother, driven to suicide by hunger and destitution. He finds friends and allies among the poor: Theresa herself, the student, and the people living in the working-class quarter, who refuse to hand him over to the police because, writes Kafka, 'the workers had no liking for the authorities'.[53]

A typical detail shows to what point certain bureaucrats in *America* are still related to personal/paternal authority: in one of the hotel offices, porters throw things on the ground, which are then picked up and put back in their place by exhausted messengers. In 'Letter to His Father', Kafka describes his father's behaviour to his employees as follows: 'the way you would push goods you did not want to have mixed up with others, knocking them off the counter . . . and the assistant had to pick them up.'[54]

The authoritarian aspect of American civilization had been much less evident in Holitscher's *Amerika heute und morgen*; it was Kafka himself who highlighted the ubiquitousness of domination in social relationships. This difference is particularly noticeable in Holitscher's chapter 'Hotel Athenäum, Chautauqua'. In that modern grand hotel, the young lift boy is a high-school student, exactly like Karl Rossmann in the Hotel Occidental. However, far from being oppressed by a ruthless bureaucratic hierarchy, like the hero of *America*, the *Liftjunge* converses with a rich client about Latin grammar – which suggests to Holitscher that the difference between social classes is less pronounced in America than in Europe.[55]

Shortly after *America*, Kafka wrote the short-story 'In the Penal

Colony', which, of all his writings, presents Authority with
the most murderous and unjust face. Traditional and Personal
authority (of patriarchal origin) is still found in the shape of the
Commandants (the Old and the New). But these characters play
a relatively minor role: the essential manifestation of authority
shifts to an impersonal mechanism.

It has frequently been suggested that this short-story was
Kafka's most prophetic, since it pointed forward, to the concentration camps of the Second World War. That may be so.
But when he wrote it, he had in mind a quite definite reality
of his time: namely, colonialism, and more specifically, French
colonialism. The officers and commandants of the 'colony' are
French; the common soldiers, the dockers, and the victims
marked down for execution are 'natives', who 'do not understand
a word of French'. Kafka uses this colonial background to make
more understandable the extraordinary violence of domination,
which is here much more direct and brutal than in *The Castle* and
The Trial. However, what is at stake in the story goes far beyond
its specific context.

In 'In the Penal Colony', Kafka tells of the monstrous vengeance of offended authority. A poor soldier is condemned to death
'for undisciplined and insulting behaviour towards a superior'.
Having failed to accomplish an exaggerated and ridiculous
task, and having been struck in the face by the Captain's
whip, the soldier dared to revolt against authority. Without
any chance to defend himself – in accordance with the officers' legal doctrine that 'guilt must never be doubted!' – the
man is condemned to execution by a torture machine that
slowly writes on his body with piercing needles: 'Honour thy
superiors'.

The central character of this story is neither the explorer who
indignantly observes the events, nor the prisoner, nor the officer,
nor (as is usually thought) the Commandant of the colony. It is
the Machine.

The entire narrative revolves around this death-dealing machine,
its origins, its mode of operation, its significance; all the other
characters are structured in relation to that central axis. As the
officer gives his explanation, the Machine appears more and
more as an end in itself. The Machine is not there to execute
the man, but rather the man is there to provide the Machine

with a body on which it can write its aesthetic masterpiece, its bloody inscription illustrated with 'many ornaments and embellishments'. The Commandant himself is nothing but a servant of the Machine, and he ultimately sacrifices himself to that insatiable Moloch.

Here authority appears in its most alienated and reified form, as an 'objective' mechanism, a fetish produced by men which enslaves, dominates and destroys them.

What specific 'machine' of human sacrifice was Kafka thinking of? 'In the Penal Colony' was written in October 1914, three months after the First World War broke out.

For Kafka, the First World War was an inhuman mechanism not only because its blind gear wheel escaped anyone's control, but also – in a more immediate sense – because it involved an immense confrontation between killing machines. In a text written in 1916 (a public appeal for the construction of a hospital for war victims with nervous disorders), Kafka directly referred to this aspect:

> This great war which encompasses the sum total of human misery is also a war on the nervous system, more a war on the nervous system than any previous war. . . Just as the intensive industrialization of the past decades of peace had attacked, affected, and caused disorders of the nervous systems of those engaged in industry more than ever before, so the enormously increased mechanization of present-day warfare presents the gravest dangers and disorders to the nervous system of fighting men.[56]

In *The Trial* and *The Castle*, it is impersonal and hierarchical authority that takes centre stage: in Benjamin's words, Kafka wrote from the point of view of the 'modern citizen, who knows he is at the mercy of vast bureaucratic machinery, whose functioning is steered by authorities who remain nebulous even to the executive organs themselves, let alone the people they deal with'.[57] Contrary to what has often been claimed, Kafka's two great novels were not a criticism of the old Austro-Hungarian Imperial state, that 'mixture of despotism and negligence' which Victor Adler spoke of. Rather, they focus precisely on the state apparatus in its most modern and most anonymous dimension as an autonomous 'thing-like' system that has been transformed into a goal in itself. Many critics have interpreted *The Trial*, too, as a prophetic work in which Kafka, with his visionary imagination, foresaw the laws of totalitarian States, Nazi or Stalinist trials, and so on. Bertolt Brecht, though a loyal fellow-traveller of the Soviet Union, noted in conversation with Benjamin in 1934 (even before the Moscow Trials):

> Kafka had one problem, and one only, and that was the problem of organization. He was terrified by the thought of the empire of ants: the thought of men being alienated from themselves by the forms of their life in society. And he anticipated certain forms of this alienation, e.g. the methods of the GPU.[58]

This kind of remark may be considered a justifiable homage to the Prague author's clairvoyance, but it sheds very little light on Kafka's own motivations or on what *The Trial* meant to him. Moreover, such attempts to read back into Kafka the so-called 'emergency forms of the State' obscure one of the novel's most important key ideas: namely, the alienated and oppressive nature of the 'normal', legal and constitutional state. From the very first pages, Kafka says quite clearly: 'K. lived in a country with a legal constitution (*Rechtsstaat*), there was universal peace, all the laws were in force; who dared seize him in his own dwelling?'[59] Like the anarchists, Kafka seemed to consider any form of State, the state as such, to be an authoritarian hierarchy founded upon illusion and falsehood.

The inspiration for the plot of *The Trial* must be sought not in an imaginary future but in contemporary historical facts.[60] The great anti-Semitic trials of that era were a particularly flagrant example of State injustice: the most famous were the Tisza Affair (Hungary, 1882); the Dreyfus Affair (France, 1894–9); the Hilsner Trial (Czechoslovakia, 1899–1900); and the Beiliss Affair (Russia, 1912–13). Despite differences in the form of State (absolutism, constitutional monarchy, republic), the judicial system in each case condemned innocent victims, whose only crime was that of being Jewish. Although Kafka was still an adolescent in 1899, the Hilsner Trial seems to have made a considerable impression on him. Leopold Hilsner, a young Czech was sentenced to death for 'ritual murder', despite the lack of proof. That his life was spared was due only to a campaign led by Masaryk: a review of the trial commuted his sentence to life imprisonment. In a conversation quoted by Janouch, Kafka mentioned this episode as the starting-point for his awareness of the Jewish condition.[61] But the trial against Beiliss probably shook him even more; *Selbstwehr*, the journal published by Kafka's friends in Prague, was obsessed with the affair, and it is known that, among the papers Kafka burned shortly before his death, was a narrative about Mendel Beiliss.[62] Kafka understood these trials not only as a Jew, but also from the perspective of an anti-authoritarian universal mind: in the Jewish experience, he discovered the quintessence of the human experience in the modern era. The hero of *The Trial*, Joseph K., has neither a set nationality nor a religion: he is the representative *par excellence* of the victims of the legal machinery of the state.

Joseph K. is arrested one fine morning, and no one can explain to him why. He is judged by a court that forbids him any access to his judges – haughty and mysterious officials who do not recognize the defence and only just 'tolerate' it. Their behaviour is inexplicable and unpredictable, and it is by their decision that K. is eventually condemned and executed. Titorelli's painting which depicts the goddess of Justice symbolizes the true nature of such a system: at first, it strongly suggests the goddess of Victory, but – when the painting is well lit – it looks exactly like the goddess of Hunting in full cry.

In reality, law is virtually absent from this 'trial'. It is something unknown, impossible to know and perhaps even non-existent. This theme of the mysterious law which probably does not exist, also appears in the parable 'The Problem of our Laws', where Kafka describes a people ruled by a small aristocratic caste who keep the laws secret – so much so that their very existence is in doubt. The ending seems inspired by libertarian irony: 'Any party which would repudiate, not only all belief in the laws, but the nobility as well, would have the whole people behind it.'[63]

In *The Trial*, the absence of law is complemented by the presence of a powerful legal organization, which Joseph K. indignantly denounces:

An organization which not only employs corrupt warders, oafish Inspectors, and Examining Magistrates . . . but also has at its disposal a judicial hierarchy of high, indeed of the highest rank, with an indispensable and numerous retinue of servants, clerks, police, and other assistants, perhaps even hangmen, I do not shrink from that word. And the significance of this great organization, gentlemen? It consists in this, that innocent persons are accused of guilt, and senseless proceedings are put in motion against them.[64]

In *The Trial*, Kafka the jurist considers the state's legal machine from the point of view of the victims: it is a bureaucratic structure, opaque and absurd, unpredictable and incomprehensible, impersonal and ruthless.[65]

In a first moment, Joseph K. rebels against this machine: at the beginning of the novel, he even contemplates escaping purely and simply. But he ends up giving in to the rules of the game. As Hannah Arendt notes:

In *The Trial*, subordination is not achieved through force, but rather through the growing feeling of guilt that is evoked in the defendant K. by the unfounded and empty accusation. . . The hero's internal development and the machine's functioning finally come together in the last scene of the execution, when K. allows himself without resistance or even contradiction to be led off and killed.[66]

This is why Joseph K. complains of dying 'like a dog'. For Kafka, the dog represents the one who servilely obeys authority, as did Robinson in *America*. In *The Trial*, the merchant Block is also presented as a kind of dog at the feet of the lawyer attorney, and in 'In the Penal Colony', Kafka speaks of the 'dog-like' (*hündisch*) submission of the condemned. The shame (the final word of *The Trial*) that must outlive Joseph K. is that of having yielded without resistance to his executioners.

In *The Castle*, Kafka deals directly with the state and the bureaucratic system: not the traditional and personal face of power (which is portrayed by an insignificant character, Count Westwest), but the foundations of all states, the state in general, and in particular the modern state, with its impersonal, authoritarian and alienated hierarchical apparatus. His correspondence from that time testifies to the same anxiety: in a letter to Milena on the war (although his remarks have a broader application), he states that 'events are judged and decided only by the incalculable hierarchy of the higher authorities' – an expression that seems to be taken directly from *The Trial* or *The Castle*.[67]

In the novel, the 'Castle' embodies Power, Authority, the State, against the people, who are represented by the 'Village'. The Castle is presented as an alienated, haughty, inaccessible, distant and arbitrary power, which governs the village through a labyrinth of bureaucrats whose behaviour is crass, inexplicable and utterly void of sense.

In the fifth chapter, Kafka sketches a tragi-comic parody of the bureaucratic universe, of the 'official' confusion that his character K. considers eminently ridiculous. The Mayor discloses to K. the circular and empty internal logic of the system:

> Is there a Control Authority? Only a total stranger could ask a question like yours. There are only Control Authorities. Frankly, it isn't their function to hunt out errors in the vulgar sense, for errors don't happen, and even when once in a while an error does happen, as in your case, who can say finally that it's an error?[68]

The Mayor is here suggesting that the entire bureaucratic machine is made up only of control services, which control each other. But he adds immediately that there is nothing to control, as there are not really any errors. Every sentence refutes the previous one, and the end result is 'administrative' nonsense.

While the Mayor is speaking, something in the background grows, expands and submerges everything: official paper, the paper with which, according to Kafka, the chains of tormented mankind are made. An ocean of paper covers the Mayor's room, a mountain of paper accumulates in Sordini's office.

But the height of bureaucratic alienation is reached when the Mayor describes the official apparatus as an autonomous machine that seems to work 'by itself': 'it's as if the administrative apparatus were unable any longer to bear the tension, the year-long irritation caused by the same affair – probably trivial in itself – and had hit on the decision by itself, without the assistance of the officials.'[69] Kafka thereby presents the bureaucratic system as a reified world, in which relationships between individuals become things, independent objects, blind gear wheels.

The individual human being is powerless in the face of this indecipherable and omnipotent apparatus. Not only K. as a 'troublemaker', but all those who defy Authority, even in its vilest whims (the Amalia affair), are defeated and punished with exclusion.

According to Marthe Robert, the Land Surveyor K. represents a new step (in relation to Joseph K.) in the 'hero's slow progress toward the reconquest of his self from the tyranny of "the administrative"': he dies utterly exhausted but at least he has 'dismantled, piece by piece, symbol by symbol, sign by sign, the all-powerful edifice which remains standing thanks only to the despotism of the masters, duly supported by the mental laziness and credulity of the blind subjects'.[70] The Land Surveyor is the stranger – implicitly, the Jew – who finds himself outside the relationship of domination/subordination between the Castle and the Village. As a stranger, he is capable of surprise – in the sense of the Greek *taumasein*, the beginning of all philosophical knowledge – when he encounters bureaucratic absurdity as incarnated by the Castle officials. He asks for neither grace nor favour, only his right but that is plainly impossible in the universe of administrative injustice.

Libertarian utopia never appears as such in the novels and short-stories we have been discussing in this chapter. It is present only in *negative* form, as criticism directed towards a world that is totally deprived of freedom, subject to the absurd and arbitrary logic of an all-powerful 'apparatus'. The manner in which the existing state of things is criticized reveals Kafka's anarchist viewpoint. The structural homology with *theologia negativa* is striking: in both cases, the positive reverse side of the established world (libertarian utopia or messianic redemption) is a *radical absence*, and this is precisely what defines human life as demeaned, damned or void of meaning. The subterranean elective affinity between the two 'negative' configurations results in an intimate convergence, which shapes the structure of meaning in the novels. Crushing of the individual ('like a dog') or sovereign denial of freedom are the very index of the non-redemption of the world – just as, conversely, the individual's unlimited (religious) freedom seems to announce the coming of the Messiah.

Negative theology and negative utopia tend to fuse in a reversed form of (religious) metaphysical anarchism, which may well be one of the main components of the unique and enigmatic spiritual quality of Kafka's writings.

6

Outside all Currents, at the Crossing of the Ways: Walter Benjamin

Because he sees ways everywhere, he always positions himself at crossroads.

Walter Benjamin, 'The Destructive Character', 1931

'A l'écart de tous les courants' was the French title of the last article that Adorno wrote on Walter Benjamin, in 1969. The singularity of Benjamin's work placed him apart, outside the main intellectual or political trends of early twentieth-century Europe, whether neo-Kantianism or phenomenology, Marxism or positivism, liberalism or conservativism. Strictly unclassifiable and irreducible to established models, Benjamin was at the crossing of all the ways as well as at the centre of the complex network of relationships that were woven within the German-Jewish milieu. The path that led from Berlin to Jerusalem (for Scholem and Buber) or from Berlin to Moscow (for Bloch and Lukács) intersected in Benjamin, and his subtle, esoteric thinking seemed to knot together all the political and cultural contradictions of the Jewish intelligentsia in *Mitteleuropa*: theology and historical materialism; assimilation and Zionism; conservative romanticism and nihilistic revolution; mystical messianism and profane utopia.

In order to grasp this particularity, richness and tension, the following hypothesis might serve us as a starting-point. Walter Benjamin was one of the few authors in whom the elective affinity between Jewish messianism and libertarian utopia led to an authentic *fusion* – that is, to the dawning of a new way of thinking which could not simply be reduced to its components. This form was significant not only for political or religious reasons; it implied a new way of perceiving historical temporality. For, contrary to what has usually been argued, Benjamin was not only a great literary critic or renewer of Marxist aesthetics: as some authors

95

(notably Miguel Abensour and Stephane Mosès) have pointed out, the decisive challenge of his work lay in a new conception of history. Other messianic/libertarian thinkers suggested such a conception in their writings, but in Benjamin's work it achieved its highest philosophical expression.

The following remarks seek to reconstruct the development of the elective affinity between messianism and utopia in Benjamin's spiritual itinerary. One is immediately struck both by the astonishing continuity of certain fundamental themes, and by the succession of sharp turns, unexpected reversals, forward dashes and backward jumps. Benjamin's thinking advances like the painting of an artist who never erases his strokes, but instead covers them over each time with a fresh layer of paint: at times, it seems to follow the contours of the original sketch, while at others, it seems to go beyond them and to take on an unexpected form.

Romantic culture was the point of departure for Benjamin's singular spiritual journey, as it was for many young German Jews of his generation. In one of his first published works – an article 'Romantik', from 1913 – Benjamin called for the birth of a new romanticism, and proclaimed that 'the romantic *will* for beauty, the romantic *will* for truth, the romantic *will* for action' were the 'unsurpassable' (*unüberwindlich*) facts of modern culture.[1] The letters he wrote between 1910 and 1920 contain innumerable references to Romantic writers – notably Hölderlin, Novalis, Schlegel, Tieck, Franz von Baader and Franz-Joseph Molitor (the last two, moreover, were fascinated by the cabbala and Jewish mysticism). In 1919, in a thesis on 'The Concept of Art Criticism in German Romanticism', Benjamin hailed the Romantics (in particular, Friedrich Schlegel and Novalis) for their surpassing (*Überwindung*) of 'rational dogmas'.[2]

Of course, Benjamin's own concept of romanticism could not be reduced to the classical Romantic ideas. None the less, references to cultural critiques of industrial/capitalist civilization (reminiscent of Romanticism) and to Romantic conceptions of religion, art and culture were to be found in his writings from the 1915 essay on Hölderlin to the 1930 article on E.T.A. Hoffmann. As he wrote to Gershom Scholem in June 1917, 'Romanticism is clearly the last movement that keeps tradition alive for the present (*die Tradition hinüberrettete*)'.[3]

The roots of the close association of messianic and utopian-anarchist themes lie deep within a neo-romantic critique of 'progress'. If we analyse one of Benjamin's first works, the lecture on 'The Life of Students' (1914), we can already see in outline his entire social/religious *Weltanschauung*. In opposition to 'a shapeless progressive tendency', he extols the critical power of utopian images, such as the French Revolution of 1789, or the messianic Kingdom. Technology and science are not the real questions for society to consider. Instead, it has to examine the metaphysical problems raised by Plato, Spinoza, the Romantics and Nietzsche; these must inspire students, so that their community might become 'the scene for a permanent revolution of the spirit'. Benjamin hints at anarchism when he affirms that all science and liberal arts are necessarily 'alien to the State and often inimical to the State'. But he expresses his ideas more directly when he invokes the spirit of Tolstoy, who called on people to place themselves at the service of the poor – 'a spirit generated in the conceptions of the most profound anarchists and in the Christian monastic communities'.[4] Utopia, anarchism, revolution and messianism combine alchemically and join with a neo-romantic cultural critique of 'progress' and purely scientific/technical knowledge. The past (monastic communities) and the future (anarchist utopia) are directly associated in typically romantic/revolutionary terms.

'The Life of Students' contains *in nuce* several of Benjamin's future *illuminations*, and the similarities between it and his final writings can be demonstrated in a precise and rigorous way. Its themes will later flow in all his works, sometimes openly, sometimes as a stream hidden underground. Despite this essential continuity in Benjamin's spiritual trajectory from 1914 to 1940, major changes did undoubtedly take place. In particular, after 1924 Marxism became an increasingly crucial component of his world-view. However, as I will try to show, Communism and historical materialism did not supplant his old spiritualist and libertarian-romantic convictions; rather, they amalgamated with them and, in so doing, constituted a singular and unique form of thought.

It is true that, as Benjamin's appropriation of historical materialism grew deeper in the 1930s, he referred less often to romanticism; yet several key elements of the romantic world-view remained at the heart of his religious and philosophical-political ideas. Neither his messianism nor his anarchism can be understood outside the romantic cultural field, which served as their common foundation.

It would be wrong, however, to overlook the rationalist, *Aufklärer* dimension of Benjamin's world-view, notably in relation to Kant and to neo-Kantianism (Hermann Cohen). In a certain sense, Benjamin's method drew its inspiration from a *sui generis* synthesis of romanticism and the Enlightenment: the former was most dominant in the works he wrote prior to 1930, while the latter predominated in his later materialist works. In an article from 1931 on Franz von Baader, whose 'diagnosis of the social condition of the working class was well ahead of nearly every one of his contemporaries' (at the beginning of the nineteenth century), Benjamin insisted that *Romantik* [Romanticism] and *Aufklärung* [Enlightenment] were linked in the political thinking of that conservative and mystical philosopher, who dreamed of a clergy that could embody 'the spirit of humanity' beyond national borders.[5] The same reasoning applies *mutatis mutandis* to Benjamin's own search for a possible point of convergence between Jewish messianism and proletarian internationalism, between romantic criticism of bourgeois civilization and enlightened humanism.

The link between romanticism and messianism in Benjamin is illustrated not only by his interest in the mystical cabbalistic writings of Romantic thinkers like Franz von Baader and Franz Joseph Molitor, but especially by his doctoral thesis, in which he emphasized that the true essence of the *Frühromantik* 'must be sought in romantic messianism'. He discovered the messianic dimension of romanticism in the writings of Friedrich Schlegel and Novalis in particular, and among his quotations from the young Schlegel is the astonishing statement that 'the revolutionary desire to realize the Kingdom of God is . . . the beginning of modern history'.[6]

In 'The Concept of Art Criticism in German Romanticism', one passage is crucial for an understanding of Benjamin's nascent messianic philosophy of history. In it he contrasts a *qualitative* perception of time (*qualitative zeitliche Unendlichkeit*) – 'which issues from romantic messianism', and for which the life of mankind is a process of fulfilment (*Erfüllung*) and not just of becoming – to the empty infinity of time (*leere Unendlichkeit der Zeit*) characteristic of the modern ideology of Progress.[7] There is no need to stress the similarity between this passage (which seems to have escaped the attention of commentators) and the ideas expressed in 1940 in the *Theses on the Philosophy of History*.

Benjamin's early writings on Jewish theology – particularly 'On Language as Such and on the Language of Man' ('Über die Sprache überhaupt und über die Sprache des Menschen') from 1916 – were also inspired by romanticism. This latter essay is usually thought to have been influenced by cabbalistic sources. Yet, as Gershom Scholem mentioned in his memoirs, he did not begin to discuss the cabbala with Benjamin until 1917; and it was only after then that his friend discovered the writings of the Christian cabbalist Franz Joseph Molitor.[8] Winfried Menninghaus's recent investigations show convincingly that the direct source for Benjamin's theory of 'linguistic magic' was the Romantic philosophy of language of Novalis, Schlegel, Hamman and Herder, itself inspired by themes borrowed from the cabbala.[9]

Benjamin's essay on language is imbued with a longing for paradise lost, with its 'blissful Adamite linguistic spirit', before the discovery of the Tree of Good and Evil (the original sin) and the Fall into 'chatter' and linguistic confusion (the Tower of Babel).[10] But the utopian/messianic dimension of this philosophy of language will assert itself only in a later work, 'The Task of the Translator' (1921), which already incorporates the outcome of Benjamin's discussions with Scholem on the cabbala and his readings of Molitor. According to this article, the multiplicity of languages will be abolished in the 'messianic conclusion of their history' – that is, in 'the predestined, hitherto inaccessible realm of reconciliation and fulfillment of languages'.[11]

What exactly did Scholem contribute to the mystical and messianic reflections of the young Benjamin? An unpublished letter from Scholem to Hannah Arendt, written in 1960, sheds some light on this matter by referring to an article of Scholem's, also from 1921, on the significance of the Torah in Jewish mysticism: 'These ideas were what really attracted Walter Benjamin's kabbalistic inclinations, insofar as I could explain them to him in my intuitive (rather than educated) youth.'[12] Now, one of the main aspects of Scholem's article was a description of the coming messianic era (contained in certain cabbalistic documents) as a return to a paradisaical utopia, which would go beyond the separation between good and evil: 'The entire world will be in as perfect a state as was the Garden of Eden.'[13]

The linguistic theology of the young Benjamin seems, therefore, to have been constructed on a messianic/restorative paradigm inspired by cabbalism and romanticism which longed for the restoration of Edenic harmony. This paradigm was not without its similarities to Molitor's book on the cabbala, where the task of the *Maschiach* is to 'destroy the innermost root of evil and to erase the general *P'gimah* that was a result of the fall of Adam', thereby bringing redemption and restoring the former state (*den früheren Zustand wiederherstellen*).[14]

Benjamin's libertarian utopia, too, was based on a neo-romantic structure of feeling. He explicitly affirmed this connection (albeit in reference to other authors) in a highly illuminating letter to Scholem from 1918; designating romanticism as 'one of the most powerful movements of our time', and adding that the ideal aspect of Catholic romanticism (as opposed to its political side) 'was developed, through incorporation of social elements, in anarchism (Leonhard Frank, Ludwig Rubiner)'.[15] As we have already seen in Benjamin's talk on students (1914) the Catholic-romantic restorative dimension was closely tied to libertarian ideas: monastic communities and anarchist groups were presented as the two most significant models of social action.

In general, Benjamin's political conceptions were influenced by the libertarian, anarchist or anarcho-syndicalist thinkers closest to anti-capitalist romanticism and its restorative aspirations: Georges Sorel, Gustav Landauer, Tolstoy, Strindberg.[16] However, Benjamin's ideas were far from being 'political' in the usual sense of the word. When in 1919 Scholem defined the doctrine they shared as 'theocratic anarchism', the term had an exclusively religious meaning.[17] According to Werner Kraft, a close friend of Benjamin's at the time, Benjamin's anarchism had a certain 'symbolic' quality; he was neither on the left nor on the right, but 'somewhere else'.[18] Benjamin himself – with obvious delectation – used the term 'nihilism' to refer to his own political (or rather anti-political) ideas during the 1920s. For example, in a letter to Scholem from 1924, he spoke of 'my nihilism', a term which Scholem interpreted as being synonymous with anarchist convictions.[19] Scholem certainly contributed to the development of these convictions in Benjamin, for example by providing him with the writings of Landauer and other libertarian literature;[20] but the tendency had already been there before they met, as can be deduced from the 1914 talk on 'The Life of Students'.

The key to the particular nature of Benjamin's anarchism is its relationship to Jewish messianism, a relationship that can be grasped only through the concept of elective affinity. Starting from the same neo-romantic roots, the two cultural figures shared a utopian-restorative structure, a revolutionary/catastrophist perspective of history, and a libertarian image of the Edenic future.

The essay 'Critique of Violence' ('Zur Kritik der Gewalt'), written in 1921 under the direct inspiration of Sorel's *Reflections on Violence*, was one of the first works in which Benjamin expressed his libertarian and revolutionary views in all their explosiveness. In this essay, Benjamin voices his utter scorn for state institutions, such as the police ('the greatest conceivable degeneration of violence') or Parliament ('a woeful spectacle'). He gives unreserved approval to the 'annihilating and on the whole apt' critique of parliaments made by the Bolsheviks and anarcho-syndicalists (a highly revealing association), as well as to the Sorelian idea of a general strike which 'sets itself the sole task of destroying state power'. It seems to Benjamin that this conception, which he himself calls anarchist, is 'deep, moral and genuinely revolutionary'. However, Benjamin parts with Sorel at this point and enters the completely different realm of messianic theology. Revolutionary violence, pure and immediate, is a manifestation of divine violence, the sole form capable of breaking the 'cycle maintained by mythical forms of law' (including state power) and thus of founding 'a new historic epoch'. Divine/revolutionary violence is 'law-destroying' and is therefore opposed both to law-making mythical violence and to law-preserving violence.[21]

Benjamin's *sui generis* dialectic of anarchy and messianism, revolution and theology, is also present, in a particularly dense form, in the hermetically mercurial piece entitled 'Theologico-Political Fragment' ('Theologisch-politisches Fragment'). Written at approximately the same period, this 'metaphysical anarchist' text (Scholem *dixit*) sets the sphere of historical evolution completely apart from that of the messianic: 'nothing historical can relate itself on its own account to anything Messianic'. But immediately afterwards, it erects over this seemingly infinite abyss a dialectical bridge, a subtle passageway, a strange route, which appears to be directly inspired by certain paragraphs from Franz Rosenzweig's *The Star of Redemption* (1921). The *dynamis* of the profane – or to be more precise, the 'order of the profane . . . through being profane' (the equivalent of Rosenzweig's 'human order of the world') – which Benjamin defines as 'free mankind's pursuit of happiness' (as opposed to Rosenzweig's 'great deeds of liberation') 'assists the coming of the Messianic Kingdom'. Benjamin's phrasing is less imperative than Rosenzweigs – 'assist the coming' (or 'category of its quietest approach') as opposed to 'indispensable preconditions of its advent [the Kingdom of God]' – but the thought processes are the same: they both seek to mediate between the emancipatory, historical and 'profane' struggles of man and the accomplishment of the messianic promise.[22] At the end of the fragment, Benjamin expresses his desire for a temporal and spiritual *restitutio in integrum* – a task he assigns to a unique form of world politics, 'whose method must be called nihilism' (a term that replaces anarchism, which Benjamin may have judged to be too profane). *Restitutio in integrum* (or *restitutio omnium*) is a figure from Christian theology, which refers both to the resurrection of the dead at the Last Judgement and to the eschatological return of all things to their original perfection. The term had appeared in two works by Ernst Bloch: *The Spirit of Utopia* (1918), which Benjamin cites in the 'Fragment', and *Thomas Münzer* (1921); Benjamin probably took it from these sources.[23]

A paradoxical echo of Benjamin's libertarian problematic is found in *The Origin of German Tragic Drama* (written in 1924 and published in 1928). From the conservative lawyer Carl Schmitt, Benjamin borrows the notion that, in the final analysis, sovereignty is founded upon the dictatorial powers of the state of emergency.[24] In a recent commentary on this essay, Norbert Bolz noted that Benjamin was interested in Schmitt because of the 'physiognomic analogy between the reactionary critic and the anarchist': both men rejected liberal myths and viewed the state of emergency as the core of political order. The extreme situation had a historical-philosophical index: it defined the 'time of the final fight between Authority and Anarchy'.[25]

Benjamin's first written reference to Bolshevism comes in the 1921 essay on violence, where it is directly associated with anarcho-syndicalism as an anti-parliamentarian revolutionary doctrine. Throughout his political evolution, he will link Communist and libertarian ideas in one way or another. His Marxism, far from replacing anarchism, will to a large extent be dyed with libertarian colours.

After Benjamin simultaneously discovered Marxism (through Lukács' *History and Class Consciousness*) and Bolshevism (through Asja Lacis in 1924), his political reflections gave a central place to Communism and, later, to historical materialism. Aware of the tensions between what he called 'the foundations of my nihilism' and the Hegelian-Marxist dialectic represented by Lukács' work, Benjamin was, nevertheless, greatly attracted by the 'political praxis of Communism' as a 'stance that binds' (*verbindliche Haltung*). What interested him the most about Lukács' book (which he discovered through Ernst Bloch when the two met in Capri in 1924), was the unity of theory and practice that made up 'the hard philosophical core' of the work and gave it such superiority that 'any other approach is nothing but demagogic bourgeois phraseology'.[26]

In a letter to Scholem two years later (29 May 1926), Benjamin said that he was considering joining the Communist Party; but he insisted that this did not mean he was thinking of 'abjuring' his former anarchism. (Note that this was the first time that Benjamin explicitly referred in writing to his own convictions as being anarchist rather than simply 'nihilist'.) In Benjamin's opinion, anarchist methods were 'certainly inappropriate' and Communist goals were 'meaningless'; but that 'in no way detracts from the value of Communist action, because it is the corrective of Communist goals – and because there are no meaningful *political* goals.'[27] From these obscure and essentially negative remarks, two 'positive' suggestions may perhaps be deduced: anarchist goals were significant because they were not political goals, but Communist action provided the best method for achieving those goals. In an attempt to interpret this enigmatic passage, the American researcher Richard Wolin wrote that in the final analysis, the only worthwhile goals for Benjamin were the messianic ends.[28] That is true, provided we do not forget that, in Benjamin's mind, messianic and anarchist goals were closely linked. In the same letter to Scholem, Benjamin spoke of an identity between religious and political observance, 'which shows up only in the paradoxical transformation (*Umschlagen*) of one into the other (in both directions)'.²⁹ The paradoxical reversal/transformation (*Umschlagen*) of anarchism (or 'nihilism') into messianism and *vice versa*, may be one of the most important keys for understanding Benjamin's esoteric social/religious world-view, from the 'Theologico-Political Fragment' to his *Theses on the Philosophy of History*.

The first work in which the impact of Marxism can be felt is *One Way Street* (*Einbahnstrasse*), written in 1925, and published in 1928. The change that took place in Benjamin's thinking as a result of the economic crisis (the collapse of his father's business in Berlin!), the rejection of his university accreditation in 1925, and the discovery of Communism can be illustrated by a comparison between the first and last drafts of the manuscript. Thus the first version of the chapter 'Imperial Panorama', written in 1923, contains the following remark about man as a victim of poverty (resulting from the economic crisis and inflation): 'Then he must be alert to every humiliation done to him and so discipline himself that his suffering becomes no longer the downhill road of hatred, but the rising path of prayer (*den aufsteigenden Pfad des Gebetes*).' In the 1925 version, the sentence is repeated word for word until the radically different ending: 'Then he must be alert to every humiliation done to him and so discipline himself that his suffering becomes no longer the downhill road of grief, but the rising path of revolt (*den aufsteigenden Pfad der Revolte*).'³⁰ In the flash of those few words, we can glimpse the astonishing change that took place in Benjamin's political ideas over the course of those two years.

Benjamin's earlier neo-romantic criticism of progress did not disappear, but it became charged with a Marxist revolutionary tension. In a fragment from *One Way Street* significantly entitled 'Fire Alarm', he sounded the tocsin:

If the abolition of the bourgeoisie is not completed by an almost calculable moment in economic and technical development (a moment signalled by inflation and poison-gas warfare), all is lost. Before the spark reaches the dynamite, the lighted fuse must be cut.

Could the proletariat achieve this revolutionary interruption in time? 'The continuance or the end of three thousand years of cultural development will be decided by the answer.'[31] This was the first text in which Benjamin contrasted revolution with the catastrophic continuation of a technological progress dependent upon the ruling classes. What his criticism called for was not the negation of technology but its complete redefinition: mastery not of nature but 'of the relation between nature and man'.[32]

It is also interesting to note that, in spite of his interest in Communism, the only revolutionary political movement that Benjamin mentioned in this work was anarcho-syndicalism. Unlike the conservative politician, who does not hesitate to set his private life in contradiction with the principles he defends in public, the anarcho-syndicalist mercilessly subjects his private life to the standards that he seeks to make into the laws of a future society. These two figures are presented in the fragment 'Ministry of the Interior' as the two ideal forms of political behaviour.[33]

An attempt to articulate Communism and anarchism was the leitmotiv of Benjamin's essay 'Surrealism' (1929). Locating himself ('the German observer') in the 'infinitely perilous [position] between anarchistic insurrection and revolutionary discipline', he hails the Surrealists as the most remarkable inheritors of the libertarian tradition: 'Since Bakunin, Europe has lacked a radical concept of freedom. The Surrealists have one.' It is true that Benjamin's concept of anarchism had a broad metaphorical dimension. For example, he referred to Dostoevsky, Rimbaud and Lautréamont as 'great anarchists', who, between 1865 and 1875, 'independently of one another [. . .] set its clock at exactly the same hour'; forty years later (when Surrealism came into being), their writings exploded at the same moment. Benjamin also applied the term 'nihilism' to Breton, singling out his 'revolutionary nihilism' for praise. Moreover, he drew attention to a passage from *Nadja*, in which the Surrealist poet congratulated himself on the 'delightful days spent looting Paris under the sign of [the anarchist martyrs] Sacco and Vanzetti'.[34]

It is true that Benjamin was concerned about the danger of overemphasizing the 'anarchist component' of the revolution, at the expense of 'methodical and disciplinary preparation' (in

other words, Communism). However, he believed that, with
respect to the cardinal questions of the era, Surrealism and
Communism had come ever closer to each other. In opposition
to the dilettantish and complacent optimism of social democracy,
they both shared the same perception of the fate of mankind in
Europe: 'pessimism all along the line.' And if the *Communist
Manifesto* demanded that reality transcend itself (through 'revolutionary discharge'), 'the Surrealists have understood its present
commands'.[35]

After 1930, references to anarchism seem to disappear from
Benjamin's writings, as does any mention of the messianic era;
but their hidden presence can be detected, like a secret furnace
or an underground fire, actively shaping developments on the
surface. For example, it is probable that Benjamin's sympathy
for Communism between 1925 and 1935 had something to do
with the clearly 'apocalyptic' orientation of the Comintern at that
time: the so-called 'Third Period', with its doctrine that world
revolution was imminent. In a letter to Scholem from April 1931,
Benjamin referred to the 'Bolshevik revolution in Germany' as an
event that would probably take place in the near future! In his
response, Scholem saw a danger in Benjamin's intense yearning
for a community, 'even if it is the apocalyptic community of the
revolution'. In July 1931, Benjamin replied: 'I doubt that we will
have to wait any longer than Autumn for civil war to break out.'[36]
Already in 1930 Benjamin had written an article on theories of
Fascism whose famous last paragraph (which Adorno wanted to
exclude from a new edition in the 1960s) made a call to turn world
war into civil war (in Germany).[37] On the other hand, Benjamin
remained sceptical of the Popular Front in France – a position
in keeping with his previous anti-parliamentarian convictions.
In a letter to Fritz Lieb from July 1937, he complained that the
left-wing papers 'cling only to the fetish of a "left-wing" majority,
and no one cares that it is carrying out policies which, if practised
by the Right, would lead to rioting'.[38]

There are also more direct signs that Benjamin's esoteric
anarchist faith persisted during the 1930s. In a letter he wrote
to Alfred Cohn in February 1935 – still during the period in which
he seemed closest to orthodox Communist doctrine – he stated
that, while reading Drieu La Rochelle's short-story 'The Deserter',
'to my great astonishment, I found the very representation of my

own political attitude'.[39] An analysis of this story (published in 1934) might therefore give us a vital lead to Benjamin's hidden political philosophy. The hero (or anti-hero) of the book is a French deserter from the First World War, a cosmopolitan internationalist exiled in Latin America for whom 'nationalism was the most ignoble aspect of the modern mind'. The traveller who converses with him, probably expressing Drieu's own opinions, treats him at times as an 'old reactionary', and at other times as a 'wandering Jew', 'an anarchist', or a 'harmless utopian'. The deserter responds: 'I don't want your European state of war, your perpetual mobilization, your militarist socialization. Call it any name you fancy: anarchism, if you like. But I know that I've nothing to do with theories in books I haven't read.' However, there is a type of spontaneous libertarian spirit in the deserter's anti-political and anti-state philosophy: 'Politics is the vilest of the games that this planet has to offer. Everything coming from the State is a job for lackeys.'[40] If this literary figure represents, to use Benjamin's own words, the 'very representation' of his own political position, there is no doubt that his position was much closer to anarchism than his works written during the 1930s would seem to suggest.

The more or less hidden persistence of some anarchist themes may be one of the reasons for Benjamin's critical attitude towards the Soviet Union, in spite of all his sympathy for the Soviet experiment. In his *Moscow Diary*, which he wrote in late 1926 and early 1927, we find opinions broadly similar to those of the left-wing Opposition within the Bolshevik Party (Trotsky-Zinoviev-Kamenev). The Soviet government was seeking to

> bring about a suspension of militant Communism, to usher in a period free of class conflict, to de-politicize the life of its citizens as much as possible. . . An attempt is being made to arrest the dynamic of revolutionary progress in the life of the state – one has entered, like it or not, a period of restoration. . . .[41]

Benjamin's interest in Trotsky's writings, even after his expulsion from the Soviet Union, is further evidence of this critical distance. After having read the autobiography of the founder of the Red Army and his *History of the Russian Revolution*. Benjamin stated in a letter to Gretel Adorno in 1932: 'It has been years since I have taken in anything with so much tension that it takes my breath away.'[42]

However, after the triumph of Nazism in Germany in 1933, there began a short period in which Benjamin seemed to draw much closer to the Soviet model of Communism. It was also the period in which he seemed to rally to a 'progressive' conception of technology.

In Irving Wohlfarth's remarkable essay 'On the Messianic Structure of Benjamin's Last Reflections', he argues that Benjamin saw the revolution at times as accelerating the dialectic of historical progress and at other times as pulling its emergency brake.[43] This is a very illuminating remark, but it should be made clear that the first variant was a brief intellectual experiment in which Benjamin engaged during the mid-1930s, while criticism of the ideology of 'progress' was an essential component of most of his writings.

How can Benjamin's brief excursion into 'progressivism' be explained? The usual argument has been 'the influence of Brecht'. That may be true, but as a general rule influence itself, far from explaining anything, requires an explanation. One might put forward the following hypothesis. The articles that Benjamin wrote between 1933 and 1935, which contain a highly favourable evaluation of technological progress – notably 'Erfahrung und Armut' [Experience and Poverty] (1933), 'The Author as Producer' (1934), and 'The Work of Art in the Age of Mechanical Reproduction' (1935) – are also those in which Benjamin displays uncritical support for the Soviet Union, whose ideology at that time (the second Five-year Plan) was more than ever a wildly industrialist and productivist version of Marxism. It was not by chance that the beginning of Benjamin's 'progressive interlude' coincided with the rise of Hitler in Germany, which, in the eyes of many left-wing intellectuals, made the Soviet Union look like the last bulwark against Fascism.

However, the significance of these writings, which seemingly contradict Benjamin's entire way of thinking, must not be exaggerated. On the one hand, during the same period he wrote works that were consistent with his traditional concerns: the essays on Kafka (1934) and Bachofen (1935); the article 'Paris, Capital of the Nineteenth Century' (1935), among others. On the other hand, the three works at issue are themselves extremely ambiguous.

In 'Erfahrung und Armut', Benjamin hails the end of culture as a healthy *tabula rasa*, but the words he uses to refer to the new civilization – 'sombre and cold', like glass and steel – are hardly joyful: 'a new barbarism'. As for Benjamin's essay on the work of art, Scholem already emphasized the deep tension between the first part (the loss of the aura) and the second (the celebration of film).[44] And its openness to different, if not contradictory, interpretations is confirmed by a recent commentary which concludes that, far from praising modernity, it 'echoes the reactions of indignation in the face of the rising up of the masses and the preponderance of technology'![45]

The end of Benjamin's experiment in support for Soviet-style progressivism and technology as such seemed to coincide with the 1936 Moscow Trials, which Benjamin found truly perplexing.[46] Among Benjamin's papers recently discovered by Giorgio Agamben (and now on file in the Bibliothèque Nationale in Paris) is a short note on Brecht – probably written in 1937 – in which he goes so far as to compare the practices of the GPU with those of the Nazis in Germany. In this note, Benjamin scorns Brecht's poem, 'Lesebuch für Städtebewohner' [Manual for City Dwellers] for its 'poetic glorification of the dangerous errors which the praxis of the GPU brought upon the workers' movement'. He also criticizes his own commentary on the poem as a 'pious falsification' (*fromme Fälschung*).[47]

Another sign that Benjamin was distancing himself from Stalin's Soviet Union was his renewed interest, around 1937, in Trotsky's critique of Stalinism. He met Pierre Missac and discussed with him Trotsky's *Revolution Betrayed* – a work about which Missac had written very favourably in the journal *Cahiers du Sud* (No. 196, August 1937). The following year, while Benjamin was with Brecht in Denmark, the 'Trotsky' problem came up again in their conversations; according to Brecht, Trotsky's writings 'prove that there exists a suspicion – a justifiable suspicion – demanding a sceptical appraisal of Russian affairs'. A few days later, Brecht spoke of the Soviet Union as a 'workers' monarchy', and Benjamin compared this organism to certain 'grotesque sports of nature dredged up from the depths of the sea in the form of horned fish or other monsters'.[48] After the German-Soviet Pact was signed in 1939, Benjamin broke for good with the monstrous Stalinist variant of Communism; he alluded to it clearly in the *Theses on the*

Philosophy of History, when he condemned the 'politicians in whom
the opponents of Fascism had placed their hopes [and who] are
prostrate and confirm their defeat by betraying their own cause'.[49]
Parallel to his move away from the Soviet Union – and particularly
after 1936 – criticism of the ideology of technological 'progress'
once more became a major theme of his reflections, culminating
in the *Theses on the Philosophy of History*.

This is not to say that after 1936 Benjamin simply rejected
science and technology, or that he denied the advance in mankind's 'abilities and knowledge' (which he explicitly recognizes
in his *Theses*). What he rejected – with passion and tenacity –
was the life-threatening myth that technological development
would of itself bring about better social conditions and freedom for mankind, or that in order to establish a free society,
socialists merely had to follow the inexorable course of material
progress. Benjamin was firmly convinced that, without a revolutionary interruption of technological progress as it existed under
capitalism, mankind's very existence was in danger. Moreover,
he was increasingly inclined to think that capitalist/ industrial
'progress' entailed a considerable degree of social 'regression'
and made modern human life exactly the opposite of a paradise
lost; in fact, it made it a Hell. In 'Zentralpark', which he wrote in
1938, he penned the following extraordinary passage, quivering
with the energy of despair: 'The concept of progress must be
founded on the idea of catastrophe. The catastrophe is that things
continue to "go on as they are". . . . Strindberg's thoughts: Hell is
not what awaits us – but *the life we are living*.'[50]

Criticism of the doctrines of progress is a central component
of the essay 'The Storyteller', (1936), where Leskov is hailed
(in the words of Tolstoy) as the first writer 'who pointed out
the inadequacy of economic progress', and as one of the last
storytellers who remained faithful to the Golden Age in which
men could believe themselves to be in harmony with nature.[51]
In the article that Benjamin wrote on Fuchs in 1937, this kind
of critique inspired his polemics against positivism (including
positivist social democracy), which 'was able to see the progress
of natural science only in the development of technology, and
failed to recognise the concomitant retrogression of society'.
To Darwinist social-democratic evolutionism – whose insipidly
optimistic illusions ignored the dangers of modern technology,

particularly in relation to war – Benjamin contrasted the 'vision of emergent barbarism, as Engels perceived it in *The Condition of the Working Class in England*, and which Marx glimpsed in his prognosis of capitalist development'.[52]

These quotations illustrate the fact that Benjamin's abandonment of the materialist/progressivist outlook he had held between 1933 and 1935 did not in any way entail a break with Marxism. Nothing could be further from the truth than to identify – as is too often done – Benjamin's Marxism with the works of the 'Brechtian' period alone. The essays that Benjamin wrote between 1936 and 1940 were also inspired by Marxism; but their interpretation of historical materialism (sustained by Jewish theology and romantic culture) was radically different from the orthodoxy of the Comintern.

Taking Marxism as his starting-point – as well as the writings of such authors as Turgot and Jochmann – Benjamin formulated what he described in the 'Passagenwerk' (1935–9) as the critical theory of history, whose viewpoint stressed regression (*der Rückschritt*) in history at least as much as it did any type of progress. Benjamin recognized that the concept of progress might originally have had a critical function, but when the bourgeoisie took over positions of power in the nineteenth century, that critical function disappeared. Hence the need to subject it to immanent critique through historical materialism, 'whose basic concept is not progress, but actualization'.[53]

In an important article on Benjamin, Habermas declared without any hesitation that Benjamin's philosophy of history was incompatible with historical materialism. Benjamin's mistake, he argued, was to try to endow historical materialism – 'which takes account of progress not only of the productive forces but also of domination' – with an 'anti-evolutionary conception of history'.[54] The fact is, however, that within historical materialism there does exist a dialectical and anti-evolutionary interpretation which takes account of progress as well as regression. It can be found from Antonto Labriola to the Frankfurt School itself, and it is also supported by numerous texts of Marx. Can one speak of progress within relationships of domination, as Habermas suggested? Was Benjamin so wrong to place the state of emergency and Fascism at the centre of his reflections? In an essay on Benjamin and Blanqui, Miguel Abensour made the following pertinent remark:

To think of Fascism from the point of view of progress is to
see it merely as an interlude, a temporary regression, or a relic
destined to fade away and give free rein once more to progress,
as if nothing had happened. To think of Fascism from the point
of view of the victims (Jewish or proletarian) of the state of
emergency is to construct a permanent place for barbarism in
history.[55]

If Benjamin, in the 'Passagenwerk', linked together Baudelaire and
Blanqui, it was because of their common hostility to progress.
In his essay on the 1855 World Exhibition, Baudelaire angrily
denounced the idea of progress as a 'treacherous beacon', a
'grotesque idea, which has flourished on the rotten ground of
modern self-complacency', and because of which people 'will
fall asleep on the pillow of fate in a drivelling sleep of decay'.
Benjamin carefully studied this text and quoted the following
excerpt in the 'Passagenwerk': 'The disciples of the philosophers of
steam and chemical matches understand it so: progress appears
to them only as an indefinite series. Where is this guarantee?' If
Baudelaire could dominate Paris in his poetry – unlike the great
city poets who followed him – it was, according to Benjamin,
because of the critical distance he maintained from his subject,
which was a result of his 'frenetic hostility towards progress'; in
reality, his spleen was 'a feeling that corresponds to permanent
catastrophe'. As for Blanqui, one of his great merits was to
have 'armed the revolutionary class with a healthy indifference
towards speculations on progress'.[56]

There is no doubt that Benjamin largely shared the feelings of
the author of *Les Fleurs du Mal*. In a note on Baudelaire probably
written around 1938, he gave an anti-capitalist colour to this
critique of progress: 'This devaluation of the human environment
by the market economy had a profound impact on his experience
of history. . . Nothing is more contemptible than to bring the idea
of progress into play against that experience. . . History has since
shown how right he was not to trust technological progress.'[57]

In my opinion, it would be wrong to link Benjamin's conception
of history only to the specific events he was living through at the
end of the 1930s: the irresistible rise of Fascism, the preparation
and unleashing of the Second World War. His was a fundamental
reflection on modernity, whose roots can be found in his first

writings, and whose scope was much broader and more significant than a mere commentary on political events. This said, it is obvious that in his works – perhaps more than in any of his contemporaries – there is a feeling that catastrophe is about to crash down on Europe and the world, and a lucid intuition that it will assume proportions unprecedented in human history, above all because of the extraordinary technological perfection of the means of war.

It is within the overall context of Benjamin's philosophy of history, based on the most radical and profound critique of the illusions of progress, that his observations on the decline of experience in the modern world must be analysed. In Benjamin's mind, *Erfahrung* – 'experience' as a cultural trait rooted in tradition – did not at all mean the same as *Erlebnis* – immediate psychological 'experiencing'. In 'Spleen' and 'La Vie antérieure', Baudelaire held in his hand 'the scattered fragments of genuine historical experience'; by contrast, the bad infinity of Bergson's *'durée'*, which excluded tradition, represented, in Benjamin's eyes, all the passing moments (*Erlebnisse*) 'that strut about in the borrowed garb of experience [*Erfahrung*]'. It was in his essay on Baudelaire that Benjamin provided the most precise definition of what he meant by *Erfahrung*: 'Experience is indeed a matter of tradition, in collective existence as well as private life. It is less the product of facts firmly anchored in memory than of a convergence in memory of accumulated and frequently unconscious data.'[58]

The idea that modernity produces a decline or loss of experience appeared very early on in Benjamin's writings. In 'Programme of the Coming Philosophy', written in 1918, he already spoke of 'experience virtually reduced to nadir, to a minimum of significance' during the Age of Enlightenment, and more generally, during all modern times.[59] This theme was taken up again and developed between 1936 and 1940, particularly in 'The Storyteller' (1936) in which he argued that in the modern age 'experience has fallen in value. And it looks as if it is continuing to fall into bottomlessness'. Storytelling and fairy tales (which he contrasted to myth) were rooted in the collective pre-capitalist experience of the popular and artisan milieux; their 'liberating magic [*befreiender Zauber*] . . . does not bring nature into play in

a mythical way, but points to its complicity with liberated

man'.[60] In Benjamin's opinion, the disenchantment of the world (*Entzauberung der Welt*), which Max Weber analysed in relation to the advent of the capitalist era, meant the decline of collective *Erfahrung* and the breaking of the 'liberating magic', so that the mythical nightmare, destructive of man's accord with nature, was unleashed anew.

In the 'Passagenwerk', Benjamin linked the beginning of the atrophy (*Verkümmerung*) of experience to the advent of manufacture and commodity production. But it was evidently with the rapid development of modern industry that this impoverishment reached its nadir. In the Baudelaire essays of 1936 to 1939 – which, along with the 'Passagenwerk' and the 1940 *Theses*, form a whole with inseparable parts – Benjamin analysed the 'inhospitable and blinding experience that was likely in the major industrial age' and leaned directly on Marx's analyses in *Capital*. In working with machines, workers learn to co-ordinate their own 'movements to the uniform and unceasing motion of an automaton'. The worker suffers a deep loss of dignity, and 'his work has been sealed off from experience'. Benjamin thus closely linked the loss of experience with the transformation of the worker into an automaton: his gestures as he works the machinery are repetitive, devoid of meaning and mechanical, as automatic as those of the passers-by in the crowds described by Edgar Allen Poe and E.T.A. Hoffmann. Both no longer know *Erfarhrung* – only *Erlebnis*, and particularly the *Chockerlebnis* (shock experience) which causes them to react as automatons 'whose memory has been completely erased'.[61]

In a lecture Benjamin gave in 1930, he had already shown his interest in the 'decidedly religious' duality between Life and Automaton that was to be found in tales of the supernatural by Hoffmann, Poe, Kubin and Panizza.[62] Benjamin was probably referring, among other works, to 'Maelzel's Chess Player' by Edgar Allen Poe. This story is about an automaton chess-player, 'habited as a Turk', in whose 'left hand is a pipe'. If it were a pure machine 'it would always win'; but that does not happen. One of the hypotheses put forward by Poe to explain its lack of complete success is that 'a dwarf actuates the machine' while hidden inside it. Poe's story obviously inspired 'Thesis I' of Benjamin's *Theses on the Philosophy of History*, in which he describes an automaton puppet 'in Turkish attire', 'with a hookah in its mouth', who 'was to win all the time' so long as a little hunchback guided the puppet's hand by means of strings. In my opinion, the relationship between Poe's story and Benjamin's *Theses* is not merely anecdotal. The philosophical ending to 'Maelzel's Chess Player' is as follows: 'This fact proves that . . . its movements are regulated by *mind*' and nothing else. In Benjamin's work, Poe's 'mind' becomes 'theology'; in other words, the messianic spirit, without which the revolution could not triumph, nor could historical materialism 'win all the time'. The automaton image refers to the vulgar ('mechanistic') materialist conceptions of social democracy or Stalinist Communism, which perceive the development of the productive forces and economic progress as 'automatically' leading to the final crisis of capitalism and the victory of the proletariat.[63]

As to E.T.A. Hoffmann, Benjamin noted that his Tales were based on an identity between the automatic (*Automatischen*) and the satanic; man's daily life was "the product of a vile, artificial mechanism, which Satan regulated from within'.[64] The classic example of such an identity was, of course, the character of Olympia, the automaton doll (created by the diabolic Doctor Coppelius) with whom poor Nathanael falls madly in love, not noticing that 'her playing and her singing are unpleasantly perfect, . . . [and] seem to stem from some kind of clockwork'.[65] A section in the 'Passagenwerk' on the doll and the automaton refers in particular to the 'deadly automatons' of mythology. Thus, Benjamin mentions an essay by Caillois which analyses the myth of Pandora, 'an automaton made by the god of iron for the loss of mankind' and other figures of 'female-machinery, who were artificial, mechanical . . . and most notably deadly'.[66] The theme of the two quotations standing at the head of this section of the 'Passagenwerk' is the general transformation of human beings into dolls or automatons in the modern world. This is the meaning, for example, of Franz Dingelstedt's phrase: 'Eyes instead of clocks will tell the time.'[67] The allegory of the automaton, the keen and hopeless perception of the mechanical, uniform, empty and repetitive life of individuals in industrial society, is one of the great illuminations that permeate Benjamin's last writings.

If, for Benjamin, the automaton is the human being who has lost all experience and memory, then the link between *Erfahrung*, theology and historical materialism is 'remembrance' (*Eingedenken*)

– as distinct from memory (*Andenken*), which is linked to the simple 'lived moment' (*Erlebnis*).[68] According to a fragment from the 'Passagenwerk', in remembrance (*Eingedenken*) 'we have an experience (*Erfahrung*) which keeps us from conceiving history in a radically untheological way';[69] and in one of the notes for the *Theses*, remembrance is presented as the 'quintessence' of the *Jewish* 'theological conception of history'.[70] Remembrance has a special link to two realms of lost experience: the struggle of the defeated generations (the victims of progress), and in the more distant past, the 'lost paradise' – the experience of early classless societies – that the storm of progress has removed us from. In 'Paris – the Capital of the Nineteenth Century' (1936), Benjamin referred to dreams of the future as always being 'coupled' (*vermählt*) with elements coming from prehistory (*Urgeschichte*) – that is to say, from 'a classless society'. The experiences of this society, like a sediment in the collective unconscious, 'interact with the new to give birth to the utopias'.[71]

What exactly did this prehistoric, archaic or primitive classless society mean to Benjamin? His main reference in this context is to the works of Bachofen. Indeed, an article that he wrote (in French) on Bachofen in 1935 is one of the most decisive keys to his entire philosophy of history. Bachofen's work, Benjamin argues, was inspired by 'romantic sources', and it has attracted the interest of Marxist and anarchist thinkers (such as Elisée Reclus) because it 'evokes a Communist society at the dawn of history'. Refuting conservative and Fascist interpretations (Klages and Bäumler respectively), Benjamin shows that Bachofen 'examined to unexplored depths the sources that sustained the libertarian ideal throughout the ages, from which Reclus drew his inspiration'. For their part, Engels and Lafargue were interested in Bachofen's study of matriarchal societies, in which there existed a high degree of democracy and civic equality, as well as forms of primitive communism which signified a true 'subversion of the concept of authority'.[72] This article – as well as the reference during the same period to Drieu's anarchist 'Deserter' – is evidence for the persistence of Benjamin's libertarian sympathies, which he always regarded as complementary (and not contradictory) to Marxism.[73]

The archaic societies of *Urgeschichte* were also those of the harmony between man and nature – a harmony broken by 'progress'

which would have to be recovered in the liberated society of
the future. In Benjamin's eyes, one name represented the future
promise of reconciliation: *Fourier*. In his essay on Jochmann from
1937, Fourier is mentioned as a dialectician who discovered that
'all partial improvements in the social constitution of mankind
throughout "civilization" were necessarily followed by a deterio-
ration in his general status'; and in 'Paris – the Capital of the
Nineteenth Century', Fourier is compared to Paul Scheerbart
(a libertarian writer whom Benjamin greatly appreciated) as a
paradigmatic example of the convergence between the old and
the new, in a utopia which brings new life to the primal symbols
(*Uralte*) of desire.[74]

In the *Passagenwerk*, Benjamin closely links the abolition of
man's exploitation of man to the end of man's exploitation of
nature, and he refers to Fourier and Bachofen as emblematic
figures of the new and the ancient harmony. Fourier's 'passionate
work', in which play becomes a model of non-exploited and
non-exploiting labour, appears to Benjamin as capable of creating
a new world where action is finally sister to dream. The ancestral
image of this reconciliation — discovered by Bachofen in prehistoric matriarchies – is that of Nature as a giving mother.[75]
Similar ideas are discussed in the 1939 (French) version of the
Introduction to the 'Passagenwerk' and in the *Theses on the Philosophy
of History*. In these works, Benjamin explicitly criticizes vulgar
Marxism and contrasts it with 'Fourier's fantastic imaginings' –
which, for Benjamin, exemplify a kind of labour which 'far from
exploiting nature, is capable of delivering her of the creations
which lie dormant in her womb as potentials'.[76]

This in no way implies that Benjamin advocated a return to
some primitive age (real or imaginary). On the contrary, he
clearly maintained in the 'Passagenwerk' that the metamorphosis
of work into play 'presupposed highly developed forces of
production, which are only now available to humanity for the
first time'.[77] Benjamin's method, characteristic of revolutionary
romanticism, was to weave dialectical relationships between the
pre-capitalist past and the post-capitalist future, between archaic
and utopian harmony, between lost ancient experience and future
liberated experience.

By placing his Golden Age in the prehistoric past, Benjamin
set himself apart from the mainstream of German Romanticism,

for which the Middle Ages were the nostalgic fatherland. In doing so, he was very close to Marx and Engels – more than he himself thought. For in a letter to Engels dated 25 March 1868, Marx wrote that whereas the first reaction against the ideology of the Enlightenment had been 'to regard everything medieval as romantic', the second reaction, corresponding to the socialist orientation, 'is to look beyond the Middle Ages into the primitive age of every nation', where 'what is newest [can be found] in what is oldest – even egalitarians, to a degree which would have made Proudhon shudder'.[78] It is very unlikely that Benjamin knew of this letter, but one cannot help being struck by its similarity to his own references to a primitive era, in which the oldest and the newest were intimately linked. Of course, there is no doubt that nostalgia for an archaic past is part and parcel of romanticism (Rousseau!).

For Benjamin, it was not a matter of restoring primitive communism, but rather of finding again – through collective remembrance – the lost experience of the ancient anti-authoritarian and anti-patriarchal egalitarianism, and of turning it into a spiritual force within the revolutionary struggle to establish a future classless society. As we know, the ideas expressed in the first version of the 'Passagenwerk' were harshly criticized by Adorno, who in his letter to Benjamin dated August 1935, insisted that the entire text was marred by its 'overestimation of the archaic', comparable to the mythical thought of a Klages or a Jung. He refused to associate the archaic past with the 'Golden Age', or the present money-making age with 'Hell'.[79]

Swayed by Adorno's criticism, Benjamin toned down the 'archaic' aspect in his next writings for the 'Passagenwerk'. However, it is still present, implicitly or explicitly, in his essays on Baudelaire from 1939, and if we analyse the texts closely enough, we can find a new version of the opposition between the 'Hell' of the capitalist present and the prehistoric 'Paradise'.

Modernity is characterized as 'Hell' in 'Zentralpark' (in the previously mentioned reference to Strindberg) as well as in the 'Passagenwerk' – and notably in the new version (in French) of 'Paris – the Capital of the Nineteenth Century' (1939), where Benjamin discusses Blanqui and the work he wrote in prison as an old man, *Eternity through the Stars*. This work, for Benjamin, was 'an appalling indictment . . . of society', a 'vision of Hell'

which unveiled, through an astral phantasmagoria, the essence
of the modern (capitalist) world. Dominated by the commodity, it
was *par excellence* the universe of repetition, of the 'Ever-the-same'
(*Immergleiche*) disguised as newness, of the agonizing and infernal
myth of the eternal return. In Blanqui's book, newness 'appeared
as the attribute of what belongs to the realm of damnation'
– an idea that Benjamin closely associated with Baudelaire's
poem on the seven old men, the 'infernal procession' that
does nothing but multiply the same repulsive image. In the
kingdom of commodities, for which Blanqui's astronomic work
and Baudelaire's poem were the supreme image, 'mankind . . .
plays the part of the damned', because the repetitive and artificial
'newness' of commodity production is 'as incapable of providing
it with an emancipatory solution as a new fashion is of renewing
society'.[80]

In what sense, then, does Benjamin see Hell as the allegory
condensing the essential features of modernity? On the one hand,
it is a permanent catastrophe (Strindberg); on the other hand, it
is the hopeless repetition of 'eternal and ever-new punishments'
(an expression taken from the vaudeville *Ciel et Enfer* [Heaven
and Hell], which Benjamin quotes in his 1939 essay). Seen from
this angle, the worst Hell is that of Greek mythology, where
Sisyphus, Tantalus and Danaides suffer eternal return of the
same punishment. Such as the lot of the worker who is a
prisoner of the assembly line, whom Benjamin (quoting Engels)
compares to Sisyphus. This is why the inscription at the factory
gates (mentioned in Marx's *Capital*) is the same as that which
adorned Dante's Gates of Hell.[81]

In the face of this 'damned' universe, doomed to the *Immergleiche*
of industry, machine/ production, commodities, fashion and
Chockerlebnis, this universe which reduces men to the condition
of automatons stripped of memory and *Erfahrung*, Benjamin's
hermeneutics discovers in the poetry of Baudelaire a subtle form
of resistance to the ravages of 'progress': a liberating evocation of
lost experience and the 'Golden Age'.

In primitive or pre-capitalist societies, 'where there is experience in the strictest sense of the word, certain contents of the
individual past combine with material of the collective past. The
rituals with their ceremonies, their festivals . . . kept producing
the amalgamation of these two elements of memory over and

over again'.[82] It is exactly this aspect of *Erfahrung* that lies at the heart of Baudelaire's correspondences and enables him to be radically opposed to modern catastrophe: 'The important thing is that the *correspondances* record a concept of experience which includes ritual elements. Only by appropriating these elements was Baudelaire able to fathom the full meaning of the breakdown which he, a modern man, was witnessing.' In this context the figure of the past Edenic reappears: 'The *correspondances* are the data of remembrance – not historical data, but data of prehistory. What makes festive days great and significant is the encounter with an earlier life.' In Baudelaire's correspondences, 'the murmur of the past may be heard in the correspondences, and the canonical experience of them has its place in a previous life'.[83] Once again, in these words is found the dialectical image of the classless community (Bachofen), which the 1935 essay designated as the source for socialist utopias. As Tiedemann rightly notes, 'the idea of the *correspondances* is the utopia by which a lost paradise appears as projected into the future'.[84] For Benjamin, this prehistoric 'paradise', this 'previous life' are also characterized by harmony, reciprocity, and complicity between man and nature – totally missing from modern life.[85]

Benjamin's linking of 'feast days' and the remembrance of the 'Golden Age' may have been inspired by a lecture on 'The Feast' which Roger Caillois gave at the Collège de Sociologie in May 1939. It is known that Benjamin had ties to the Collège, and in a letter to Gretel Adorno from February 1940, he mentions the article which Caillois wrote up for the *Nouvelle Revue française* in December 1939.[86] According to Caillois,

> the feast presents itself as a bringing-up-to-date of the early times of the universe, of the *Urzeit* (primeval times), the eminently creative original age. . . The Golden Age, the childhood of the world as the childhood of man, corresponds to the concept of an earthly paradise in which everything is given at first, and at the end of which one had to earn one's bread with the sweat of one's brow. It is the reign of Saturn or Kronos, without war or commerce, without slavery or private property.[87]

There is a striking analogy with Benjamin's problematic, in spite of the undeniable differences in approach.

The lost experience that Benjamin sought, whose remembrance he found in Baudelaire, is therefore that of a classless society living in a state of Edenic harmony with nature – an experience that has disappeared in the modern, industrial/capitalist civilization, and whose heritage must be saved through socialist utopia. However, remembrance as such is powerless to change the world: in Benjamin's eyes, one of the great merits of Baudelaire was in fact his despairing recognition of that powerlessness. Analysing Baudelaire's poem in *Les Fleurs du Mal*, 'Le Printemps adorable a perdu son odeur!' (Spring, the Beloved, has lost its scent!), Benjamin wrote: 'The word "*perdu*" acknowledges the present state of collapse of that experience which he once shared. . . This gives a sense of measureless desolation to Baudelaire's verse. For someone who is past experiencing, there is no consolation.' The poems that Baudelaire wrested from 'the inefficacy of the same consolation, the breakdown of the same fervour, the failure of the same effort . . . are in no way inferior to those in which the *correspondances* celebrate their triumphs.'[88] How can this powerlessness, this infinite despair be overcome, and how can the lost springtime of humanity be regained?

In 'Zentralpark', Benjamin noted: 'Baudelaire's deepest desire was to interrupt the course of the world.' But Baudelaire's inability to achieve this caused his impatience and anger.[89] Who could take on such a decisive mission? The answer to that question is found in the 1940 *Theses* (and in their preparatory notes): it is the proletarian revolution that can and must carry out the messianic interruption of the course of the world. It alone has the capacity, by sustaining itself on the forces of remembrance, to restore the lost experience, to abolish the 'Hell' of the commodity, to break the baleful circle of the *Immergleiche*, to free humanity from mythical anguish and individuals from becoming automatons. By reconciling human beings once more with nature, the world revolution will establish a classless society, a secularized form of the messianic age, of paradise lost/ regained. Revolution is not a continuation of 'progress', but rather its interruption and the bringing-up-to-date of prehistoric and/ or pre-capitalist *Erfahrung*.

Revolution is therefore both future utopia and messianic redemption (*Erlösung*). It is in this sense that Benjamin's sibylline remark in the 'Passagenwerk' must be interpreted: 'The true conception of historical time rests entirely on the image of redemption (*Erlösung*).'[90] Benjamin's search for the lost experience might seem to have been turned towards the past, but it was ultimately directed towards the messianic/revolutionary future.

It was again in the *Theses on the Philosophy of History* (and their preparatory notes) that Benjamin most cogently formulated his vision of the revolution as a redemptive interruption of the continuity of history, as the pulling of the emergency cord by humanity as it travelled in the train of history. This idea was radically opposed to the liberal, social democratic and vulgar-Marxist myths of progress as an automatic, irresistible and unlimited improvement, and of technological development as a current that one need only follow to move forward.[91] In Benjamin's eyes, Blanqui, the legendary revolutionary fighter whose name 'had been the rallying sound that had reverberated through the preceding century', incarnated this vision: the basic presupposition of his activity had never been an illusory belief in progress (which he held in ridicule), but rather the decision to put an end to present injustice. Of all revolutionaries, he had been the most determined to 'tear humanity away at the last moment from the catastrophe that continually threatened it'.[92]

There are practically no explicit references to anarchism in Benjamin's last works – unless we consider Blanqui, for whom 'regular Anarchy is the future of humanity', as a libertarian thinker.[93] But Rolf Tiedemann has accurately shown that these writings 'can be read as a *palimpsest*: his old anarchism can be seen beneath the explicit Marxism, and his path risks leading to the abstraction of anarchist practice'.[94] The word *palimpsest* may not be exact enough: the relationship between the two messages is less a mechanical link of superimposition than an alchemical blending of previously distilled substances.

This holds particularly true for the *Theses on the Philosophy of History*. According to Tiedemann, 'Benjamin's idea of political *praxis* in the 1940 *Theses* has more of the enthusiasm of the anarchists than the sobriety of Marxism'.[95] However, this too seems inadequate, in so far as it qualifies as mutually exclusive the two political philosophies that Benjamin fuses in the 'hard core' of his theory. Habermas also perceives an 'anarchist conception of the Present (*Jetztzeiten*)' in the *Theses*.[96] Moreover, in the preparatory notes to the *Theses*, Benjamin directly refers to an anarchist figure, Nechaev (whom he links to Dostoevsky's 'Devils', as well as to Marx) when he speaks of the attempt to 'weave revolutionary destruction with the idea of Redemption'.[97] Once again, messianism and anarchy are welded together.

Analysing the normative ideas that governed Benjamin's thought, Scholem noted with remarkable insight:

> An apocalyptic element of destructiveness is preserved in the metamorphosis undergone in his writing by the messianic idea, which continues to play a potent part in his thought. The noble and positive power of destruction . . . now becomes an aspect of redemption, related to the immanence of the world, acted out in the history of human labor.[98]

Scholem's main textual references for this problematic are Benjamin's essay 'The Destructive Character' (1931) and the literary works written in the 1930s. But the preparatory notes for the 1940 *Theses* are the most forceful expression of this messianic/revolutionary concept of destruction, which 'weaves together' or 'interlaces' (*verschränkt*) class struggle with redemption, Marx with Nechaev, historical materialism with Dostoevsky (whom Benjamin regarded in 1929 as one of the 'great anarchists' of the nineteenth century).

The 'principle of destruction' was not the only terrain on which a convergence between messianism and libertarian/Communist revolution took place in Benjamin's last works. The elective affinity between the two was also based on their common restorative/utopian structure: that of the redeemed future as a restoration of paradise lost (*Tikkun*). This is expressed in the epigram by Karl Kraus, *Ursprung ist das Ziel* (Origin is the Goal), which serves as the heading to 'Thesis XIV' of *Theses on the Philosophy of History* – the one which defines revolution as a 'tiger's leap into the past'.

In the *Theses*, the revolution of the oppressed is linked to the figure of the Messiah, who 'comes not only as the redeemer' but 'as the subduer of Antichrist' (whose embodiment at the time, in Benjamin's eyes, was the Third Reich).[99] His mission is to accomplish the task that the Angel of History, its wings trapped in the storm of progress, cannot fulfil: 'wake the dead and restore what [has] been destroyed' – a phrase which, according to

Scholem, refers to the cabbalistic concept of *Tikkun*.[100] Historical messianism is situated at the polar opposite of all progressive historicism: 'The Messiah breaks history; the Messiah does not come at the end of an evolution.'[101]

There is a mysterious link, a correspondence in the Baudelearean sense, between each expression of the profane revolutionary utopia and of the sacred messianic sphere, between the history of redemption and the history of class struggle. To Paradise Lost corresponds the prehistoric, egalitarian (classless), democratic and non-authoritarian communist society, living in Edenic harmony with nature; to the expulsion from the Garden of Eden, or to the tempest which removes men from Paradise and towards Hell, corresponds 'progress', industrial civilization, capitalist/mercantile society, the modern catastrophe and its accumulation of debris; to the Coming of the Messiah corresponds the revolutionary/proletarian interruption of history; and to the Messianic Age and the re-establishment of Paradise with its Adamic language, corresponds the new classless and stateless society with its universal language. *Ursprung ist das Ziel* and *restitutio in integrum* are the spiritual quintessence of Benjamin's Marxist/libertarian 'theology of revolution'.[102]

Many analysts view the relationship between messianism and revolution in Benjamin's writings as a movement of 'secularization', while others (such as Gerhard Kaiser) speak of a 'theologization of Marxism'.[103] During the bitter polemical battles over Benjamin's work during the 1960s in Germany, the stress was laid either on his religious metaphysics or on his communist materialism. Benjamin himself described his thinking as 'Janus-faced', but it seems that critics or followers prefer to look at only one of the faces, while ignoring the other. In order to supersede such styles of argument, it may be useful to recall that the Roman god had two faces but only one head: Benjamin's 'faces' were manifestations of one and the same way of thinking, which had simultaneously a messianic and a secular expression.

In fact, Benjamin had already explained in 1926 (in the previously mentioned letter to Scholem) that he was interested in a form of identity between religion and politics which showed up only 'in the paradoxical reversal (*Umschlagen*) of the one into the other'. The *Theses on the Philosophy of History* were precisely such a paradoxical reversal of the Jewish religion into Marxist class

struggle, or conversely, of revolutionary utopia into apocalyptic
messianism.

The first type of reversal – from the messianic into the political
– cannot be understood with the category of 'secularization'
in its strict sense, for here the religious dimension does not
disappear as in true secularization. It can be said, however,
that this dimension has secular implications and consequences.
In his preparatory notes for the *Theses*, Benjamin wrote: 'In his
representation of the classless society, Marx secularized the representation of the Messianic Age. And he was right.' However,
social democracy made its own use of this secularization to
present classless society as the end goal of 'historical progress',
thus stripping it of its true meaning: 'that interruption of historical continuity which, having failed thousands of times, will
be accomplished in the end'. Consequently, 'its true messianic
face (*echtes messianisches Gesicht*) must be restored to the concept
of classless society, in the interests precisely of the revolutionary
politics of the proletariat'.[104] Criticizing these notes, Tiedemann
considered that for Benjamin

> the revolutionary politics of the proletariat are not to be
> practised in the interests of establishing a classless society,
> but rather the other way around: classless society is only an
> occasion for bringing revolutionary politics back into play;
> the real purpose is to make revolution for its own sake. . .
> Ends and means – classless society and revolution – are
> reversed. . .[105]

In my view, rather than a 'reversal', there is in Benjamin a
dialectical unity between ends and means: there will not be a
classless society without a revolutionary interruption of historical
continuity ('Progress'), nor will there be revolutionary action of
the proletariat if the end (a classless society) is not understood
in all its messianic explosiveness, as a breaking point. Benjamin's
ends are not 'revolution for revolution's sake', but he does believe
that without a revolution there can be no redemption, and that
without a messianic/redemptive view of history there can be no
truly radical revolutionary *praxis*.

In a recent article on socialist/religious utopians (such as
Leroux), Miguel Abensour has shown that their religious dimension was not a flight from politics into mysticism, but rather a

form of 'search for absolute differentiation' which 'would enable utopia to overturn the classic political issues and to situate itself in relation to the question of revolution'.[106] Something analogous happens with Walter Benjamin: the profane consequence of the messianism in his last writings is to increase their explosive charge: it helps to lend them their unique subversive quality, which makes the *Theses on the Philosophy of History* one of the most radical, innovative and visionary documents of revolutionary thought since Marx's 'Theses on Feuerbach'.

The distinction that Benjamin drew between the chemist/commentator and the alchemist/critic must be applied to the study of his own works. Looking beyond the 'wood' and the 'ashes' of his writings, the alchemist must focus his attention on the burning spiritual flame of the work: the revolutionary redemption of mankind.

7

The Religious-Atheist and Libertarian Assimilated Jews: Gustav Landauer, Ernst Bloch, Georg Lukács, Erich Fromm

This next group of authors falls outside the realm of religious Judaism. Their religious concerns do refer to Jewish sources, but they do not belong to any denomination or to religion in the usual sense of the word. In fact, they tend to elude the traditional distinctions between religion and the secular world, sacred and profane (Durkheim), natural and supernatural (Weber), transcendent and immanent (Eliade). The provisional term *religious atheism* – which Lukács used to describe Dostoevsky – allows us to define this paradoxical spiritual form which seems to seek out, with the energy of despair, the point of messianic convergence between the sacred and the profane.

Some of the authors in this group (such as Erich Fromm) received a Jewish religious education in their youth, but the majority did not discover Judaism until later in life. Irrespective of their particular path, however, they all shared a strange and contradictory outlook, one that combined a rejection of actual religious beliefs with a passionate interest in mystical and millenarian currents, both Jewish and Christian. At any event, theirs was a messianic/revolutionary spirituality which inextricably wove together the threads of religious tradition and social utopia.

Having been close to the libertarian ideal between 1914 and 1923, most of these authors (with the exception of Landauer) gradually drew nearer to Marxism and – in the case of Lukács and, to some extent, Bloch – even embraced Communism after an intermediary stage of anarcho-Bolshevism. Other Jewish figures of this period, such as Ernst Toller, Manes Sperber and Eugen Leviné, were not far from the world-view of this group.

127

Gustav Landauer was born on 7 April 1870 into an assimilated bourgeois Jewish family in south-west Germany. A writer, philosopher, literary critic, friend of Buber and Kropotkin, and editor of the libertarian journal *Der Sozialist* from 1909 to 1915, Landauer was the only politically active anarchist of all the authors studied in this chapter. In April 1919, he became People's Commissar of Culture in the short-lived Councils Republic of Bavaria; he was murdered by the Army on 2 May 1919, after the defeat of the revolution in Munich. His profoundly original works have been defined by modern researchers as 'an anarchist form of Jewish messianism'.[1]

Landauer was first and foremost a revolutionary romantic, and it is only in terms of this source that his messianism and his libertarian utopia can both be properly understood.[2] In fact, his world-view represents revolutionary romanticism in an almost 'ideal-typical' way. It would be hard to imagine an author for whom past and future, conservatism and revolution, were so deeply and directly entangled. If there ever was a perfect model of restorative/utopian thought in the twentieth-century cultural universe, it was surely that which is to be found in Landauer's writings.

In an autobiographical article written in 1913, Landauer described the atmosphere of his youth as one of revolt against the family milieu, as a 'continual clash between romantic nostalgia and the cramping barriers of Philistinism (*enge Philisterschranken*)'.[3] What did romanticism mean to Landauer? In a note found among his papers in the Landauer Archives in Jerusalem, he explained that romanticism must be understood neither as 'political reaction' (Chateaubriand) nor as 'patriotic German medievalism', nor as a 'literary school'. What Romanticism, Goethe, Schiller, Kant, Fichte and the French Revolution had in common was that they were all anti-Philistine (*Anti-Philister*)[4] – a term which, in the cultural language of the nineteenth century, denoted hostility to bourgeois narrow-mindedness, pettiness and vulgarity.

Apart from the Romantic poets – notably Hölderlin, whom he compared in a lecture in 1916 to the biblical prophets! – the author mentioned most often in Landauer's writings is Nietzsche. However, unlike the author of *Zarathustra* and most other romantic critics of modern civilization, Landauer's orientation was socialist and libertarian right from the start. For that reason, he identified with Rousseau, Tolstoy and Strindberg, in whom he found a harmonious blending of 'revolution and romanticism, purity and fermentation, sainthood and madness'.[5]

Medieval *Gemeinschaft* held a place of honour in Landauer's restorative problematic, just as it did in the works of the 'classical' Romantics. For Landauer, the Christian Middle Ages (in their universal 'Catholic' and not their 'patriotic German' dimension) were an era of 'lofty radiance', in which the 'spirit gave meaning, sanctity and consecration to life'. Medieval towns, guilds, brotherhoods, corporations and associations, expressed a social life that was genuine and rich in spirituality, as opposed to the modern state, 'the supreme form of Non-spirit' (*Ungeist*). Landauer criticized Marxism for its denial of the affinity between future socialism and certain social structures of the past, such as the city republics of the Middle Ages, the *Mark*, the old German rural community, and the Russian *Mir*.[6]

Landauer expressed his romantic philosophy of history most systematically in the pamphlet 'Die Revolution', which appeared in 1907 in a series of sociological monographs under the direction of Martin Buber. In this essay, the Christian Middle Ages were depicted as 'a cultural summit', a period of blossoming and fullness. Landauer did not deny the obscurantist aspects of the period, but he did his best to play them down. 'If someone were to raise the objection that there was also one form or another of feudalism, clericalism, inquisition, and so on, I could answer only: "I know full well – but. . ."' On the other hand, the entire modern era since the sixteenth century was 'a time of decadence and therefore of transition', a time when the spirit disappeared and was replaced by violence, authority, the state. In the long path stretching from the decline of the (medieval) Christian communal spirit to the blossoming of a new communal spirit of the socialist future, revolutions were the only genuine moment, the only true 'spiritual bath'. 'Without this brief period of regeneration, we could no longer continue to live, we would be condemned to founder.' In Landauer's view, the first and most important modern revolution was that of Thomas Münzer and the anabaptists, who 'tried one last time, and for a long time, to change life, all of life', and 'to re-establish what had existed during the time of the spirit'. Landauer also expressed sympathy for the Christian anti-monarchists (*monarchomachen*), the

Holy League (the sixteenth-century Catholic confederation), the Fronde and all anti-centralist movements, which were evidence of 'attempts by tradition to restore and enlarge the old institutions belonging to the federation of orders and parliaments'.[7]

In *Aufruf zum Sozialismus* [Summons to Socialism], which Landauer wrote in 1911, he launched a direct attack on the philosophy of progress common to liberals and Second International Marxists: 'No progress, no technology, no virtuosity can bring us salvation and happiness.' Rejecting the German Marxists' 'belief in evolutionary progress (*Fortschrittsentwicklung*)', Landauer presented his own vision of historical change:

> To my mind, human history is not made up of anonymous processes, nor is it merely an accumulation of countless small events. . . When something noble and grandiose, deeply moving and innovative, has happened to mankind, it has turned out that it was the impossible and the unbelievable . . . that brought about the turning point.

Revolution was precisely the special time of the eruption of the new, a time when 'the unbelievable, the miraculous moves towards the realm of the possible'.[8]

Karl Mannheim was, therefore, correct to regard radical anarchism, and Landauer's thought in particular, as the heir of anabaptist millenarianism and even as 'the Chiliastic mentality . . . preserved in its purest and most genuine form'. This form of thinking precluded any concept of evolution and any representation of progress; within a '*qualitative* differentiation of time', revolution was perceived as a breakthrough (*Durchbruch*), an abrupt moment (*abrupter Augenblick*), an experience lived in the here-and-now (*Jetzt-Erleben*).[9] Mannheim's analysis was all the more impressive in that that it applied not only to Landauer but also, with a few subtle differences, to Martin Buber, to Walter Benjamin (his messianic concept of *Jetztzeit*), and to many other German-Jewish thinkers.

Landauer's primary criticism of 'progress', modernity and the industrial age was that they led to absolute domination by the 'true Antichrist', by the 'mortal enemy of what had been true Christianity or the spirit of life'; in other words, by the modern state.[10] As a convinced anarchist, he invoked the legacy of Proudhon, Kropotkin, Bakunin and Tolstoy when he proposed as an alternative to the centralized state a *regeneratio* of society through the formation of a network of autonomous structures inspired by pre-capitalist communities. Landauer did not advocate a return to the medieval past, but he wanted to give the past a new form and to create a *Kultur* with the means available in modern *Zivilisation*.[11]

More concretely, Landauer held that the medieval forms of community, which had been safeguarded over centuries from social decay, should become 'the seeds and life crystals (*Lebenskristalle*) of a future socialist culture'. The rural villages, with their vestiges of communal property and autonomy *vis-à-vis* the state, would serve as the fulcrum for the reconstruction of society. Socialist militants would settle in the villages and help to revive the spirit of the fifteenth and sixteenth centuries – the spirit of the heretical and rebellious peasants of the past; they would re-establish the unity (broken by capitalism) between agriculture, industry and handicrafts; between manual and mental labour; and between education and apprenticeship.[12]

In an essay on Walt Whitman, Landauer compared the American poet to Proudhon and emphasized that the two men combined 'conservative and revolutionary mentalities, individualism and socialism'.[13] This characterization fully applied to his own social vision of the world, in which a utopian dialectic joined together ancestral tradition and hope in the future, romantic conservation and libertarian revolution. As Martin Buber wrote in the chapter entitled, 'Landauer' in *Paths to Utopia*: 'Revolutionary conservatism was exactly what Landauer had in mind: a revolutionary choice of those elements of social being which deserve to be preserved and are viable in the building of a new structure.'[14]

Certain mystical and heretical religious traditions were high up on the list of 'elements of social being which deserve to be preserved'. Christian traditions came first of all: until 1908, nearly all of Landauer's religious references were taken from Christianity. He was drawn in particular to the heretics and mystics. In 'Die Revolution' (1907), he extolled Peter Chelcicky, the fourteenth-century Hussite prophet, 'a Christian anarchist who was well ahead of his time, and who had recognized that the Church and State were mortal enemies of Christian life'; Landauer also hailed the Peasant War and the true Christian spirit that inspired it.[15] Of the Christian mystics, Landauer was most interested in Meister Eckhart; during a one-year prison term which Landauer served in 1899 (for 'insulting behaviour towards the authorities'), he translated a collection of Eckhart's writings into modern German. In a special Preface he wrote: 'Meister Eckhart is too good for a historical homage; he must be raised from the dead.'[16] There is an obvious parallel here with Martin Buber, who around the same time was studying the mystics of the Renaissance period, and who in 1901 published an essay on Jakob Böhme. Moreover, a common interest in Christian mysticism was one of the first things that brought Landauer and Buber closer together on a personal level after they met for the first time in 1900.[17]

More generally, Landauer's concept of religion was that which the Romantics had taken from Goethe and Spinoza. Was it a form of pantheism? In an essay from 1901, Landauer identified God with *natura naturans* and referred in this connection to Meister Eckhart, Spinoza and Goethe.[18] At any event, Landauer's religion was radically different from (and in certain respects, the direct opposite of) that of the Churches or denominations. In a letter Landauer wrote in 1891 (which can be found among his papers at the Institute of Social History in Amsterdam), he stated: 'A rabbi . . . cannot have a true religion; if he did, he would not be the cleric of an established denomination.'[19] Elsewhere he endorses a remark made by the Romantic theologian Schleiermacher: religion must be an accompaniment to life, like music. Everything must be done *with* religion, nothing *by* religion. Like the Romantics, Landauer looked on the supreme heights of *Geist* for the point of unity between Religion, Science and Art.[20]

One of the central themes of Landauer's pantheist or atheist romantic religiosity was that of man becoming God. In one of his first published articles – an essay he wrote in 1891 entitled 'Die religiöse Jugenderziehung' (The Religious Education of the Young) – he declared that the only God in whom one should believe was 'the God whom we want to become and whom we shall become'.[21] This heterodox problematic can be found in several of Landauer's other writings, notably in a long (and still unpublished) commentary on the Gospel according to Saint John, which invoked the promise of the Scriptures: 'Ye shall be as gods'.[22]

Landauer felt close to religious libertarians like Tolstoy ('the new Jesus' as he called him), who had come to bring a message of social redemption, a religion opposed to Churches, without mythology or superstition. As an enemy of Pharisaism, Tolstoy loved criminals and sinners, but he hated duplicity; his religion was the religion of love, 'as defined by Plato, Jesus and Spinoza'.[23]

Landauer, like several other romantic Jews of his generation, was fascinated by the person of Christ: he regarded him, along with Moses and Spinoza, as one of the three great prophetic figures of the Jewish people.[24] The following remark appears in a note at the Landauer Archives in Jerusalem: 'Jesus, the greatest of all orators, could make *but a single* speech today: immediately afterwards, he would be thrown into prison for the *crime of high treason*! . . . If he were to *return, which Temple* would he drive the *Pharisees* out of?'[25]

Prior to 1908, there are very few references to Judaism in Landauer's writings – or even in his letters. In an essay from 1907, 'Volk und Land. Dreissig sozialistische Thesen' (People and Land: Thirty Socialist Theses), he mentions spiritual figures from every nation: from France, Rabelais, Molière and Voltaire; from Germany, Goethe, and so on. He then adds: 'The Jews, too, have their unity and their Isaiah, Jesus, and Spinoza' – a very characteristic choice, in which two of the highest representatives of Judaism are, to say the least, removed from the orthodox religious tradition. In reality, Landauer's deepest sympathies in this essay are still not for Judaism but for another culture that goes beyond the boundaries of states and languages: that of 'Christianity, with its Dante and its Gothic, which spread from Moscow to Sicily and Spain'.[26]

What caused Landauer to turn towards Judaism was his discovery through the writings of Martin Buber – in particular, *The Legend of the Baal-Schem* (1908) – of a new conception of Jewish spirituality, a romantic Jewish religiosity.

In October 1908, shortly after *The Legend of the Baal-Schem* was published, Landauer hailed in a letter 'the marvellous stories and legends (from the tradition of eighteenth-century Polish-Jewish mystics of the Baal-Schem and Rabbi Nachman'.[27] Landauer also wrote a review of the book – which was not published until 1910 – which brought to the fore its romantic/messianic aspects: 'The extraordinary thing about these Jewish legends is . . . that not only must the God who is sought after free people from the boundaries and illusions of the life of the senses, but he must first and foremost be the Messiah who will lift the poor, tormented Jews from their suffering and oppression.' The Hasidic tales were the collective work of a *Volk* (People) – which did not signify something 'popular' or trivial, but rather 'living growth: the future within the present, the spirit within history, the whole within the individual. . . The liberating and unifying God within imprisoned and lacerated Man; the heavenly within the earthly'.[28]

On the other hand, in the same review Landauer also registered the change in his own attitude towards Judaism as a result of having read Buber's book:

> Nowhere can a Jew learn, as he can in Buber's thoughts and writings, what many today do not know spontaneously and discover only when there is an outside impulse: namely, that Judaism is not an external accident (*äussere Zufälligkeit*) but a lasting internal quality (*unverlierbare innere Eigenschaft*), and identification with it unites a number of individuals within a *Gemeinschaft*. In this way, a common ground and a common situation of the soul (*Seelensituation*) is established between the person writing this article and the author of the book.[29]

Landauer himself was one of those Jews for whom Judaism had been an 'external accident'. In a letter to the editor of the magazine *Zeit*, which he had written some years before in response to an anti-Semitic article by a certain von Gerlach, Landauer qualified his belonging to Judaism as 'chance' (*Zufall*).[30]

In another article on Buber from 1913, Landauer stressed that as a result of his work, which had saved a buried and underground tradition from oblivion, 'the image of the Jewish essence (*des jüdischen Wesens*) became different for Jews and non-Jews'.[31] So it was that Buber's *The Legend of the Baal-Schem* constituted for Landauer, as it did for many other Jewish intellectuals of German cultural origin, 'the external accident' which allowed them to discover their own Jewish identity. It would, however, be too one-sided to suggest that Buber's influence alone accounted for this 'Jewish turn' – especially since his religious ideas were themselves deeply influenced by Landauer's social philosophy and by his writings on Christian mysticism.[32] In reality, the two men drew from the same source of German neo-romantic culture, and it was from this common base that they influenced each other.

What set Landauer's thinking apart from Buber's – beside their different political leanings – was their attitude towards religion. Whereas Buber's spirituality fell within the realm of religious faith in the strict sense, Landauer's anarchist philosophy belonged instead to the ambiguous domain of religious atheism. The prophetic, mystical or Jewish messianic themes were secularized, to a certain degree at least, in Landauer's socialist utopia. But this was not secularization in the usual sense of the word: the religious dimension remained at the very heart of his political imaginary. It was not simply nullified but rather preserved/ suppressed – in the dialectical sense of *Aufhebung* – in utopian revolutionary prophecy. In Landauer's mystical secularization – some authors speak of his 'mystical atheism'[33] – a religious symbolic universe explicitly entered his revolutionary discourse and imbued it with a *sui generis* spirituality which seemed to escape the usual distinctions between faith and atheism. Landauer refused to believe in a God 'beyond the earth and beyond the world' (*überirdischen und überweltlichen Gott*); following Feuerbach, he affirmed that it was man who created God, and not the other way around. But still that did not keep him from defining socialism as a 'religion'.[34]

Landauer's attitude towards the Jewish religion was inspired by the romantic dialectic of utopia; it linked up the millennial past and the liberated future, tradition preserved in collective memory and revolution, within the same spiritual movement. In an article on the Jewish question from 1913, he wrote: 'the arch-ancient, which we keep in our soul, is the path taken by mankind towards the future, and the tradition of our martyred and nostalgic heart is nothing other than the revolution and the regeneration of mankind.'[35]

One characteristic example of Landauer's revolutionary traditionalism was the way in which he interpreted Moses' institution of the Year of Jubilee, which re-established social equality every fifty years through the redistribution of land and goods. In *Aufruf zum Sozialismus* (1911), he wrote:

> The uprising (*Aufruhr*) as a Constitution, transformation and
> upheaval as a rule expected to last for ever . . . were the
> grandiosity and sacredness (*Heilige*) of the Mosaic social order.
> We need that once again: new regulations and a spiritual
> upheaval which will not make things and commandments
> permanently rigid, but which will *proclaim its own permanence*.
> The revolution must become an element of our social order, it
> must become the basic rule of our Constitution.[36]

A note in the Landauer Archives takes up the theme from
another angle: in other religions, the gods help the nation and
protect its heroes, while in Judaism, 'God is *eternally opposed*
to servility; he is, therefore, the insurrectionary (*Aufrührer*),
the arouser (*Aufrüttler*), the admonisher (*Mahner*)'. The Jewish
religion is evidence of the 'people's holy dissatisfaction with
itself'.[37]

Jews held a special place in Landauer's messianic conception
of history: their mission (*Amt*), vocation (*Beruf*) or task (*Dienst*)
was to help transform society and create a new humanity. Why
the Jew?

> A voice, like a wild cry resonating throughout the world and
> like a sigh in our heart of hearts, tells us irrefutably that the
> redemption of the Jew can take place only at the same time as
> that of humanity; and that it is one and the same to await the
> Messiah while in exile and dispersed, and to be the Messiah of
> the nations.[38]

This was, of course, a typical form of pariah messianism, which
reversed in the spiritual domain the 'negative privilege' (to quote
Max Weber) of the pariah people. In Landauer's mind, the Jewish
vocation dated back to the Bible itself. In a commentary on
Strindberg written in 1917, he maintained that there had been
two great prophecies in history: 'Rome, world domination; Israel,
world redemption.' The Jewish tradition, which never forgot
God's promise to Abraham – the redemption of the Jew along
with all nations – was evidence of 'a messianic conception, a
messianic faith, a messianic will'.[39]

    The Jewish mission of redemption in modern times has taken
the secular form of socialism. Landauer regarded the present

condition of Jews as the objective foundation for their international socialist role. Unlike other nations, Jews had the unique particularity of being a people, a community, but not a state, which gave them the historical chance to escape the statist delirium. Taking this as his starting-point, Landauer the anarchist rejected the two dominant currents within the German-Jewish community: assimilation – which implied joining the German Imperial State – and Zionism, which sought to establish a Jewish State.[40] Landauer radically dissociated the nation from the state, and himself claimed to have roots in three nationalities: German, South German and Jewish![41] He even rejected the designations 'German Jew' or 'German-Jewish' because he did not want any one of his national identities to be reduced to an adjective. This explains the conclusion to his 'heretical' article on the Jewish question, 'Sind das Ketzergedanken?': while other nations delimit themselves from their neighbours by means of state borders, 'the Jewish nation carries its neighbours in its bosom'. Landauer regarded that singularity as the surest sign of the Jews' mission towards humanity.[42]

When Landauer was invited in 1912 by a West Berlin branch of the German Zionist movement to give a speech on 'Judaism and Socialism', he put forward the provocative idea that the *Galuth* (the Exile, the Diaspora) was exactly what linked Judaism to socialism – a theme that logically ensued from his entire analysis of the Jewish condition.[43] This is where Landauer's path parted from that of his Zionist friend Martin Buber, leading him to the revolution in 1918–19.

Landauer reacted with impassioned hope to the October Revolution in Russia, which he regarded as an event of utmost importance, including for the future of the Jews. In a letter to Buber dated 5 February 1918, Landauer contrasted his own position with that of his friend:

> My heart has never lured me to Palestine, nor do I believe that it necessarily provides the geographical requirement for a Jewish *Gemeinschaft*. The real event of importance, one that may even be decisive for us, is the liberation of Russia. . . It seems preferable to me – despite everything – that Bronstein is not teaching at the University of Jaffa, but is Trotsky in Russia.[44]

As soon as the revolution broke out in Germany in November 1918, Landauer fervently hailed 'the Spirit of the Revolution' and compared its actions to those of the biblical prophets.[45] In January 1919, he wrote a new Preface for a reissue of *Aufruf zum Sozialismus*, which expressed his messianism in all its dramatic intensity – both apocalyptic/religious and utopian-revolutionary: 'Chaos is upon us. . . The Spirits are awakening . . . may Revolution give birth to Religion – a Religion of action, life, and love, a Religion that engenders happiness, brings redemption and overcomes all.' In Landauer's eyes, the workers' councils that were spreading in Europe were 'organic sections of a self-determining (*selbstbestimmendes*) people'; he may indeed have regarded them as a latter-day version of the autonomous communities of the Middle Ages.[46]

It thus becomes understandable why in April 1919, Landauer committed himself to the short-lived Councils Republic of Bavaria, in which he served – for only a few days – as People's Commissar for Public Education. When the Republic fell on 2 May 1919, Landauer was imprisoned and murdered in Munich by the White Guards. In an article written immediately after Landauer's death, Martin Buber dedicated a final homage to him: 'Landauer fell like a prophet and a martyr of the human community to come.'[47]

Although Gustav Landauer is virtually forgotten today, his spiritual influence left its mark on the majority of the Jewish intellectuals of the romantic generation. The signs can be traced not only in Martin Buber, but also in Hans Kohn, Rudolf Kayser, Leo Löwenthal, Manes Sperber, Gershom Scholem, Walter Benjamin, Ernst Bloch and Ernst Toller.

'Theologist of revolution' and philosopher of hope, a friend of Lukács and Benjamin, Ernst Bloch himself defined his thought as revolutionary romantic.[48] Bloch was born in the industrial city of Ludwigshafen, headquarters for IG Farben, and he looked with wonder upon the neighbouring city of Mannheim, an old cultural and religious centre. As Bloch later said in an autobiographical interview, the contrast between 'the ugly, naked and uncaring face of late capitalism' – a symbol of the 'railway-station nature' (*Bahnhofshaftigkeit*) of our modern life – and the old city on the other side of the Rhine – a symbol of the 'most shining medieval history' and of the 'Germanic Holy

Roman Empire' – had made a deep impression on him.[49] An avid reader of Schelling since adolescence, Bloch studied in Berlin under Georg Simmel, the Jewish neo-romantic sociologist. For a few years, along with Lukács, he participated in the Max Weber Circle at Heidelberg, one of the main centres of anti-capitalist romanticism within German academic circles. Contemporary accounts describe Bloch as a 'semi-Catholic apocalyptic Jew', or as 'a new Jewish philosopher . . . who obviously believed that he was the precursor of a new Messiah'.[50]

Between 1910 and 1917, there was a deep spiritual communion between Bloch and Lukács, traces of which can be found in their early writings. According to Bloch (in the interview he granted me in 1974), 'we were like communicating vessels; the water was always at the same level in both.' Lukács was responsible for initiating Bloch into the religious universe of Meister Eckhart, Kierkegaard and Dostoevsky – three decisive sources in Bloch's spiritual evolution.[51]

Geist der Utopie [Spirit of Utopia] may be considered – alongside the writings of Gustav Landauer, with which Bloch was very familiar – as one of the most characteristic works of modern revolutionary romanticism, particularly in its first version published in 1918. From the very start of the book, there is a bitter critique of machinery and 'technological coldness', followed by a hymn to the glory of Gothic art, that 'lofty spirit' which becomes 'organic-spiritual transcendence', superior to Greek art itself, because it makes of man as Christ 'the alchemical measure of all construction'.[52] In the final chapter Bloch presents an astonishing vision of the future utopia as a hierarchical, neo-medieval society: at the bottom, there is 'nothing but peasants and artisans'; and at the top, 'nobility without serfs or war', a 'spiritual aristocracy' of 'chivalrous and pious' men – all, of course, after the socialist revolution, which will do away with the profit economy and the state that protects it.[53] During our interview in 1974, Bloch insisted: 'The new aristocracy that I spoke of was not profitable economically – that is, not based on exploitation – but on the contrary, it had ascetic and chivalrous virtues.' These virtues were a 'moral and cultural heritage that can be found in Marx and Engels', for whom the rejection of capitalism as a fundamentally unjust system implied values that dated back 'to the code of the Knights, to the Code of King Arthur's Round Table'.[54] The passage in question was not, however, included in the second edition of the book in 1923, which was greatly re-worked and more Marxist. Another significant change was the distinction that Bloch now made between the 'authentically Christian' idea of humanity held during the Middle Ages and the 'romanticism of the new reaction', which was 'spiritless and un-Christian' (*geistlos und unchristlich*), which left out Thomas Münzer and the Peasant War and venerated only 'heraldic plunderers'.[55] In other words, in 1923, Bloch did not foresake his romantic problematic, but was concerned to distinguish it more clearly from conservative or reactionary romanticism, by appealing to revolutionary (millenarian) historical references.

The passages quoted above already disclose what constituted the dominant aspect of Bloch's romanticism: religiosity. He definitively rejected 'the Philistine ideals' of the free-thinking and 'banally atheistic' bourgeoisie, and he looked upon the establishment of a new Church – the 'space of a still-flowing tradition and a link with the End' – as one of the necessary outcomes of the socialist revolution.[56]

Bloch used words charged with religiosity to develop his political ideas and his Marxist/libertarian, anarcho-Bolshevik utopia. The state was for him, as for the anarchists, the mortal enemy, and he denounced 'its satanic and heathen coercive essence'. The state claimed to be 'God on earth', but the false God who lived within it emerged immediately in war and white terror. In the final analysis, the state as an end in itself, and 'world omnipotence through worship of the demonic', were 'the conscious expression of anti-Christianity' (*Antichristentum*). Bloch therefore insisted that the socialist free association of the future, as Marx and Engels had also perceived it, should not be confused in any way with all forms of 'state socialism'. At the same time, however, he recognized that the need to use violence and force in the struggle against the established order was inevitable:

> Domination and power are in themselves evil, but it is necessary to oppose them with means of power (*machtgemäss*), as a categorical imperative with gun in hand, so long as the demonic shuts itself off so fiercely against the (still lost) amulet of purity.[57]

This led Bloch to admit in 1923 that the state could be, as it was in Bolshevism, a temporary 'necessary evil' – a theme that set him apart, of course, from anarchist views properly so called. Never the less, Bloch emphasized that, from a socialist point of view, the state had to wither away and be replaced by a simple 'international organization of production and consumption'.[58] In *Geist der Utopie*, Bloch did not mention any anarchist author, but in an essay written around the same time as the first edition (1918), he hailed Hugo Ball the 'Christian Bakuninist', and the idea of anarchy as 'the multi-coloured, multiform and direct word of Christ'. In Bloch's eyes, the most radical utopia of the future was that of Bakunin: 'the confederation, freed of all "states" and of all authoritarian "organizations".'[59]

Bloch's religiosity drew its inspiration from Christian sources – the Apocalypse, Joachim de Flore, the mystics and heretics of the Middle Ages – as well as from Jewish texts such as the Old Testament (notably the books of Deuteronomy and Isaiah), the cabbala (and Christian cabbalists), Hasidism, and the writings of Buber.[60] In an interview that he gave to Jean-Michel Palmier in 1976, Bloch hinted that his interest in the cabbala and in the philosophy and tradition of German Romanticism began at the same time.[61] This would be typical of members of the intelligentsia who came from completely assimilated families, and who discovered messianism and Jewish mysticism through writers like Baader, Schlegel or Molitor.

According to Emmanuel Levinas, Bloch's Jewish culture 'probably involved no more than a reading of the Old Testament (in translation) and various elements of folklore imported from Eastern European Jews, with their Hasidic tales that were greatly appreciated in the West'.[62] It seems to me, however, that Levinas's assessment is far from accurate. Bloch's early writings showed a fairly good knowledge of the cabbala and of literature on Jewish mysticism. Thus, the first edition of *Geist der Utopie* (1918) contains numerous references to the cabbala and cabbalistic themes (Schechina, Adam Kadmon), to Jewish (Meir ben Gabbai, Eyebeschütz) or Christian (Molitor) cabbalists – and, of course, to the Baal-Schem.[63]

Bloch's attitude towards Judaism was complex. One of the few texts in which he expressed his views on the subject was the chapter 'Symbol: die Juden' ('Jews: A Symbol'), which was published in the first edition of *Geist der Utopie*, but not in the

1923 edition. (It was, however, included in the collection *Durch die Wüste*, also published in 1923.) In that chapter, Bloch rejected both the assimilationism of the free-thinking, non-religious Jewish bourgeoisie and the preservation of the traditional ghetto in Eastern Europe. As for Zionism, he suggested that 'in using the concept of nation-state – which had rather fleeting currency in the nineteenth century – it wanted to change Judea into a type of Asiatic Balkan State'. Bloch did, however, value the historical continuity of the 'people of the Psalms and of the prophets', and he was delighted at the 'awakening of Jewish pride' that was taking place at the time. In his view, the Jewish religion had the basic virtue of 'being built on the Messiah, on an appeal to the Messiah'. He therefore assigned to the Jews, along with the Germans and Russians, a crucial role in 'preparing for the absolute era', as these three peoples were destined to receive 'the birth of God and messianism'.[64]

Adorno was correct when he wrote that the 'perspective of the messianic end of history and the thrust towards transcendence' formed the centre around which everything in *Geist der Utopie* was organized.[65] In that central knot, Bloch combined and entangled Jewish as well as Christian references. Like Landauer and Buber, he regarded Jesus as a Jewish prophet who should 'return to his people' and be recognized as such by the Jews. But he did not look upon Jesus as the Messiah; the true Messiah, the 'distant Messiah', the Saviour, the 'final Christ, as yet unknown', had still to come.[66] In *Geist der Utopie*, Bloch hailed the Russian workers' and soldiers' councils of February 1917, not only as enemies of the money economy (*Geldwirtschaft*) and 'mercantile ethics', ('the crowning of all that is wicked in man'), but also as 'praetorians, who, in the Russian Revolution, for the first time established Christ as Emperor'.[67]

After the October Revolution, there is a 'shift in emphasis' (as Arno Münster puts it) in Bloch's writings towards the historical realization of utopia.[68] The first consequence was *Thomas Münzer als Theologe der Revolution*, published in 1921, when Germany still seemed on the eve of a new revolutionary wave.

There is no doubt that Bloch was greatly inspired by Landauer's remarks on Münzer – even if he did not quote from the relevant work 'Die Revolution', 1907.[69] This can be seen in his explicitly anarchist interpretation of the anabaptist message.

According to Bloch, that heretical movement 'denied State authority' and

> proclaimed, almost anticipating Bakunin, freedom of association beyond states; an International of the meek in spirit and the elect; a nihilistic negation of any law imposed from outside; freedom for each to adopt the moral code they have chosen and understood.

In spite of his support for the Russian Revolution, Bloch still seemed to retain a deeply 'mystical-libertarian' approach.[70] He regarded Münzer as the incarnation of the Christian ideal of a 'pure community of love, without judicial and State institutions', as against the deification of the State by its machiavellian theologian, Luther, and against the 'hard and impious materiality of the State'. In Bloch's view, Münzer also represented a central link in the 'subterranean history of the revolution', made up of past heretical and millenarian movements: the Brethren of the Valley, the Catharists, the Albigenses, Joachim of Calabria, the Brethren of Good Will, the Brethren of Free Spirit, Meister Eckhart, the Hussites, Münzer and the Anabaptists, Sebastian Frank, the Illuminati, Rousseau, Weitling, Baader, and Tolstoy. That entire vast tradition now 'knocks at the door in order to put an end to fear, to the State, and to all inhumane power'.[71]

Bloch's anarcho-Bolshevik revolutionary outlook cannot be separated from his messianic conception of temporality, which was opposed to all gradualism of progress: Münzer and his friends 'did not wage the battle for better times, but for the end of all time . . . the eruption of the Kingdom'. It was characteristic of Bloch's 'synchretic' (Judeo-Christian) religious approach that in the same passage he linked together the Third Gospel of Joachim of Floris, the chiliasm of the Anabaptists and the millenarianism of the (sixteenth-century) Safed cabbalists, who, north of Lake Tiberias, waited for 'the messianic avenger, the destroyer of the existing Empire and Papacy . . . the restorer of "*Olam-ha-Tikkun*", the true Kingdom of God'.[72]

Bloch was particularly sensitive to the restorative aspects of messianism. Thus, the anabaptist ideal meant 'escape from the curse cast on work, and the final return to Paradise'; and Münzer's dream had been of *restitutio omnium* – the eschatological return of all things to their original perfection (analogous to the *restitutio in integrum* mentioned in *Geist der Utopie* and taken over in Benjamin's 'Theologico-Political Fragment').[73]

It would, however, be wrong to regard Bloch's *Thomas Münzer* as nothing more than an exercise in the history of religions or as a more romantic version of Kautsky's *Vorläufer des Sozialismus*. In Bloch's eyes, in a Germany prey to revolutionary fever the whole question was a burning issue of the times. (In March 1921, workers influenced by the Communist movement had launched a semi-insurrectionary offensive.) In the conclusion to the book, Bloch heralded the 'time that is to come' – 'in Germany and in Russia, it will come into full being' – and believed he could perceive that 'a new messianism was in preparation'. The Princess Sabbat would appear, still hidden behind a thin, cracked wall, while 'from on high, upon the rubble of a civilization in ruins . . . would rise the spirit of an ineradicable utopia'. Bloch's faith in the imminence of millennial utopia is the focal point that put his entire work in its true perspective: 'It is impossible for the time of the Kingdom not to come now; it is for that time that a spirit shines in us, a spirit that refuses to resign, a spirit that will not be disappointed in any way.'[74]

Bloch's later works – notably *Das Prinzip Hoffnung* [The Principle of Hope], published in 1949 and 1955 – fall beyond the time-span of this study. Although for the most part he maintained his romantic-revolutionary and messianic orientation, the libertarian problematic tended to disappear. Bloch never rallied to Stalinist *diamat*, but the influence of the 'State socialism' of the GDR (which he left in 1961) cannot be ignored, particularly in certain political passages in *Das Prinzip Hoffnung*. Thus, he rejected anarchist ideas as 'a bogey of the bourgeoisie', and he criticized Bakunin's 'abstract hatred of power' and his 'unconsidered sense of freedom'.[75]

Born into an assimilated Jewish upper-class family in Budapest, Georg Lukács was essentially more at home in German culture.[76] He was fascinated by romanticism, and between 1907 and 1908, outlined the draft of a book to be entitled *Nineteenth Century Romanticism*. His first major work, *Soul and Form* from 1910, focused primarily on writers linked to Romanticism or neo-romanticism: Novalis, Theodor Storm, Stefan George, Paul Ernst, among others. An 'anti-capitalist romantic' dimension

(Lukács himself coined the phrase) was present in his writings even after he joined the Communist Party: for example, his essay 'Old Culture and New Culture' (1919) was permeated with deep nostalgia for pre-capitalist cultures, which Lukács contrasted to the 'culture-destroying' nature of capitalism. An amusing but quite characteristic detail illustrates the persistence of Lukács' romantic sensibility: in April 1919 one of his first decrees as People's Commissar of Public Education was that fairy tales should be read in every school and children's hospital in Hungary.[77]

Lukács' interest in mystical thought – be it Christian, Jewish, or even Hindu! – developed within this romantic spiritual framework. Like many other intellectuals, Jewish or non-Jewish, of German cultural origins, he probably discovered the spiritual universe of mystical Jewish religiosity through Buber's books on Hasidism. In 1911, Lukács wrote to Buber and expressed admiration for his work – which had been 'a great experience' (*ein großes Erlebnis*) for him – and in particular, for the *The Legend of the Baal-Schem* from 1908, which he hailed as an 'unforgettable' book. Buber and Lukács continued to correspond until 1921, and their letters between November and December 1916 suggest that they met in Heppenheim, the village where Buber lived at the time.[78] In 1911, Lukács published an article on Buber's books in a Hungarian journal of philosophy, where he compared the Baal-Schem to Meister Eckhart and Jakob Böhme. This piece, entitled 'Jewish Mysticism', was the only one that Lukács ever wrote on a Jewish theme (and he never had it translated or re-published). Attributing great importance to Hasidism in the history of religions of the modern age, Lukács wrote:

> The Hasidic movement, whose first major figure was the Baal-Schem, and whose last one was Rabbi Nachman, was a primitive and powerful mysticism, the only great and authentic movement since the German mysticism of the Reformation and the Spanish mysticism of the Counter-Reformation.[79]

One of the aspects that most attracted Lukács to Hasidism (such as Buber presented it) was its messianic aspiration. In his notebook from 1911, he copied several passages from Buber's works, including an excerpt from *Geschichten des Rabbi Nachman* [Tales of Rabbi Nachman] (1906) which discusses waiting for the Messiah in Jerusalem.[80] Several years later, in another notebook on Dostoevsky, Lukács referred to the idea that the *Shabbat* was 'the source of the world to come', or the reflection of redemption, and quoted a passage to this effect from *The Legend of the Baal-Schem*.[81]

Several contemporary accounts reveal that the young Lukács harboured an ardent apocalyptic messianism. Marianne Weber, the wife of the sociologist, described Lukács between 1912 and 1917 as a thinker who was 'moved by eschatological hopes of a new emissary of the transcendent God', seeing 'the basis of salvation in a socialist social order created by brotherhood'.[82] Bloch may have contributed to this eschatological dimension of the young Lukács. Paul Honigsheim, who was then attending the Max Weber Circle, described the two in the following terms: 'Ernst Bloch, the semi-Catholic apocalyptic Jew, with his follower at the time, Lukács.'[83] One of the spiritual elements that Lukács shared with Bloch was a fusion of Jewish and Russian mysticism. The Hungarian intellectual Emma Ritoök knew both philosophers very well between 1910 and 1914, before falling out with them and becoming an anti-Semite and an anti-Communist. In the 1920s, she wrote a *roman à clef*, *The Adventurers of the Spirit*, in which one of the characters, 'Ervin Donath' (most probably based on Lukács), declares:

> I often suspected that we would have to orient ourselves toward the East, but until now, I was missing the sure connection [with Jewish mysticism]. Is it possible that Slavic mysticism could prepare the way for a new mission for the Jewish spirit?[84]

Another source, this one less suspect, confirms Lukács' attraction to Jewish messianism. Béla Balázs, one of Lukács' best friends at the time, wrote in his diary in 1914:

> Gyuri's [Lukács'] great new philosophy (. . .) *Messianism.* Gyuri has discovered the Jew in him! The search for ancestors. The hasidic sect, the Baal-Schem. Now he, too, has found his ancestors and his race, but me, I am alone and abandoned. . . Gyuri's theory on the emergence or re-emergence of a Jewish type, the anti-rationalist ascetic, the antithesis of what is usually described as Jewish.[85]

Like other German-Jewish intellectuals, Lukács was primarily interested in the 'romantic' aspects of Judaism, as opposed to the rationalist image of the Jewish religion conveyed by the *Haskala*, the liberal Jewish establishment and German sociologists (such as Max Weber and Werner Sombart). Most notably in his notes on Dostoevsky from 1915, Lukács seemed to distinguish two radically different aspects in the Jewish religion: on the one hand, what he called 'the Jehovaic', to denote punitive authoritarianism and the metaphysics of the State; and, on the other hand, messianism, which bore from within a true 'ethical democracy'. Lukács paid special attention to 'heretical' Jewish messianic movements – like Sabbatai Sevi and Jakob Frank – the very ones that were to fascinate Gershom Scholem several years later.[86]

It would be wrong to view the messianism of the young Lukács as exclusively Jewish in origin. His knowledge of Jewish texts other than the Old Testament was very limited, and his apocalyptic tendency owed as much, if not more, to Slavic mysticism and to Dostoevsky, in particular. Balázs's comment ('Gyuri has discovered the Jew in him') is interesting, because in Lukács' many autobiographical writings and conversations, he always denied any link between his thinking and Judaism.[87] In any event, Lukács' return to his Jewish roots was much more restricted than Bloch's or Benjamin's.

Max Weber, who discussed ethical and religious questions with Lukács on several occasions, placed him directly within the German spiritual context as 'one of the types of German "eschatologism", at the opposite pole from Stefan George'.[88] In fact, Stefan George, the conservative bard of German ancestry, was considered by his followers as a veritable religious guide. Lukács did not share that opinion, and in a letter he wrote in 1913 to Félix Bertaux, he stressed that George was not 'a true prophet, a true envoy and herald of God' – thereby implying that the advent of a true messianic prophet was possible.[89]

Lukács's apocalyptic sense was heightened by the war which he saw as the lowest point in the abyss, 'the age of absolute sinfulness (*Zeitalter der vollendeten Sündhaftigkeit*)', to use Fichte's expression which Lukács adopted in *The Theory of the Novel*. In a note on Dostoevsky, he linked Fichte's expression to the Jewish doctrine that 'the Messiah could come only in an age of absolute (*vollendeter*) impiety'.[90] Sometimes, his messianic hope showed through in his writings; for example, in 'Ariadne auf Naxos', an essay from 1916, he spoke of a new God who was to come, and suggested that his dawning could already be felt.[91]

Nevertheless, it must be emphasized that Lukacs' messianism remained within the framework of 'atheist religiosity', far removed from religion in the usual sense. In Lukács' eyes, the symbolic figure of this form of spirituality was the Russian *Narodnik* poet and martyr, Ivan Kaliaev who in February 1905, having overcome his moral and religious scruples, assassinated the Grand Duke Sergei, Governor General of Moscow, and was executed shortly after by the tsarist authorities. In Lukács' notes on Dostoevsky, he wrote that Kaliaev appears as the representative of believers who consider themselves atheists, and whose faith is directed to 'a new, silent God, who needs our help'.[92] This comment outlines the political dimension of Lukács' eschatology (inspired by both Christianity and Judaism) whose spiritual trajectory is expressed in an astonishing summary: 'knowledge of the prophets: the advent of the Messiah – but not the Messiah himself. . . It is a lie that Christ has already been here – his advent: the Revolution.'[93]

Unlike the other authors of the neo-romantic movement who were close to him (such as Paul Ernst and Thomas Mann), Lukács manifested a radically anti-statist tendency, particularly after the outbreak of war. In a letter he wrote to Paul Ernst, he referred to compulsory military service as the 'most vile slavery that has ever existed' and denounced Hegel's capital sin against the spirit in covering State power with a metaphysical halo. Of course, Lukács added, the State is a power, 'but so are earthquakes and epidemics'.[94] A wonderfully outrageous variant of this comparison can also be found in his notes on Dostoevsky, when he refers to the State as *'organisierte Tuberkulose'* ('organized tuberculosis'): 'The victorious are right. The State as organized tuberculosis; if the germs of the plague were to organize, they would found the world Kingdom.'[95] As Ferenc Feher shows very clearly in a remarkable essay on the young Lukács, the entire draft of the book on Dostoevsky (of which there remains nothing but a collection of notes) was structured as the story of an immense decline: the institutionalization/alienation of the spirit in the Church and the State. The whole of human history was a victory parade for the State, a tale of ever greater depravity.[96] In discussing Kierkegaard, Lukács characterized the triumph of the Church and State as 'Satan's ruse'; and in a section on Nietzsche, he defined the State as 'organized immorality – internally, in the form of the police, punishment, social orders, commerce and family; and externally, in the form of a Will for Power, for war, for conquest and vengeance'.[97]

In one of Lukács' notebooks that I was able to consult in the Lukács Archives, there is a bibliography (probably written around 1910 or 1911) of works on French anarcho-syndicalism: Sorel, Berth, Lagardelle, Pouget.[98] There is also a semi-anarchist reference to Sorel among Lukács' notes on Dostoevsky; following a quotation from the Apocalypse of Saint John on the need to abolish all trade comes the following text: '*State*, Sorel: no correction is possible so long as that power is not reduced to a secondary role in social relations.'[99] The choice of Sorel, also found in Walter Benjamin, is understandable given the romantic anti-capitalist and apocalyptic nature of the theoretician of the general strike.[100]

The Sorelian problematic played an even greater role in Lukács' political radicalization after his return to Budapest in 1917 – when he was deeply attracted by Ervin Szabó, the eminent Hungarian historian and anarcho-syndicalist leader (of Jewish origin). In an autobiographical text from 1969, Lukács recalled: 'At that point in my development, I was considerably influenced by French anarcho-syndicalism.'[101] His political views at the time (1917–18) were in fact characterized by anti-parliamentarianism, subordination of politics to ethics, and rejection of all dictatorship, even revolutionary; it was a semi-anarchist, ethical socialist vision.

During 1918, probably under the influence of the Russian Revolution, Lukács' messianism became more political and linked with his revolutionary ideology. In a lecture from 1918, he paid homage to the Anabaptists and made his own their categorical imperative: 'Bring the Kingdom of God down to earth at this very moment'.[102] Finally, in December 1918, Lukács published an article ('Bolshevism as a Moral Problem') in which the proletariat was presented as the 'bearer of social redemption for mankind' and the 'Messiah-class of world history'.[103] Messianism, thus 'secularized', tended to merge with social revolution, which Lukács then conceived as a total upheaval on a world scale.

To a certain extent, Lukács maintained his world-view even during the first period after he joined the Communist Party. The first Bolshevik work he read (at the end of 1918) made the transition easier for him; it was Lenin's *State and Revolution*, whose radically anti-statist problematic was in some ways similar to anarchism. Certainly, this book seems to have played a role in Lukács' decision to join the Hungarian Communist Party in December 1918.[104] One of his first articles in the Communist press, 'Party and Class' (1919), was still permeated by the influence of Ervin Szabó's anarcho-syndicalism.[105] Another significant example was his well-known anti-parliamentarian article 'Zur Frage des Parlamentarismus' (1920), which was sharply criticized by Lenin. In a conversation on the eve of his death (1971), Lukács recalled that in 1919, he was convinced that the proletarian revolution would soon lead 'to Heaven on Earth', which he understood in a profoundly sectarian-ascetic manner.[106]

It was only little by little, between 1920 and 1923, that Lukács really rallied to Bolshevism. *History and Class Consciousness*, his great work from 1923, was already the *Aufhebung* (negation/preservation/supersession) of messianism and libertarian utopia within a Marxist-dialectical problematic. However, in (probably sincere) self-criticism made in 1967, he referred to the 'utopian messianism' of the book.[107]

Of all the thinkers that we have examined so far, Lukács was one of the least touched by the Jewish problematic: his relationship to Jewish messianism remained largely 'subterranean', showing up only indirectly in his writings. His reflections and his utopian/revolutionary aspirations always remained within a universal-humanist and world-wide framework. Of all the authors analysed in this book, Lukács represents the polar opposite of Scholem, whose anarchist utopia disappears from the surface and can be perceived only in a 'hidden' and mediated way, through his writings on Jewish messianism.

Erich Fromm is known chiefly for his works published in the United States in the 1940s and after: *Escape from Freedom* (1941), *Man for Himself* (1947), *The Sane Society* (1955), among others. In the 1950s, Marcuse severely criticized them as 'conformist' works, whose 'cultural revisionism' robbed Freudian psychoanalysis of its critical force.[108]

Whatever judgement one may have of those criticisms (in my view, they are both important and questionable), there was another, much less known period, between 1927 and 1934, when Fromm's early psychoanalytical writings had an undeniably critical and even revolutionary power. This was the time when Fromm was beginning to explore a possible convergence between psychoanalysis and Marxism, and when he was associated with the *Institut für Sozialforschung* (the Frankfurt School) by writing articles and book reviews for its journal and participating in its collective research projects.

In spite of their thematic diversity, these works have several common characteristics: a messianic dimension of Jewish origin; a radically critical attitude to capitalism as a socio-economic system and as a psychological or character structure; and an anti-authoritarian political orientation. These three elements together shaped an original and subversive mode of thinking, similar in many ways to the thought of Walter Benjamin or Ernst Bloch.

In an autobiographical note published in 1966, Fromm observed, not without pride, that he had studied the Old Testament and the Talmud since he was a child. His masters were remarkable rabbinical scholars: Ludwig Krause, his mother's uncle and a Talmud traditionalist of strict observance; the well-known rabbi, Nehemia Nobel, 'whose thinking was permeated as deeply with Jewish mysticism as with Western humanism'; and Salman Rabinkow, the expert in Hasidism who was also a socialist intellectual.[109] What had struck Fromm the most in the Bible – especially in light of the catastrophes of the First World War – were the messianic prophecies of Isaiah, Hosea and Amos, the promise of an 'end of times' which would establish everlasting peace between nations and men.[110] Starting from this cultural context, Fromm became interested in Marx's philosophy, which he saw as the expression, in secular language, of the tradition of prophetic messianism.[111]

In the early 1920s, Fromm helped to create the *Freies Jüdisches Lehrhaus* (Free House for Jewish Studies) in Frankfurt, an institution animated by Franz Rosenzweig and Martin Buber. Along with Ernst Simon and Nahum Glatzer, he attended Gershom Scholem's seminar on the apocalypse of the Book of Daniel.[112]

At the same time, he studied in Heidelberg with Rickert, Jaspers and Alfred Weber; and in 1922, he presented his doctoral thesis, 'Das jüdische Gesetz, ein Beitrag zur Soziologie des Diasporajudentums' (Jewish Law: A Contribution to the Sociology of Diaspora Judaism), which analysed, among other themes, the socio-psychological structure of Hasidism.[113] According to Scholem, Fromm at that time was a religious Jew *shomer mitzvot* – 'faithful to the Commandments of the Law' – and a member of the Association of Zionist Students.[114]

In 1924, Fromm settled in Heidelberg, where he was psychoanalysed by Frieda Reichmann, an orthodox Freudian whom he married in 1926. It was probably the impact of his analysis that made him lose his religious faith at this moment – even if his thinking always remained deeply tinged with religiosity. According to Scholem, in 1927 Fromm had become 'an enthusiastic Trotskyite', who was convinced of the superiority of his new faith and filled with pity for the petty-bourgeois, Zionist narrow-mindedness of his former teacher.[115]

In 1927, Fromm published his first psychoanalytical work in the journal *Imago*, which Freud edited. The article 'Der Sabbath', is a quite astonishing piece with a powerful messianic impetus. Its problematic is typically restorative/utopian, and still filled with a religious spirit, in spite of its scientific language and the direct influence of Otto Rank's *The Birth Trauma* (1924), as well as the works by Reik and Abraham on the psychoanalysis of religions. Fromm begins with an analysis of the meaning of the work interdiction imposed during the Jewish Sabbath, showing that the biblical concept of 'work' referred primarily to the relationship between man and nature – or more precisely, man and the earth. Therefore, a ban on work implied a suspension during the Sabbath of 'Man's incestuous violation of Mother Earth and Nature in general'. The deep psychological significance of this practice was that the Jewish religion, by strictly and harshly prohibiting all industrious activity during the Sabbath, sought 'the re-establishment (*Wiederherstellung*) of the paradisaical state without work; the harmony between man and nature; and the return to the maternal womb (*der Rückkehr in den Mutterleib*)'. From which stemmed the talmudic promise that the Messiah would come once Israel kept the Sabbath in its entirety. According to Fromm,

the prophets regarded messianic time as a condition in which
the fight between man and nature would reach an end. . . The
paradisaical state would be established once more. If man was
expelled from Paradise because he wanted to be like God – that
is, the father's equal, capable of conquering the mother – and
if work was punishment for that primal breach (*Urverbrechen*),
then, according to the prophets, in the messianic period man
would live once more in complete harmony with nature, in
other words, without having to work, in Paradise – the
equivalent of the mother's womb.[116]

Fromm took up those same ideas several times after the Second
World War, but he toned down the restorative aspect and
endowed the ideas with a more rationalist and 'progressive'
dimension.[117]

It is interesting to compare Fromm's essay on the Sabbath with
Walter Benjamin's ideas – both in his text on language from
1916 and in the later theological works – on the theme of
re-establishing the Edenic harmony between man and nature.
The point is not that there was a 'influence', but rather that the
same vein of thought ran through different personalities within
German-Jewish culture.

Fromm's concern to combine Marxism and psychoanalysis lies
at the heart of his subsequent works. What is striking about his
interpretation of Marxism is its directly anti-authoritarian charge
– which also emerges in his interpretation and application of
the Freudian method. One very revealing example is his article
from 1931, 'Contribution to the Psychology of the Criminal and
of the Punitive Society (*der strafenden Gesellschaft*)'. According
to Fromm, the true goal of legal punishment is not, as is
usually claimed, to prevent crime, and still less to reform
the criminal, but 'to educate the masses so that they tie and
subordinate themselves to the rulers'. Every class society has
been characterized by a small stratum of property-owners who
dominate a great mass of the dispossessed. Physical violence
(the police and the Army) represents the most visible means
of maintaining that domination, but in the long run, it cannot
effectively guarantee it. For this reason, psychological means
acquire a crucial importance: their role is 'to lead the masses
into attachment and spiritual dependence on the ruling class

or its representatives, so that the masses will submit and obey without the use of violence'. Penal justice is one such means; it allows the ruling-class State to impose itself on the masses like a father-figure who punishes and demands obedience; it is 'an indispensable psychological precondition of class society and has nothing to do with any supposed prevention of criminality'.[118] It is hard not to see in these words a premonition of the future that was awaiting Germany in the next few years.

Fromm's first major work was *The Dogma of Christ*, published in Vienna in 1931. This combined psychoanalysis and Marxism but was not at variance with his Jewish-religious concerns, because it saw early Christianity as the direct successor of Jewish messianism struggling against the Roman Empire.

In Fromm's view, Christianity was originally 'a messianic-revolutionary movement', bearing the message of eschatological expectation, the nearness of the Kingdom of God. The early Christian community was 'a free brotherhood of the poor', intensely hostile to all authority or 'paternal' power. The original Christian myth depicted Christ as the suffering Messiah who was elevated to the dignity of God; it bore a concealed hostility to God the Father, the Emperor and authority in general. Christianity was the expression of the revolutionary tendencies, the expectations and longings of the oppressed masses (first Jewish and then pagan), who grouped together in 'a community organization without authorities, statutes or bureaucracy'.[119]

From the third century, however, the social foundations of Christianity were transformed when it became the religion of the dominant upper classes of the Roman Empire. Beliefs about Christ were then deeply modified: man elevated to the dignity of God became the Son of Man who had always been God (dogma of consubstantiation). At the same time, the eschatological hope for real historical deliverance was gradually replaced by the idea that salvation would be an internal, spiritual, non-historical and individual liberation. Finally, in close association with this disavowal of messianism, a growing reconciliation took place between Church and State. In short, 'Christianity, which had been the religion of a community of equal brothers, without hierarchy or bureaucracy, became the "Church", the reflected image of the absolute monarchy of the Roman Empire'. Together with this transformation of a free confraternity into an authoritarian, hierarchical organization, there was also a psychic change: hostility towards the father, and the early Christian contempt for the rich and the rulers, for all authority, was replaced by reverence and subordination to the new clerical authorities. Aggressive impulses, originally directed against the father, were then turned against the self in a manner that posed no danger for social stability; they thereby induced a general feeling of guilt – along with a masochistic need for atonement.[120] If Scholem was correct when he referred to Fromm's 'Trotskyism' in 1927, it is not out of the question that Fromm's analysis of the evolution of Christianity was, in his mind, analogous to that experienced by Soviet Communism after Lenin's death.

It might be said that Fromm's historical research, like Scholem's writings on the history of religions, did not project his own feelings onto history, but that his attitudes, concepts and values (his world-view) made him more sensitive to some aspects of historical reality than to others; in Fromm's case, to the messianic and anti-authoritarian dimension of early Christianity. In spite of its scientific nature, it is clear that the *The Dogma of Christ* was not 'neutral', since the author did not hide his sympathy for the revolutionary eschatology of the early Christians.

The Dogma of Christ was hailed in the *Zeitschrift für Sozialforschung* – the journal of the Frankfurt Institute of Social Research – as the first concrete example of a synthesis between Freud and Marx.[121] Although not actually a member of the Institute, Fromm was associated with the Frankfurt School during the 1930s and published several essays and articles in its journal, which was edited by Horkheimer.

Fromm's article on the Sabbath from 1927 contains, at least implicitly, a romantic-type critique of the bourgeois work ethic and of the domination of nature – a theme also present, in a more intense form, in one of his first articles for the *Zeitschrift für Sozialforschung* (in 1932). In this latter piece, Fromm uses the novels of Defoe and Benjamin Franklin's autobiography to analyse the capitalist/bourgeois spirit (as defined by Sombart and Weber), comparing it to the 'anal character' studied by Freud and his disciple, Karl Abraham. The pre-capitalist spirit – for which the search for pleasure and satisfaction was a self-evident goal superordinate to economic activity – is contrasted with the spirit of capitalism, for which saving and acquiring are the essential goals. In the Middle Ages, the individual (in accordance with his social class) derived great satisfaction from sumptuous festivities, beautiful paintings, splendid monuments as well as numerous religious holidays.

> It was understood that man had an innate right to happiness, blessedness or pleasure; this was viewed as the proper goal of all human activity, whether it was economic or not. The bourgeois spirit introduced a decisive change in this respect. Happiness or blessedness ceased to be the unquestioned goal of life. Something else took first place on the scale of values: duty.[122]

Fromm's essay – whose theme was deeply linked to the article on the Sabbath, even if the messianic aspect was missing – displays a romantic idealization of pre-capitalist (notably medieval) ways of life.

A similar perspective inspired another article that Fromm published at that time, dedicated to Bachofen's writings on matriarchy. He begins by noting that Bachofen's works were enthusiastically received by two opposing political camps: the socialists (Marx, Engels, and Bebel) and the counter-revolutionary antisocialists (Klages and Bäumler).

> One common element in the opposing attitudes to matriarchy is their common distance from bourgeois-democratic society . . . whether they had looked back to the past as a lost paradise, or looked forward hopefully to a better future. But criticism of the present was about the only thing that the two opposing adherents of matriarchy did share.

Fromm emphasizes that the matriarchal society of which Bachofen spoke included many features that were similar to socialist ideals: democracy, equality, liberty, fraternity, harmony with nature, absence of private property. He quotes the view of the socialist Kelles-Krauz that Bachofen dug beneath the bourgeois renaissance so that precious seeds of a new revolutionary renaissance might spring from the ground: the renaissance of the communist spirit. Basing himself on Bachofen and Freud, Fromm then draws a distinction between two types of social character: 'patricentric' and 'matricentric'. Patricentrics are characterized by feelings of guilt; an obedient love of paternal authority; a wish to dominate the weakest, and pleasure in so doing; acceptance of suffering as punishment for one's own wrongdoings. Bourgeois society and the Protestant work ethic are the modern expression of this patricentric character. Matricentrics, on the other hand, do not experience anguish and submission, but feel maternal love for the weak; a greater aptitude for pleasure and happiness; far less intense feelings of guilt, and so on. The present-day representatives of matricentric tendencies are the working class and the Marxist social programme.[123]

This article should be compared with Fromm's 1927 essay on the Sabbath: Bachofen's primordial matriarchal society appears as the anthropological equivalent of the Edenic and maternal paradise, freed from the curse of work. The socialist revolution corresponds on a secular level to the advent of the Messiah, who will re-establish the Garden of Pleasures.

Fromm's article on Bachofen, which was also published in the *Zeitschrift für Sozialforschung*, had a profound influence on Walter Benjamin; in his own essay on Bachofen from the following year, he developed similar themes and explicitly referred to Fromm's 'remarkable study'.[124]

After Fromm left for the United States in 1934, he toned down the libertarian/revolutionary radicalism of his Marxism, and his thinking took a more moderate turn. The first signs of this change can be detected as early as 1936, in his contribution to the Frankfurt School study on authority and the family. Although Fromm reaffirmed his anti-authoritarian perspective, he rejected anarchism as a form of inconsequential revolt and hailed nineteenth-century bourgeois democracy as a form of authority based on the (unequal, but real) satisfaction of the interests of all social layers.[125]

When all is said and done, however, Fromm's cultural critique of industrial civilization, his messianic aspiration to a new world, and his anti-authoritarian tendency remained throughout his later works. *You Shall be as Gods* (1966), for example, a book that offers a humanist/socialist interpretation of biblical prophecy, follows the 1927 essay nearly word for word (except for the references to the lost paradise, which disappear completely) when it insists that the Sabbath is the expression of the central idea of Judaism: 'The idea of freedom, the idea of complete harmony between man and nature, man and man; the idea of the anticipation of messianic time and of man's defeat of time, sadness and death.'[126] The eschatological references strewn throughout the work no longer have the subversive explosiveness of Fromm's writings from the 1920s and 1930s, but they are evidence that he maintained his politico-religious concerns as well as his critical attitude towards the established order.

8

Crossroads, Circles and Figures:
A Few Examples

The scope of this study has been limited to approximately a dozen authors, but many other Jewish intellectuals of German cultural origins undoubtedly shared the libertarian orientation and the romantic messianic concept of history that we have examined.

Let us now look briefly at some of the cultural crossroads, and some of the literary, political and religious circles and movements within Central Europe which created the most favourable environment for the elective affinity between utopia and messianism to emerge. We shall also consider several examples – not necessarily 'exemplary' or representative – of writers, thinkers or militants from these circles.

Der Jude [The Jew], the magazine that Martin Buber edited, was one of those propitious cultural milieux. Franz Rosenzweig, Gershom Scholem, Franz Kafka, Ernst Simon and Hugo Bergmann were among its contributors. During its nine years of publication (1910–24), it was one of the main intellectual centres of religious sensibility within German-Jewish culture.

Among the authors associated with *Der Jude*, a few stood somewhere between Buber and Landauer; but since their main identification was with Judaism, they essentially belonged to the spiritual universe of the semi-anarchist religious Jews. I am speaking, above all, of Hans Kohn and Rudolf Kayser.

Between 1912 and 1914, Hans Kohn was one of the main driving forces behind the *Bar-Kochba* Circle in Prague, in which Hugo Bergmann, Robert Weltsch, Max Brod and – more sporadically – Franz Kafka were active. *Bar-Kochba*, as is well known, was a Zionist cultural club influenced by Martin Buber, Achad Ha-am (Asher Ginsberg, the theoretician of cultural Zionism who opposed Herzl and the idea of a Jewish state) and Gustav Landauer. In a work published in 1930, Kohn described the state of mind in his milieu:

> During the first decade of the twentieth century, interest in romanticism revived once again. Novalis and Hölderlin in particular were the 'classics' we read the most when we were young. . . For the new generation, specialized and mechanized science seemed cold, lifeless and sterile. We wanted to return to the obscure and primordial sources (*Urquellen*) of Being. . . Mysticism was the fountain of youth into which plunged the religious nostalgia of the time.[1]

This was the context for what Kohn in his autobiography (written in 1965) called the transfer of concepts from German nationalism to Jewish nationalism or Zionism – concepts such as the 'organic popular community' or *Volksurträume* (ancestral folk dreams). Kohn was one of the few protagonists of his time who openly recognized the relationship between his Jewish neo-romantic thinking and Germanic sources:

> Our Zionism was not a reaction to persecution but, under the influence of the German thought of the period, a search for 'roots', a turning inward toward the supposed center of our true self, which dated back, so we believed, over two thousand years to biblical times.[2]

In Prague in 1913, he published a collection *Vom Judentum* which, in addition to his own essay 'Der Geist des Orients' [The Spirit of the East], included contributions from Buber, Landauer and Karl Wolfskehl: a Zionist, an anarchist and a conservative partisan of Stefan George. Around the same time, Kohn tried (in vain) to edit a selection of texts by German Christian mystics. From the very beginning, his Judeo-Christian religious and spiritual interests were closely associated with libertarian themes. Thus, in his view, Jesus was

> one of the greatest Hebrew prophets, a religious ethical anarchist, to whom the powers and ambitions of the age meant little compared with the approaching *Malkhut Shamayim*, the Kingdom of Heaven, whose coming he announced to the Jews and which would put an end to the injustices on this earth.[3]

Kohn was mobilized during the First World War and taken prisoner by the tsarist army. He hailed the October Revolution with great enthusiasm – 'the most powerful guiding experience for mankind since 1793' – and in 1919 he sent a piece from the Soviet Union for publication in *Der Jude*. According to this article – which is an impressive document of the radicalization of certain religious Jewish circles at the crest of the revolutionary wave in *Mitteleuropa* – the real answer to the Jewish question was possible only simultaneously with a solution to the 'question of mankind' (*Menschheitsfrage*) through world revolution, which would destroy the State – that 'sinister phantom . . . enemy of the spirit'. Kohn believed in the messianic vocation of the Jews, as a people who bore the *Ol Malkhut Hashamayim* (Yoke of the Kingdom of Heaven), from which would come the words of redemption for all mankind: libertarian socialism, 'the doctrine of our prophets and Jesus', inspired by the 'spirit of Gustav Landauer'. The goal of the struggle, which would be achieved in a distant future, was to establish 'a power which would no longer be "power", but rather An-archia'.[4]

After a brief stay in Paris in 1920, Kohn discovered the writings of Péguy and, in a book on nationalism published in 1922, took up Péguy's distinction between mysticism and politics. The nation had to be separated from the State: it did not need a State in order to develop socially and culturally, and national sentiment had to be dissociated from the concept of a territorial State.[5] Armed with these ideas, Kohn left for Palestine and in 1925 became one of the founders and leading members of the *Brit Shalom*. At that time, in an essay entitled *Die politische Idee des Judentums* [The Political Idea of Judaism], he wrote that 'the prophets conceived the advent of the messianic reign as a historical act, to take place among living generations' – unlike the late apocalypse, which transformed it into a metaphysical event centred on the resurrection of the dead. In the Jewish tradition, the messianic world 'is not to be found in the beyond, but rather in the time that is unfolding, that is going to come, *olam haba*'. It was the time when all men would be united in a brotherly alliance, a kingdom of universal peace.[6]

Ever Buber's faithful follower, Kohn worked in Jerusalem from 1927 to 1929 on a biography of his spiritual master, which also stands as an intellectual portrait of an entire German-Jewish generation. Certain remarks in this book suggest that Kohn was searching at the time for a (romantic) synthesis between anarchism and

Marxism. After mentioning that Tönnies, 'as a student of Marx' (a questionable judgement, to say the least!), and the neo-romantics under Nietzsche's influence had always contrasted the true community with the modern sovereign nation state, 'the typical form of bourgeois/capitalist socialization', he concluded: 'Marx's socialism has the same end goal as the anarchism to which Gustav Landauer subscribed. . . Marx, too, wanted a free, non-political, and state-less association, a true *Gemeinschaft*, a society achieved by all mankind.'[7]

In 1929, an Arab rebellion broke out in Palestine, and was brutally put down by the British authorities. Traumatized by the events, Kohn broke with Zionism and left Palestine. In 1933, he moved to the United States, where he soon became known as a historian of nationalism. The works he published there – especially after 1945 – were radically anti-romantic and anti-messianic; they were written from a 'classic' liberal point of view.[8]

Unlike Hans Kohn, Rudolf Kayser was not a Zionist. His doctoral thesis of 1914 focused on Romantic literature, notably Arnim and Brentano, but he was also interested in the Jewish religion. In 1921 he published 'Moses Tod' [The Death of Moses], and in 1922 an essay on Franz Werfel dealing with the religious Jewish dimension of the Prague poet and his goal of universal redemption.[9] In 1919 he contributed to *Der Jude* a quite astonishing article which situated him (somewhat like Hans Kohn) within a political-religious field whose magnetic poles were Buber and Landauer. Whilst rejecting Zionism, Kayser advocated the establishment of a 'new Alliance (*neue Bund*)', a 'Jewish Association (*jüdische Genossenschaft*)' – which he compared to the fifteenth-century Hussite Taborites – whose mission was to 'prepare the time of the Messiah' by helping mankind to pass from 'the Hell of politics' to the 'messianic paradise'. This mission implied the abolition of the State, a task in which the Jews were called upon to play a major role, in so far as 'there is no community imaginable that is further removed from the State than the ethical-religious community of the Jews. . . The idea of the State is an un-Jewish (*unjüdisch*) idea'. It is the absence of domination, Kayser argued, which demarcates the Hebraic religious community from the State; power appertains only to the divine idea. In that sense, it is 'theocratic': only divine law rules. In conclusion, 'This is the mission of the Jews: to make earth the homeland of mankind, while remaining stateless themselves'.[10]

In that same year, Kayser published an ardent tribute to Kurt Eisner and Gustav Landauer, entitled 'The Jewish Revolutionary'. Though exaggerated by anti-Semites and denied by the Jewish bourgeoisie, the participation of Jews in modern revolutionary movements was undeniable. Jews such as Trotsky, Radek, Axelrod, Eisner, Leviné, Toller and Rosa Luxemburg became leaders of the revolution; several paid for it with their lives, like 'martyrs for the idea, Christs and messengers for a new mankind'. Their ancestral figure was the prophet who proclaimed the imminent eruption of the messianic age: *Sabbatai Sevi*! The Jewish revolutionary sought neither to reform the State nor to distribute wealth; what he wanted, by overthrowing thrones, General Staffs or economic powers, was to change human feelings completely, to awaken religiosity, love and the spirit.

> For that reason, every revolutionary-spiritual Jew today must really be a socialist, an adversary of capitalism, of its vile quest for profit and its materialistic nature. For the same reason, however, his ultimate goal is anarchy, and an end to all relationships of power.

Eisner and Landauer fell for that ideal: 'they died like Jesus of Nazareth and like all the other Jewish martyrs'.[11] These two articles by Kayser were virtually typical of the link or fusion between Jewish messianism and anarchist revolution; biblical religiosity and modern utopia seemed to form a single system of communicating vessels, fed by one and the same spiritual fluid.

Rudolf Kayser knew Walter Benjamin, and was probably the 'protector' at the Fischer publishing house of whom Benjamin spoke in a letter to Scholem dated 26 May 1921.[12] In 1923, Kayser became the editor of *Die Neue Rundschau*, the leading literary magazine in Germany. In *Die Zeit ohne Mythos*, a book published at this time, he wrote that 'anarchy is our final dream', and that 'the significance of any revolutionary eruption into political and cultural life is to ascend from the legal towards the metaphysical. . .'[13]

The ideas of Martin Buber and Gustav Landauer also had a significant influence on socialist/Zionist youth movements,

particularly on the *Hapoel Hatzair* (The Young Worker) and the
Hashomer Hatzair (The Young Guard), which sought to achieve
a federation of collectivist rural communities in Palestine. These
movements had their main roots in Eastern Europe, but they
were also quite active in Vienna, particularly among the young
Ost-Juden (Eastern Jews). That is where the writer Manes Sperber
served his political apprenticeship.

Manes Sperber was born in 1905 in the Zablotow *shtetl* in
Galicia, the Polish province of the Austro-Hungarian Empire. It
was an environment in which the Hasidic Jewish tradition and
German culture – disciples of the miraculous *Zaddik* and admirers
of Schiller, Goethe and Heine – rubbed shoulders. Sperber's early
reading attested to this 'cultural cross-breeding': the Bible in
Hebrew, Grimm's fairy tales and newspapers from Vienna.[14] In
this poverty-stricken Jewish village, 'there were always people
who . . . would demonstrate that the very excess of deprivation
and suffering confirmed the inevitable and imminent approach
of the Messiah'. Not only adults, but children as well knew that
the Messiah might descend on earth at any moment. Sometimes,
as evening came on, Sperber's great-grandfather, a venerable
Hasidic rabbi, would hurry to a hill to scan the horizon 'in
the hope of seeing the Messiah come'. When the First World
War brought its procession of atrocities, this feeling intensified
within the *shtetl*: the Hasidim confidently declared that

> redemption was approaching with giant steps; the era of the
> Messiah had already begun – for otherwise, it would make no
> sense that this war kept spreading further and further every
> day, so that ultimately all the nations on earth would be driven
> together to the slaughtering block. . .

The young Sperber shared the faith of his ancestors: 'Long before
I learned how to translate the words of the prophet Isaiah, I knew
that injustice would vanish from the earth only after the coming
of the Messiah.'[15]

In 1916, his family settled in Vienna, and from that time on, he
received his *Bildung* in the German culture of the Imperial capital
at its apogee. As an adolescent, Sperber discovered Romantic
poetry ('I was never filled with as much admiration for a poet
as I was for Hölderlin'); Nietzsche's philosophy, whose 'subversive and revolutionary' side seduced Sperber (as it did many

anarchists); and the Expressionist plays of Toller, Hasenclever and Georg Kaiser[16] – in a word, the universe of anti-capitalist romantic culture.

The cultural shock soon prompted a religious crisis. Towards the end of the war, Sperber lost his faith – a 'break that remained forever irreparable'.[17] Yet his crisis did not at all cause him to turn away from Judaism, quite the contrary: in 1917 he joined the *Hashomer Hatzair*, a Zionist/socialist youth organization. In reality, he entrusted his messianic faith to revolutionary utopia: 'I had long given up obeying the countless laws that govern the everyday life of pious Jews. But my faith in the Messiah was still as powerful as ever. Our Messianic equivalent was revolutionary activity.'[18]

The *Hashomer Hatzair*, whose centre at the time was in Vienna, was variously influenced by the German *Jugendbewegung* (notably Gustav Wyneken, to whom Benjamin had been close around 1914); by Buber's ideas on the renewal of Judaism; by Landauer's libertarian socialism; and by the romantic culture in Vienna.[19] The October Revolution would soon blow on these glowing embers, but according to Sperber, it 'nurtured our interest in the Social Revolutionaries, the descendants of the Narodniki, and in the anarcho-communist theory of Kropotkin, the revolutionary prince, far more than in Marxism'.[20] Libertarian anti-authoritarianism, then, was at the heart of their socialist utopia: 'We did not want to exert power within the State, but rather to make the State and power superfluous.' Sperber referred with great reverence to 'the noble person of Gustav Landauer', who was murdered in Munich, and he expressed his sympathy with the Soviets of Bavaria and Hungary. But his preferred heroes were the Russian revolutionaries from the turn of the century: Sophia Perovskaya, Vera Figner, Kaliaev. What attracted him so irresistibly to the martyrs of the *Narodnaya Volya* was their sacrifice and complete devotion to the 'preparation of an inaccessible state of things' (the same dream of 'sixty generations of my ancestors'), and their heroic struggle for 'a messianic future'. Like them, the young Sperber 'believed that only revolutionaries would bring about the advent of a sublime world'.[21]

As we have seen, among the Jews of the Polish and Russian *shtetl* a commitment to the revolution nearly always implied complete abandonment of religious references in favour of a materialist and thoroughly atheist rationalism. This was not the case, however, with Manes Sperber and his friends from the *Hashomer*. Caught up in the neo-romantic whirlwind of the youth in Vienna, they continued to refer in their revolutionary politics to the Jewish messianism of their ancestors. While this usually proved to be a transitional phase before the embracing of Marxism and Leninism, Sperber and a number of others were still marked during their Communist period by certain utopian, millennial and libertarian aspirations.

During the 1920s, Sperber rallied both to historical materialism and to the individual psychology of Alfred Adler. The parallel with the spiritual itinerary of Erich Fromm is impressive, but apparently their paths never crossed. In 1926, Sperber published a pamphlet in tribute to Adler, in which the messianic idea underwent a strange Christian transmutation; the author revolted against the First World War, the unprecedented massacre which took place '1,914 years after the birth of he who wanted to establish the Kingdom of Heaven on earth through a feeling of community (*Gemeinschaftsgefühl*) and love for one's neighbour.' What attracted Sperber to Adler's doctrine was both its romantic theme of *Gemeinschaft* and the idea – inspired by a libertarian interpretation of Nietzsche – of the fight against authoritarianism. In his conclusion to the pamphlet, Sperber celebrated his master as a genius driven by the 'pathos of community' and by an ardent desire to 'destroy the Will for Power'.[22]

It was around 1927, during his stay in Germany, that Sperber joined the Communist Party; but even at that time, he stayed in contact with a circle of anarchists, to whom he gave lectures. He admired the 'radicalism of these rebels who, devoid of any will for power, were fighting against all those who held power'. In his autobiography, Sperber asked himself: 'Why did I remain sympathetic to anarchists throughout my life, although I had always refused to follow them on the path of individual terrorist acts and in their voluntarist conception of history?'[23]

Even Sperber's support for the Soviet Union was based on the belief – or the illusion – that there the poor, the exploited, the 'water carriers' 'had put an end once and for all to the exercise of power and oppression'. After 1929, a new momentum was added by the catastrophic economic crisis and the apocalyptic atmosphere in the ranks of the Comintern, whose militants believed that the advent of the world revolution was imminent: 'soon, very soon, in a moment that is ever approaching, like the coming of the Messiah, for which my great-grandfather waited.'[24]

A subdued echo of Sperber's libertarian leanings can be found in the works he wrote during his Communist period. In his lectures from 1933, which were later published as *Individuum und Gemeinschaft* [Individual and Community], he used Marxist terms to reaffirm his radical anti-authoritarian convictions: 'The broader the masses in whose interest the order exists, the more limited will be the authority needed to maintain that order. Order for all would be based on the *authority of all*. Thus, it would be an order without authority (*autoritätslose Ordnung*).'[25]

Between 1934 and 1935, while exiled in Paris, Sperber worked at the Institute for the Study of Fascism (INFA), which was headed by the German Communist leader, Willi Münzenberg. Sperber arrived in Paris in June 1934, a few months after Benjamin had given his lecture 'The Author as Producer' in the Institute's premises, but it was probably not until later that the two met.

In 1937, disgusted by the Moscow Trials, Sperber broke with the Communist Party. He then wrote an essay entitled 'Zur Analyse der Tyrannis' [For an Analysis of Tyranny], which unveiled the seed of tyranny in every authoritarian leadership that separated itself from the community and became autonomous (*verselbständigt*) from it. None the less, Sperber never lost faith in a communitarian future, in which 'there will no longer be a place in men's lives for the struggle for power and domination'.[26] These ideas were also found in his post-war political writings, such as *The Achilles Heel* (1957), in which he contrasted the political philosophy of the Right (including Stalinism) – 'the State is reason' – with the true goal that the Left has always sought: 'a society in which man shall not be governed but shall be master of his own liberty, and where government shall be finally replaced by the administration of things' – a phrase that unites the libertarian ideal and the Marxist utopia in a harmonious synthesis.[27]

A subterranean atheist religion sometimes shows through in the trilogy of novels that Sperber wrote between 1949 and 1952 (*The Wind and the Flame, To Dusty Death* and *The Lost Bay*) as well as in his numerous philosophical, literary and political essays. In any event, he never ceased to draw inspiration from Judaism, whose cultural/millennial religious specificity he defined in the following terms: 'Without forgetting its past, Israel alone among nations, drew its force from an eschatological hope, the expectation of a future, near or far . . . Israel still held the Promise. Without prophetic messianism, Israel would inevitably be lost.' This was not just a historical reference for Sperber: in another text from the 1950s he proclaimed the political actuality of the heritage: 'It may be doubted whether the left can continue without drawing sustenance from an eschatological hope'.[28]

In the autobiography he wrote during the final years of his life, Sperber seemed to acknowledge the failure of his messianic/revolutionary hope: the Redeemer in which he had believed 'had come; however, he was not a true Messiah, but an anti-Messiah'.[29] Never the less, a secularized version of this hope continued to be the source of inspiration for his socialist/humanist dream of changing the world. As he wrote in one of his final essays: 'No sacrificial death, no grace from redemption, will bring about the change that is so desired, because the advent of the Messiah depends on us, on all of us, on the acts of each one of us.'[30]

Landauer's writings, and libertarian ideas in general were also very influential on the Jewish writers and poets active in the Expressionist movement, particularly in pacifist literary magazines published during the First World War: *Die weißen Blätter*, *Die Aktion*. Among the writers one can mention are: Carl Einstein, Ludwig Rubiner, Walter Hasenclever, Alfred Wolfenstein, Ernst Weiss, and Elsa Lasker-Schüler. Sometimes, their work displays apocalyptic and messianic themes linked to their revolutionary aspirations. For example, in *Briefe an Gott* [Letters to God], written in 1922, Albert Ehrenstein implores God to send a 're-organizer of the world (*Weltordner*), a slayer of demons (*Teufelstöter*), a shaper of souls who will create the communist community at a planetary level'.[31]

Of all the Jewish personalities active in German Expressionism, it is perhaps Ernst Toller who represents the utopian-millenarian sensibility in all its force.

Poet, dramatist and disciple of Gustav Landauer, Toller belongs with twentieth-century *Spätromantik* by virtue of his literary style and his religious/idealist sensibility.[32] His romantic tendency, as well as his pacifist opposition to the war, made him receptive to Landauer's work, and in particular to *Aufruf zum Sozialismus* which made a 'decisive impact' on him.[33] In a letter to Landauer dated 20 December 1917, Toller outlined the core of his nascent *Weltanschauung*: 'I believe that our most important mission is to struggle against war, poverty and the State, . . . and in their place to establish . . . a community of free men which exists through the spirit.'[34] At the end of 1918, Toller and Landauer met their mutual friend, Kurt Eisner, in Munich and were then active together in the Councils Republic of Bavaria (March–April, 1919). Under Landauer's influence, Toller regarded the socialist revolution as a negation of the State and of industrialization, and as a return to decentralized rural communities. As a pacifist, he regarded the capitalist State, which had been responsible for the First World War, as a *Golem*, a false idol, which demanded limitless sacrifice in human lives.[35] In Toller's first major Expressionist play, *Die Wandlung* [Transfiguration], which he wrote in 1917–18, he condemned 'castles and prisons', governed by men 'who serve neither God nor humanity, but a ghost, a malevolent ghost', and he called on the people to destroy them.[36] In the play *Masse Mensch* (*Man and the Masses*), written while he was imprisoned in 1919, 'The Woman' (expressing Toller's ideas) screams to her husband, a patriot and warmonger in whose eyes 'the State is holy':

> Who put up prisons . . . who cried 'holy war'? Who sacrificed a million human lives
> Upon the altars of some desperate game?
> Who threw the masses into festering holes
> In which, each day, is piled the filth of yesterday?
> Who robbed these brothers of their human features,
> Who drove them into factories,
> Debased them into parts of a machine?
> The State! . . . You! . . .[37]

This libertarian anti-statism went together with an ethic of non-violence and with passionate polemic against the (Communist) supporters of revolutionary violence – a combination that some modern literary critics have called the 'Tolstoy-like anarchism of Toller'.[38] Actually, Toller dreamed of a peaceful world revolution, of non-violent universal upheaval, which would make it possible to achieve what he called 'the holy goal': a *Gemeinschaft* of free men.[39]

Far from regarding history from the angle of progress, Toller experienced it intensely as an uninterrupted series of defeats (much like Walter Benjamin) or betrayed revolutions. In a letter to Max Beer, author of the well-known *History of Socialism and Social Struggles*, he exclaimed:

> What did I read? A history of social struggles? A history of crushed mass uprisings! A history of the never-ending suffering of thousands of years of oppression and exploitation, a history of rebellion against unbearable poverty, a history of defeat. No revolution in which the revolutionaries succeeded in achieving their goals. The only one that triumphed – the Christian revolution – did so because it betrayed its own ideas, and changed from a Communist force hostile to the State (*staatsfeindlich*) into a state power (*staatserhaltend*).[40]

In Toller's eyes, the libertarian and the communist ideal were inseparably linked and seemed to find their canonical form in primitive Christianity.

Toller was born into an assimilated Jewish family in Samotschin, a Polish town annexed by Prussia, where, as he later wrote, 'Jews looked upon themselves as the pioneers of German culture'; however, Toller was deeply affected by the anti-Semitism that surrounded him.[41] The messianic religiosity that characterized his political dramas drew on both Jewish and Christian sources; but the hero of his first play, *Die Wandlung*, is a Jew whose dilemmas probably express Toller's own torn and ambiguous position towards Judaism: that of being both at odds with the Jewish tradition and unable to assimilate completely. This character, Friedrich, exclaims: 'Me, an exiled Jew, I struggle between one shore and the other, far from the old and even farther from the new.' When Friedrich addresses his mother, he bitterly criticizes the obscurantist nature of the Jewish religion: 'What is your God, if not a narrow judge, who judges all men through worn-out laws? Still judging with the same dead laws? . . . The narrowness of your noble house of God is suffocating.' But Friedrich identifies with Ahasuerus, the mythical figure of the Wandering Jew, and feels a 'stranger' to the 'Gentile' population around him. 'Where is our country, mother? Those opposing us have a country. . . They have their

own land, in which they are rooted.'[42] In the autobiography
Toller wrote in 1933, he wondered: 'Am I, too, not Jewish? Do
I not belong to the people which for thousands of years has
been persecuted, hunted, tortured, murdered, whose prophets
have cried out to the world for Justice. . . ?' Like Landauer –
and many other Jews from Central Europe – Toller held onto
both his Jewish and German identities: Germany was 'the land
I grew up in, it was the air I breathed, the language I lived,
the spirit that formed me'. On the other hand, he considered
himself an internationalist and rejected any nationality, whether
German or Jewish, as obscurantist: 'If I were asked where I
belonged I should answer that a Jewish mother had borne me,
that Germany had nourished me, Europe had formed me, my
home (*Heimat*) was the earth, and the world my Fatherland
(*Vaterland*).'[43]

In Toller's first plays, the utopia of a libertarian/pacifist revolution is closely linked to the hope for messianic redemption,
perceived in a 'Judeo-Christian' spirit. The Christian idea of the
Messiah's redeeming sacrifice is at the heart of *Die Wandlung* –
above all, in the scene in which the choir of prisoners, guided and
inspired by Friedrich, proclaim:

Brother, you light the way for us
Through the crucifixion
We shall free ourselves
We shall find redemption
And the path towards supreme freedom.

Shot by the State, Friedrich rises from the dead to herald the
coming messianic era.

Now shall open, from within the universe
The high arched doors of the cathedral of humanity
Fiery youth of all peoples shall soar
Towards the radiant crystal shrine which it sees in the night.

But in order to gain redemption, Friedrich summons the people
to (non-violent) revolution and urges them to destroy the 'castles'
of the established order.[44] This *sui generis* unit, of revolution
and self-sacrificial religious redemption is also evident – in
particularly exalted way – in the epigraph to his second major
play, *Man and the Masses*:

World Revolution.
Bearer of New Forces.
Bearer of New Peoples.
The Century is a red glare.
Pyres are bloody with guilt.
Earth crucifies itself.[45]

We know that for Toller, these were not purely literary ideas. He tried to put them into practice by participating in the revolution of the Munich Workers Councils, on whose behalf, through an irony of history, he, the pacifist, had to command the operations of the Bavarian Red Army in April 1919. Even at that time, Toller's revolutionary practice retained a religious and messianic aura, which was echoed – negatively – in Max Weber's famous statement before the tribunal judging his former student after the fall of the Councils Republic: 'In a momentary fit of anger, God converted him into a politician.'[46]

The writer Kurt Hiller, who knew Toller well, described him as 'the prophetic and messianic type, a stranger to all party politics'.[47] However, during the 1920s, Toller moved somewhat closer to the Communist movement; in 1926 he visited the Soviet Union, where he met Radek, Lunacharsky and Trotsky, among others. In 1930, he published his impressions of the trip, which despite some reservations and criticisms, were rather favourable to the Soviet experiment, regarding it as a 'heroic example of the creative spirit', and perhaps as the 'beginning of the regeneration of culture on earth'.[48] Between 1936 and 1938 he became deeply involved in a solidarity campaign with republican Spain. But in May 1939, distraught by the defeat of the Spanish anti-Fascists, exiled in New York, isolated, unemployed and living in poverty, Toller committed suicide.

Linked to Expressionism, but outside its mainstream, was a curious esoteric/magical circle, a kind of 'Jewish sect' around Oskar Goldberg. This mysterious figure – who probably inspired the character of Chaim Breisacher in Thomas Mann's *Doctor Faustus* – combined the aspiration to a new theocracy with social-revolutionary concerns. In Scholem's opinion, some of the fascination of Goldberg's cabbalistic religious speculations was due to 'his Luciferian sparkle'.[49] Among his followers or admirers were Ernst Fraenkel, Joachim Caspary, Wolfgang Ollendorf, Ernst David, Simon Guttmann and, in particular, a young metaphysical anarchist who fascinated Walter Benjamin: Erich Unger.

In *Politik und Metaphysik*, a book published in 1921, Unger criticized the evolutionist conception of a gradual, never-ending approximation to the ideal over the generations. He contrasted this with the *immediate* achievement of ethically desirable conditions of life – the goal of a real movement, that of 'all shades of Communism and anarchism'. This goal, which had the virtue of not considering human affairs as natural, rejected any pause or any partial realization of the struggle for its ethical programme. To accept such a halt would be the equivalent of capitulating to the resistance of raw material, when the essential mission was precisely to negate it – 'a negation whose specific modalities it is the task of reason is to find'. Starting from these premises – which might be classified as nihilistic – Unger affirmed 'the inevitable and completely hopeless nothingness (*Nichts*)' of all representation by political parties, and the 'total uselessness' of all existing political forms.[50] There is clearly a similarity here with the theses that Benjamin was putting forward between 1921 and 1922. In a letter to Scholem from January 1921, Benjamin referred to Unger's work as currently 'the most significant book on politics'. Benjamin did not hide his 'extremely lively interest' in Unger's ideas, which 'were surprisingly close' to his own.[51] In his essay on violence from 1921, he quoted Unger several times; he also recommended to Scholem Unger's second book, *Die staatenlose Bildung eines jüdischen Volkes* [The Stateless Formation of a Jewish People], which was published in 1922. In this work, Unger offered a metaphysical critique of Zionism, and rejected the process that consisted in securing for the Jews a State 'like the rest': 'The Jews owe the psychic force they may now possess to their tradition and to their exceptional non-territorial position. Messianism was the Jews' true goal, and socialism – which they created and turned into a powerful force – was the empirical expression of metaphysical messianism.[52]

Political organizations or movements with a revolutionary orientation were clearly another important site for the development of utopian/messianic tendencies. For example:

(*a*) The German anarchist movement had a significant proportion of Jews in its ranks, such as Siegfried Nacht and Johannes Holzmann, not to mention the libertarian writers closest to Landauer: Stefan Grossman, Erich Mühsam, and Benedikt Friedländer.

(*b*) The Hungarian anarcho-syndicalists of Jewish origin included Ervin Szabó, who died in 1918 but was considered the 'spiritual father' of the generation that led the Workers Councils Revolution. Those of his followers who became Communists made up the group of 'ethical Bolsheviks' around Lukács in 1919; Ervin Sinkó, Béla Balázs and, to a certain extent, Ottó Korvin (who was shot by the Whites after the defeat of the Hungarian Councils Republic).

(*c*) Within the Social Democratic parties of Germany and Austro-Hungary, leading Jews generally rejected the Jewish identity and religion and adopted a world-view directly inspired by the Enlightenment, progressive rationalism, Kant and neo-Kantianism. This seemed completely to exclude any romantic or messianic dimension in leaders and thinkers such as Viktor Adler, Max Adler, Otto Bauer, Julius Deutsch, Rudolf Hilferding, Eduard Bernstein and Paul Singer. However, even in that political-cultural milieu, there appeared (rather exceptionally) themes and concerns similar to those studied in this book. For example, Julius Braunthal (the Austrian Jewish socialist known for his monumental history of the International) wrote an autobiography significantly entitled *In Search of Millennium*, which presented the final goal of the revolution as 'the New Jerusalem on earth', and spoke of socialism as a 'Messianic gospel'.[53]

(*d*) The Communist parties of Central Europe, particularly during the initial period of 1918 to 1923, included people like Lukács – or Bloch and Benjamin on the intellectual periphery of the movement; other examples could probably be found. However, most Communist leaders of Jewish origin steered clear of any reference to Judaism and were deeply hostile to any form of religion. This was especially true of those originally from Eastern Europe (such as Rosa Luxemburg, Leo Jogiches, Karl Radek or Arkadi Maslow), but others shared their thoroughly materialist and atheist outlook: Paul Levi, August Thalheimer, Werner Scholem (Gershom's brother), Ruth Fischer (also known as Elfriede Eisler), Hans Eisler, Béla Kun, Jenö Ländler, Jenö Varga, among others.

In this context, the figure of Eugen Leviné, the Spartakist leader of the Commune of Bavaria, seems relatively exceptional.

Leviné, who originally came from Russia, stood at the furthest extreme of the category outlined in this chapter, bordering on the radically different universe of East European rationalist/materialist Marxism. Born in Petrograd into a bourgeois, assimilated Jewish family of German cultural origin, Leviné went to school and university in Germany. However, he stayed in contact with Russia, and his revolutionary romanticism led him towards the Russian SR Party (*Narodniki*), in whose ranks he was active during the revolution of 1905. After a period of imprisonment when he was harshly mistreated by the tsarist police, he returned to Germany and linked up with Fedor Stepun, the Russian writer and member of the Max Weber Circle of Heidelberg, and propagator of the works of the mystic Vladimir Soloviev. Around that time, Leviné wrote a short essay on Ahasuerus, which described a dialogue between Christ and the Wandering Jew on the redemption of humanity through love. Referring to the massacre of January 1905 in Russia, Ahasuerus declares: 'He who has the strength to love, also hates. . . Look at the young people in the North [a reference to Russian revolutionaries (ML)] . . . they love their land, they love freedom . . . but hate shines in their eyes.' At the end of the dialogue, however, Christ succeeds in passing onto the Wandering Jew his faith in the redeeming power of absolute love.[54]

Leviné became a naturalized German, and in 1914 he was among the fiercest opponents of the war – which later led him to Rosa Luxemburg's Spartakist League. Around that time, he wrote an anti-war essay which took its inspiration from the pacifist and anti-authoritarian tradition of the biblical prophets:

> The same prophets who attacked the kings for their infidelity and their lust for power (*Machtgier*) also preached the idea of peace. The ancient Hebrew people received the word and dreamed of a better future, in which, according to the prophet Isaiah, 'swords will be turned into ploughshares and spears into sickles'.[55]

Leviné played a leading role in the Councils revolution of Bavaria, and after its defeat he was imprisoned, summarily tried and shot for the 'crime of high treason'. His bearing radiated an aura of sacrifice, as evidenced by the (now famous) statement he made before his judges: 'We Communists are all dead men on reprieve.'[56] No doubt, Leviné's Communism drew on Judeo-Christian romantic/revolutionary and messianic sources, and like that of Lukács (who knew him in Heidelberg and respected him greatly) it belonged to the religious-atheist wing furthest removed from Judaism.

To conclude this somewhat heteroclite enumeration, one last cultural crossroads must decidedly be mentioned: the Frankfurt School. In addition to Leo Löwenthal, Walter Benjamin and Erich Fromm, messianic and/or libertarian aspects were clearly visible in other authors associated with the school, such as Kracauer, Horkheimer and Adorno, even if the dominant element in their thought was sympathy for rationalism and (self-critical) *Aufklärung*. As proof, we need only cite the well-known passage – clearly inspired by Benjamin – at the end of *Minima Moralia*, in which Adorno declares that the sole task of thinking is to fashion 'perspectives . . . that displace and estrange the world, reveal it to be, with its rifts and crevices, as indigent and distorted as it will appear one day in the messianic light'.[57]

It is very probable, therefore, that the personalities studied in this book were only the most visible and consistent representatives of a vast subterranean movement, which traversed the whole of Central Europe and touched a significant fraction of the radical Jewish intelligentsia.

This current was as important as the more visible and better-known tendency of the rationalist-progressive Left, animated by worship of science, industry and modernity. Writing on the intellectuals of the Weimar Republic (a majority of whom were Jewish), Arthur Koestler noted that the three movements designated as 'Left' (liberals, socialists and Communists) 'differed in their attitude toward "progress" only by degree, not by type'. He explained that his own decision to join the German Communist Party was motivated by his enthusiasm for industrialization and for the Soviet Union's first Five Year Plan. In 1931, it seemed to him that 'Soviet practice [was] the admirable and ultimate fulfilment of the nineteenth century's ideal of progress. . . The greatest electric power dam in the world must surely bring the greatest happiness to the greatest number'.[58] Incidentally, his testimony illustrates that Stalinism was perfectly compatible with a progressive modernizing philosophy and with a certain (instrumental) form of rationality.

Another ground to explore would be that of similar spiritual tendencies in Christianity. Several of the authors studied in this work – particularly the most assimilated – drew abundantly on Christian eschatological, apocalyptic, heretical and mystical sources. In some cases, personal ties were woven with Christian personalities who shared the same messianic/revolutionary orientation: for example, between Walter Benjamin and the Swiss socialist preacher, Fritz Lieb; between Martin Buber and the Christian Socialist, Leonard Ragaz. Buber and Bloch, for their part, exerted a diffuse influence over the most radical movements within modern Protestant theology: Paul Tillich, Karl Barth, Jürgen Moltmann, Helmut Gollwitzer. It was not by chance that such direct relationships existed, particularly with Protestants, for whom references to Old Testament prophecy played an essential role. However, romantic/revolutionary and messianic personalities were also found in the Catholic world (Charles Péguy, for example), independent of the influence exerted by German-Jewish intellectuals – as well as in Russian Orthodoxy at the beginning of the century, notably in the religious socialist circles of St Petersburg around Merezhkovsky, Berdyaev and their friends.[59]

It would be interesting to study the convergences and the dissimilarities between these Christian milieux and the Jewish messianic/libertarian movement. It could be said that in general, messianism carried greater weight in the Jewish religious tradition than millenerianism did in the Christian tradition, where the first coming of the Redeemer had already taken place. On the other hand, as Scholem noted, Jewish messianism always placed redemption upon the stage of history, and not, as in the dominant Christian tradition, within the purely spiritual and inner domain of each individual's soul.

Never the less, in the Christian socialist/eschatological currents that we have discussed, these differences were blurred: the messianism of the prophets joined with the Apocalypse of the Gospel, and the two entered into a relationship of elective affinity with modern revolutionary ideas.

9

A French Exception: Bernard Lazare

Bernard Lazare is the exception that confirms the rule. At the turn of the century, he was one of the few, if not the only Jewish intellectual in France – and even in all of Western Europe – who came close to the romantic/revolutionary and messianic/libertarian vision of German-Jewish culture – even if there were significant differences between his type of spirituality and that of the intellectuals from Central Europe.

One outcome of the French Revolution (and of the July Monarchy) was that the Jewish community in France was much more integrated and assimilated than its counterpart in Germany. Its intellectuals shared with the Jewish bourgeoisie and notables a loyalty to the French nation, to the Republic, and to the dominant liberal ideology of reason, order and progress. In this context, Bernard Lazare could not be anything but an isolated figure rejected by the Jewish community; in fact, he was closer to certain Christian socialists (such as Péguy) than to the Jewish intelligentsia.

Bernard Lazare was born in Nîmes in 1865 into an assimilated Jewish family which had been settled in France for several centuries; his upbringing was essentially non-religious, although a number of traditional rituals were still observed. In 1886, he went to Paris. As a writer and literary critic, Lazare became involved in the Symbolist movement; he was one of the principal editors of *Entretiens politiques et littéraires* [Political and Literary Discussions], an avant-garde magazine which served as a cultural crossroads for both Symbolist poets and libertarian writers – Viellé-Griffin, Paul Adam, Henri de Régnier, Jean Grave, Elisée Reclus.

The Symbolist movement in France, as a literary and artistic reaction against narrow-minded rationalism, bourgeois positivism, realism and naturalism, had undeniable affinities with

Romanticism and German neo-romanticism – even if it was far from having the same degree of cultural influence. Jean Thorel, one of the contributors to *Entretiens*, correctly pointed out the 'striking resemblance' between the two movements, not only from a literary point of view but also in terms of their philosophical and religious orientation.[1] But the French Symbolists had points of convergence with the whole of European anti-capitalist romantic thought. Thomas Carlyle, for example, was frequently mentioned by them, and his 'Symbols' was the opening article in the pilot edition of *Entretiens*. Carlyle here claimed that the 'Imaginative faculty' was superior to the 'Logical, Mensurative faculty', and that the qualities of the heart were superior to 'Arithmetic Understanding'.[2] Given his radical anti-positivism, it was not by chance that this British author was one of Lazare's favourite authors in his youth; in the words of a friend, he 'savoured with quiet ecstasy the philosophy that Carlyle put forth in *Sartor Resartus*'.[3]

A turn towards religion was one of the components of Carlyle's philosophy that can also be found in French Symbolism. Jean Thorel noted (in the previously mentioned article) that the burgeoning of religious sentiment was 'an outcome of the principles we had recognized as being in common to the German Romantics and the Symbolists; for in this way of thinking, poetry, art, philosophy and religion very quickly became one and the same'. This turn to religion took quite diverse forms, from conversation to Catholicism (J.K. Huysmans, Villiers de L'Isle-Adam) to an attraction to mysticism and the esoteric (*Sar* Peladan, Edmond Bailly).

Unlike in Central Europe, where a great number of Jewish intellectuals were drawn to this type of neo-romantic sensibility, Bernard Lazare was one of the few Jewish writers in France who participated in the Symbolist movement and in its quest for religious spirituality. Upon his arrival in Paris in 1886, he registered at the Ecole pratique des Hautes Etudes to take classes on Christian, Indian, Semitic and Eastern Religions. Lazare was fascinated by all forms of mystical spirituality; he met Edmond Bailly, editor of the short-lived *Revue de la Haute Science*, 'a documentary magazine of esoteric traditions and religious symbolism'. In 1888, Lazare, together with his cousin Ephraïm Mikhaël, published *La Fiancée de Corinthe* [The Fiancée from Corinth], a Symbolist lyrical drama which attempted to reconcile pagan and Christian mysticism. Finally in 1891, as a literary critic for *La Nation*, Lazare hailed all books on mysticism – from the occult to the scholarly – as a legitimate reaction against positivism and rationalism.[4] Several years later, sobered up from this youthful enthusiasm, he tried to explain the motivations that had lain behind it: 'This neo-mysticism is an outgrowth of that hunger for poetry and beauty, which believes that it can find satisfaction only in religious illusion.'[5]

Judaism, on the other hand, seemed to Lazare to be an insipid, prosaic, bourgeois and anti-mystical religion *par excellence*:

> The Hebrew religion has for some time been sunk in a foolish rationalism; it appears to borrow its dogmas from the Declaration of Human Rights, but it, like Protestantism, forgets one crucial point: a religion without mystery is like a blade of wheat stripped of its grain.[6]

Such formulations already indicate which mystery-based religion the young Bernard Lazare had in view: Catholicism.

Lazare, like many other Symbolist writers, felt the allure of Catholicism – at least until the Dreyfus Affair. Approximately ten years later, in a text that was more than likely autobiographical, he described the states of mind and the hesitations of a young Jewish philosopher who had lost the faith of his ancestors:

> Catholicism took hold of him; he regarded it as a consummation of Judaism. He was seized by a kind of anger against his people, which continually proclaimed the Messiah yet had rejected him when he came. This material conception of a millennium or a golden age, this inability to understand a spiritual redemption, filled him with rage. On the other hand, while he deeply loved Catholic dogmas, and while he recognized how superior they were and how much more that religion beguiled souls, he could not turn to it, he did not have the faith. His admiration may have been that of an artist and a thinker, and the thinker in him was not sufficiently robust. He was too hemmed in by the education he had received, so rational and positivist.[7]

Lazare in fact never converted, but the works he wrote between 1890 and 1894 testify to his fascination for Jesus and his hostility towards the hard-headedness of the Jews – the straight-necked people who obstinately rejected Christ and his message. Lazare constantly penned reproaches, sometimes with a touch of regret:

> Jesus is the flower of the Semitic consciousness; in him flourishes the love, the charity and the universal mercy that burned within the souls of the prophets of Israel. . . Israel's only error was not to have understood that once Jesus was born and the Gospel written, it had only to disappear: its task had been accomplished. Had Judah abdicated, he would have lived on forever in the memory of mankind.[8]

When compared to the 'particularist and narrow' Jewish religion, Catholicism seemed 'universal and international'. The logical and natural evolution would therefore have been to convert from the former to the latter:

> true Mosaism, purified and enlarged by Isaiah, Jeremiah and Ezekiel, broadened and generalized by the Judaeo-Hellenists, would have brought Israel to Christianity, but for Ezraism, Pharisaism and Talmudism, which held the mass of the Jews bound to strict observances and narrow ritual practices.[9]

These Catholic-bearing ideas were also given literary form in a number of Symbolist tales which Lazare published between 1890 and 1891 (his most anti-Semitic period), and which were later integrated into his book *Le Miroir des Légendes* [The Mirror of Legends], published in 1892. 'L'Eternal Fugitif' [The Eternal Fugitive] re-told in its own way the story of the golden calf and the wrath of Moses at his people's fall from grace. Casting his prophetic gaze towards the future, Mosché foresaw a new transgression by the Hebrew people: their scorn of 'the one who, bearing the cross, will struggle up the hill'. As punishment for their blindness, Yahveh would scatter them all over the earth, 'like grains of wheat unable to take root'.[10] In another Symbolist fable, 'Les Incarnations', ignorance of Jesus is no longer ascribed to all Jews but only to the privileged class:

> There are two messianic currents in Israel, just as there are two sharply divided categories of souls. On the one hand, the prophetic current is characterized by intense hatred for the rich and the oppressors, represented by those who await the Anointed Oil of sweet Justice for the humble, for the pitiful shepherds of Judah, for the weak fishermen of Galilee. On the other hand, the same belief is transformed by the thick skull of the opulent and hard-hearted Pharisees. . . These merchants had an image of the Elect so different from the one given by Daniel, that when they saw the pitiable Nazarene walking and followed by a procession of publicans, sinners and healed lepers, they could not recognize the earthly monarch of whom they dreamed.[11]

In this strange text, Bernard Lazare sketched the path which several years later would help him find the spiritual heritage of his ancestors: Jewish messianism as a prophetic and libertarian manifestation of the poor and oppressed.

This type of attraction/ fascination for Catholicism was also found in several figures of the Jewish culture of Central Europe (the young Ernst Bloch, for example), but it rarely took as outrageous a form (bordering on anti-Semitism) as it did in the young Bernard Lazare. His subsequent reaction of rejection would be all the more severe.

Religion and mysticism were not the only forms of opposition that Symbolist writers and poets displayed to the prosaic and disenchanted universe of modern bourgeois society: sometimes, their hostility also expressed itself politically, or rather, anti-politically. According to George Woodcock, 'in one way or another, nearly all the major symbolist writers were tied to the literary aspects of anarchism'.[12] This may be an extreme formulation, but there is no doubt that a large number of Symbolist figures were sympathetic to anarchist ideas or contributed to anarchist-type publications: Octave Mirbeau, Richepin, Laurent Tailhade, Paul Adam, Stuart Merrill, Francis Vielé- Griffin, Camille Auclair and Bernard Lazare, to name a few. What attracted them to the libertarian movement was not only its individualism (as is usually mentioned) but also its revolutionary romanticism: in France, like everywhere else, a nostalgia for certain moral values of the past, an idealization of certain pre-capitalist (artisan or peasant) social forms, and a rejection of industrial/bourgeois civilization were essential components of the anarchist culture. In an overly enthusiastic commentary on this massive convergence between Symbolism and anarchism, Lazare wrote in 1892:

> A revolutionary socialist current is agitating the youth; not only young workers but those who think, read, and write. Art is concerned to become a social art. Poets are coming down from their ivory towers; they want to be involved in the struggle. A thirst for action has writers in its sway. If the goal of action is shrouded in fog for some, it is crystal-clear for many others.[13]

There were not many poets who became 'involved in the struggle', but real links were woven at the level of ideas and publications. For example, between 1891 and 1893, *Entretiens politiques et littéraires* became (largely thanks to Lazare) one of the main radiating centres of the Symbolist/libertarian culture, publishing alongside new-school poetry and literature, articles by Proudhon, Stirner, Bakunin, Jean Grave and Elisée Reclus.

In spite of their very different concerns, Symbolist writers and libertarian publicists shared the same rejection of bourgeois society and the same nostalgia for the heroic or poetic eras of the past. Bernard Lazare stood at the crossroads of the two movements; he was attracted both by Mallarmé's Salon (which he attended) and by Kropotkin's ideas (which he presented in *Entretiens*). With typically romantic/revolutionary intuition, he discovered affinities with libertarian utopia even in the works of the most backward-looking and reactionary Symbolist writers. For example, in an article from 1892 on Villiers de l'Isle-Adam, he hailed his 'scorn of the modern world', his 'hatred of modern social phenomena', his ability to probe 'the most secret caverns' of the bourgeois soul, 'which dominates our time, weighs it down and rots it'. True, Villiers was a 'worshipper of the gods of the past', but that took nothing away from the liberating force of his work:

> He believed that he was working to restore a dead ideal, but by killing respect for the present within an elite, he was bringing in a new ideal. He lived in a dream, which

he willingly transported to bygone days whose noble décor and sentimental, haughty chivalry he loved; he did not see what was being prepared. He did not understand that we rarely go backwards; and that whoever destroys, as he did, thereby opens new routes. . . He, who enjoyed dreaming of a re-instated Naundorf, sowed in people's hearts a revolutionary seed – the best – whose fertilizer was hatred and scorn.[14]

Thus, in Lazare's eyes, it was through their negativity that the Symbolists, though bewitched by the magic of the 'gods of the past', worked to subvert the bourgeois order. This is especially the case with the novels of Peladan, another Symbolist writer haunted by mysticism (he founded a new Rosicrucian Order) and an enemy of progress:

Of course, in his convictions, in the intransigence of his Catholicism, in his hierarchical or synarchical theories, Mr Peladan does not belong to any of the revolutionary sects active today; none the less, he has produced a work that no member of these sects could disown, for in all its negative aspects it coincides with their ideas. Mr Peladan shares the same hatred of the bourgeoisie as the Communists; he shares the same horror of militarism, justice, patriotism and democratic power as the anarchists; and in his book there can easily be found a hundred pages or so which are far more violent than any fighting leaflets, and which very actively contribute to destructive propaganda.[15]

However, Lazare's romantic ecumenicism had its limits: unlike other anarchists, he did not at all like Barrès' novels (*Un homme libre* and *L'Ennemi des Lois*), and considered that their egotism and aristocratic individualism had nothing in common with anarchism.[16]

Of all the Symbolist writers, Lazare was undoubtedly the most active in the libertarian movement: not only did he defend anarchist doctrines in literary magazines or in 'bourgeois' newspapers that allowed him to publish in their columns; he was also a regular contributor to the libertarian press itself – notably *La Révolte*, the 'anarchist-communist' weekly published by Jean Grave (and banned by the police in 1894). At Grave's trial in February 1894 for 'incitement to violence', Lazare, along with

Elisée Reclus, served as a witness for the defence. And after Grave was sentenced, Lazare organized a petition in the press to secure his freedom, and visited him in prison. In July 1894, when the Chamber of Deputies passed a law against all forms of 'anarchist propaganda' – following the assassination of President Carnot by the young anarchist Caserio – Lazare took refuge in Belgium for several weeks, fearing his imminent arrest.[17]

As Nelly Wilson observed with great insight, the anarchism of Bernard Lazare and his friends was prophetic but not 'progressive' in the Republican (or even socialist) sense; they respected the past (medieval guilds or rural communities) but disdained everything modern.[18] Besides Jean Grave (from whom Lazare distanced himself in the late 1890s) and Elisée Reclus, Georges Sorel was the libertarian thinker who most attracted Lazare. Sorel was a characteristic example of romantic anti-capitalism in all its splendid ambiguity. According to an account by Charles Péguy, Lazare had

> a secret liking, very notable, very deep, and almost very violent, for M. Sorel. . . Everything M. Sorel said so struck him that he kept talking to me about it all the other mornings of the week. They were like two great conspirators'.[19]

One aspect of this complicity was their mutual contempt for the bourgeois/parliamentary republic; it went so deep that, in a rather surprising article from 1891, Lazare freely condemned the French Revolution as a snare that had led to a regime worse than absolute monarchy:

> With the French Revolution, the people swapped an authority that was sometimes paternal, anyway susceptible to kindness and happy changes of heart, capable at a given moment of recognizing its faults . . . for the authority of an arrogant, greedy and money-grubbing bourgeois oligarchy whose soul is open to every base sentiment, intensely selfish and rapacious, incapable of any thought of generosity, of any noble idea of abnegation and devotion.[20]

However, it is highly unlikely that Lazare would have followed Georges Sorel into the royalist adventure of *Action Française* – especially after the traumatic experience of the Dreyfus Affair.

Beyond the occasional extreme statement that lent itself to

misunderstanding, Bernard Lazare had no hidden desire for restoration: he was first and foremost an anti-authoritarian, an enemy of the State in all its past, present or future forms, and a libertarian romantic whom Charles Péguy could hail with near-religious reverence:

> You must understand that here was a man, I have said with great exactness a prophet, for whom the whole apparatus of powers, reasons of state, temporary powers, political powers, authorities at every level, political, intellectual, even mental, did not weigh an ounce compared to a revolt, compared to a prompting of conscience.[21]

Despite the seduction of Catholic mysteries, Lazare ultimately identified with heretics like Thomas Münzer, who 'fought not only against the barons, bishops and the rich, those "kings of Moab", but also against the very principle of authority'.[22] Lazare's libertarian ideal was the same as that of Bakunin and Kropotkin: economic communism and political freedom; expropriation of capital and a free federation of autonomous communes; common ownership of all goods and abolition of central government. For him, anarchism meant not only categorical rejection of the State, but also refusal to submit to 'leaders, creeds, codes and laws'.[23] Hence his biting criticism of 'authoritarian socialists': that is, German Social Democracy, and people like Jules Guesde and other French Marxists. Whereas Marx's historical materialism was for him 'a philosophy, a profound view of nations and peoples', Lazare felt that the 'Marxist Party' deserved nothing but contempt:

> I know few groups of men whose average and individual mediocrity is so great. And it is rivalled only by their sectarianism. . . Their souls are narrow, their brains are stuffed with pettiness, or rather priggery, and with the derisory and pitiful vanity of a pedantic schoolmaster.[24]

Without belonging to any particular current within the libertarian movement, Lazare formed special ties at various stages in his development: first, as we have seen, with Jean Grave and his friends; later, with Fernand Pelloutier and the anarcho-syndicalists (with whom in 1896 he published his short-lived newspaper, *L'Action Sociale*); and during the final years of his life

(1901–3), with *Les Cahiers de la Quinzaine* (Sorel, Péguy). But his anarchist convictions remained essentially unchanged over the years, whether before, during or after the Dreyfus Affair.

One cannot say the same about his attitude towards the Jewish question and anti-Semitism! In these areas, there was a true upheaval in his mind – or rather, a series of quite deep and radical upheavals. Initially, between 1890 and 1892, Lazare held ideas that can only be described as anti-Semitic. This is particularly evident in an article from September 1890, 'Juifs et Israélites', where he argues that one must avoid at all costs confusing the 'Israelite of France' with the Jews, the worshippers of the Golden Calf. The 'Israelites of France' reject 'an alleged solidarity grouping them with Frankfurt money-changers, Russian usurers, Polish innkeepers or Galician pawnbrokers, with whom they have nothing in common'. The article ends with a startling appeal to the anti-Semites: 'just, at last, they should instead become anti-Jewish; on that day, they would be sure to have many Israelites on their side. . .'[25] A month later, Lazare returned to the charge in a polemic against the *Alliance Israélite universelle*:

> What do Russian usurers . . . Polish horse-traders, Prague middlemen matter to me, an Israelite of France. . . . By virtue of which supposed fraternity shall I concern myself over measures taken by the Tsar against subjects who seem to him to be doing harmful things? . . . If they are suffering, I feel for them the pity naturally owed to everyone who suffers, irrespective of who they are. . . . The Christians of Crete have as much right to move me as do the the many others who are pariahs in the world – and who are not Israelites.

Proud of his identity as an assimilated 'French Israelite', Lazare spurned any association with the unworthy throng of Ashkenazim Jews, with their 'bizarre Judeo-Germanic patois'; 'thanks to those hordes who are confused with us, people forget that we have been living in France for nearly two thousand years.'[26] This type of complicitous attitude to anti-Semitism on the part of the assimilated Jew, was exactly what Lazare would pillory once he had become a 'conscious pariah'.

As the anti-Semitic campaign intensified in France – notably through the impetus of Edouard Drumont's highly successful

book *La France juive* (1886) – Lazare began to become aware of
what was at stake and to polemicize against its spokespersons.
Determined to undertake a systematic study of the question, he
worked between 1891 and 1893 on *L'Anti-sémitisme, son histoire
et ses causes* (*Anti-Semitism, Its History and Causes*), which was
published in 1894. This book falls into two parts that are
quite distinct in both subject-matter and orientation. The first,
finished in 1892 and still quite influenced by anti-Semitism,
is historical in character. It holds Jews responsible 'in part, at
least' for their ills, because of their 'unsociable' character, their
political and religious exclusiveness, their tendency to form a
State within a State, their obstinacy in rejecting the message
of Christ, and so on. It is thus hardly surprising that the
book was received with glee by notorious anti-Semites like
Drumont, Picard and Maurras. The second part, on the other
hand (Chapters eight to fifteen), deals with the modern day.
Written in 1893, it outlines Lazare's new position that was much
more hostile to anti-Semitic dogmas and much more favourable
to Judaism. Nelly Wilson is right to use the term 'conversion'
or 'metamorphosis' to describe the spectacular shift that takes
place between the beginning and the end of the book, between
the past and the present.[27] One possible explanation for this
initial change – well ahead of the Dreyfus Affair, incidentally
– was Lazare's discovery of the great prophetic texts in the
Bible, at the very time that he was becoming aware (perhaps
from continual anti-Semitic scapegoating of Jewish subversion) of
the ubiquitous presence of the Jewish revolutionary in modern
societies:

> Opposed to the Jewish money baron, the product of exile,
> of Talmudism, of hostile legislation and persecution, stands
> the Jewish revolutionist, the child of biblical and prophetic
> tradition, that same tradition which animated the fanatic
> Anabaptists of Germany in the sixteenth century, and the
> Puritan warriors of Cromwell.[28]

This same idea is developed at length in 'The Revolutionary Spirit
in Judaism', a chapter of the book which had been previously
published as an article in the *Revue Bleue* in May 1893. Lazare's
basic theory is that the Jew, by the very nature of his religion
and his culture, is a rebel; unlike the fatalistic Muslim and the

resigned Christian, the Jew does not believe in the Beyond and cannot accept unhappiness and injustice in earthly life in the name of a future reward. Therefore, the prophets worked for the advent of justice here below and demanded an end to inequality in the conditions of life. Inspired by their words, the poor – the *anavim* and *ebionim* – did not resign themselves to poverty and

> dreamed of the day that would avenge their inequities and disgrace, of the day when the evil would be beaten back and the just exalted: the day of the Messiah. The messianic age, for all the humble, would be the age of justice.

Freedom was another aspiration that issued from the Jewish religious tradition: according to the Bible, all power belonged to God, and the Jew could be led only by Yahveh. No fellow-men could impose their will on him: 'with regard to creatures of flesh, he was free and was to be free.' No authority was greater than that of Yahveh 'and it followed inevitably that no man could rise above the others; the harsh celestial master brought earthly equality'. In other words, the Jews' concept of divinity led them to anarchy: 'theoretical and sentimental anarchy, because they always had a government, but real anarchy, because they never accepted that government, such as it was, kind-heartedly.' In fact, in the eyes of the Jews,

> all government, whatever its form, is bad, since it tends to be a substitute for the government of God; it must be fought, since Yahveh is the only leader of the Judaic republic, the only one whom the Israeli must obey.[29]

It is very clear that for Lazare, the libertarian socialist, the discovery of anarchism at the very heart of the Jewish tradition was a decisive moment in his strange process of 'conversion', which runs through the pages of his book on anti-Semitism.

According to Lazare, these three elements – justice, equality and liberty – make up the revolutionary spirit in Judaism. Of course, other nations reached these ideas, but they did not hold their complete realization to be possible in this world:

The Jews, on the contrary, not only believed that justice, liberty and equality could be sovereigns of the world, but they thought themselves specially entrusted with the mission of working for this reign. All the desires, all the hopes these three ideals gave birth to ended up by crystallizing around one central idea: that of the Messianic times, of the coming of Messiah.

The Jews' refusal to accept Christ – that obstinacy and sinfulness which seemed so incomprehensible to Lazare in 1890 – now appeared to him to be the logical consequence of their ardent messianic faith: if Israel rejected all those who said they had been sent from God, if it 'refused to hear Jesus, Bar-Cochba, Theudas, David Alroy, Serene, Moses of Crete, Sabbatai-Zevi', it was because none of them had been able to fulfill the messianic promise, by making 'chains fall, prison-walls crumble, the rod of authority rot, the ill-gotten treasures of the rich and despoilers scatter like empty smoke'.[30]

For all these reasons, and because he was a persecuted pariah without ties to established social structures, the Jew in modern society became 'a good ferment for revolution'. Jews were involved in every revolutionary movement, from Jacob Pereira – who, as a follower of Hébert, was executed on 4th Germinal, Year II – to Leo Frankel, the communard of 1871, by way of Heine, Moses Hess, Lassalle and Karl Marx in particular:

> The descendant of a long line of rabbis and teachers, he inherited the splendid powers of his ancestors. . . He was inspired by that ancient Hebraic materialism, which . . . never ceased to dream of Paradise realized on earth. But Marx was not merely a logician, he was also a rebel, an agitator, an acrid controversalist, and he derived his gift for sarcasm and invective, as Heine did, from his Jewish ancestry.

With obvious relish, Lazare listed the names of all the Jewish socialists and revolutionaries in Europe and the United States – what Maurras, in his comment on the book, called the 'World Directory' of the 'Jewish Socialist International' – as well as the specifically Jewish socialist or anarchist newspapers, published in 'a jargon which is a mixture of German and Hebrew' (Yiddish). These groups seemed particularly interesting to Lazare, because through them, 'the Jew does take an active part in revolutions; and he participates in them in so far as he is a Jew, or more correctly in so far as he remains Jewish'[31] – the first time that Lazare linked, albeit somewhat vaguely, the Jewish national identity to libertarian socialism.

The ideas presented in this chapter of Lazare's book were clearly analogous to those of romantic/revolutionary Jewish intellectuals from Central Europe: on the one hand, the affinity between messianism and revolution as a *complete* fulfillment of dreams for justice and freedom; and on the other, the correspondence between biblical theocracy and modern anarchism (Buber, Bloch, Benjamin, Scholem). But what set them apart was just as clear: the French author's approach was much more directly and immediately secularized.

This work of 1894 illustrates the path that led Bernard Lazare to regain his Jewish roots; by discovering the prophetic sources for the modern revolutionary spirit and the Jewish figures of socialism, he succeeded in reconciling the Jewish identity and libertarian utopia in his mind. However, the book was only a first step in his long journey to seek his lost identity: by reason of his initial concessions to anti-Semitism and of his contradictory and torn character, he was not able to make a full break from the illusion of the 'Israelite of France'. This is particularly apparent in the book's strange conclusion: on the eve of the Dreyfus Affair, Lazare light-heartedly foresees a gradual effacement of distinctions between Jews and Christians, the 'complete' dissolution of Jews within nations, and the disappearance of anti-Semitism in the distant future, since it was really nothing but a vestige of the past, 'one of the last, though most long-lived, manifestations of that old spirit of reaction and narrow conservatism, which is vainly attempting to arrest the onward movement of the Revolution'.[32]

It is easy to imagine Lazare's surprise when, barely a year after these lines were published, the arrest of Captain Alfred Dreyfus triggered the greatest wave of anti-Semitism in the history of France since the late Middle Ages. However, as is well known, Lazare played a major role in 'The Affair', pioneering the campaign to defend the Captain and, in 1896, publishing the first article in refutation of the official version of events: 'Une erreur judiciaire: la vérité sur l'affaire

Dreyfus' [A Legal Error: The Truth about the Dreyfus Affair]. Lazare was also the first – and for quite a long time, the only one – to denounce the effectively anti-Semitic nature of the political-judicial manoeuvres against the Captain: Dreyfus had been arrested because he was a Jew; he had been sentenced because he was a Jew; the voices of justice and truth could not be heard in his favour, because he was a Jew ('Deuxième memoire', 1897). Showered with insults and accusations, barred from the newspapers to which he had been a regular contributor, Lazare suddenly found himself in a state of total isolation: 'I was a pariah overnight', he wrote in a note to Reinach several years later.[33] He also faced isolation within the Jewish community, whose notables and intellectuals scarcely appreciated his interventions, finding them awkward or provocative, especially since they placed the Jewish question at the centre of 'The Affair'.[34]

Bernard Lazare's boldness in the Dreyfus battle was not unconnected to his anarchist ideas: his libertarian hostility towards the State, the courts and the military hierarchy was probably central to his involvement, even if his pamphlets argued solely on the ground of the defence of human rights. It was not by chance either that Sébastien Faure's *Le Libertaire* was the first newspaper to demonstrate sympathy for the Dreyfusard cause (from November 1897) and that in February 1898, Péguy wrote: 'Anti-Semitic rage has become the master of our streets . . . only the anarchists have done their duty . . . they were the only ones who dared to pit violence for justice against the violence for injustice of the anti-Semitic gangs'.[35]

If 'The Affair' confirmed Lazare in his anarchist convictions, the mass anti-Semitic hysteria against the 'traitor Dreyfus' led to a new turning-point in his ideas on the Jewish condition: his complaisant and ambivalent attitude to anti-Semitism was gone once and for all, as was his optimistic illusions about the 'Israelites of France'! He engaged in open battle against anti-Semitism, and went so far as to fight a duel with Edouard Drumont (in which neither was injured). A series of Lazare's polemical articles against the author of *La France juive* were published in 1896 in a pamphlet entitled *Contre l'antisémitisme* [Against Anti-Semitism]. From that point on, he regarded Dreyfus as the symbol of the Jews, victimized by anti-Semitic hatred throughout the world, and in particular of the East European Jews whom he had previously treated with so much contempt:

> He [Dreyfus] embodied not only the age-old suffering of the nation of martyrs, but also the present grief. Through him, I saw the Jews cooped up in Russian hard-labour prisons . . . the Romanian Jews whose human rights had been denied, the Galician Jewish proletarians starved by financial trusts.[36]

Lazare's attraction to the mysteries of Catholicism had also come to an end: the notorious participation of the Church and Catholic milieux (with a few honourable exceptions) in the anti-Semitic campaign, and the religious argument that was constantly being invoked against 'Dreyfus-Judas', led him to a violently anti-clerical and even 'anti-Christian' rejection. From that point on, he was convinced that anti-Semitism was essentially a clerical movement, a manoeuvre by the Church to re-establish a Christian State; he developed this theme with great insistence in the 1896 pamphlet and in the preparatory notes for *Job's Dungheap*.

> It has always been the Church which has whipped up anti-Semitism. The Jews always lived in peace with the rest of the population, which despised God's killer but lived on familiar terms with him. The Church constantly complained . . . that the population was living on familiar terms with the Jews. Either because it feared proselytism or the contagion of a certain lack of belief, or because it hoped to restore its prestige or to serve its own policy, the Church was always the one that threw various peoples against the Jews.[37]

But the politics of revenge was not to Lazare's taste. As Péguy put it later, he identified with 'Dreyfusard mysticism' and not with the 'Dreyfusard politics' of the new governments of Waldeck Rocheau and Emile Combes. When Combes ordered restrictive measures against the religious educational orders, Lazare showed that he was capable of generosity and libertarian consistency: in spite of his hostility to the Church, for the reasons we have seen, his essay 'La Loi et les Congrégations' (published in 1902 by the *Cahiers de la Quinzaine*) unhesitatingly defended 'freedom of education' against all State interference. Péguy wrote a deeply admiring commentary on Lazare's stance, attributing it his 'secret affinity . . . for *other* spiritual powers, even for the Catholics, whom he resolutely opposed'. But that explanation hardly seems plausible. In 1902, Lazare did not feel any affinity, even secret, for the Catholic Church – *Job's Dungheap* and the preparatory notes show that well enough. Péguy is closer to the truth when he speaks of Lazare's 'hatred of the State (and) of the temporal', of all the 'temporal apparatuses' that wanted to get 'their fat paws' into spiritual matters:

> That organs as crude as government – the Chamber, the State, the Senate – and as foreign to all that is spiritual, put their fingers into the spiritual domain was, in Lazare's eyes, not only grossly profane, but even more, an exercise and abuse of utmost incompetence.[38]

The 'Affair' brought about another major change in Lazare's ideas on the Jewish question. Like many other Jewish intellectuals of the time (Theodor Herzl), he discovered Judaism as a nationality and became a Zionist – without, however, renouncing his libertarian and revolutionary convictions. Like Martin Buber (and later Gershom Scholem), Lazare was closer to the cultural Zionism of Ahad Ha-Am than to Herzl's *Realpolitik* of compromise with the great powers. In one of his first Zionist texts, the lecture 'Le Prolétariat juif devant l'antisémitisme' [The Jewish Proletariat in the Face of Anti-Semitism], which he gave in February 1897, he declared: 'We must live once again as a nation, or more closely like a free collectivity, but only on the condition that the collectivity not be modeled after the capitalistic and oppressor states in which we live.'[39] Rather than the question of territory, it was the spiritual rebirth of the Jewish nation, a return to historical roots, that aroused his interest. 'We are still the old hard-necked people, an intractable and rebellious nation; we want to be ourselves, what our ancestors, our history, our traditions, our culture and our memories have made of us.'[40] In another lecture entitled 'Le Nationalisme juif' [Jewish Nationalism], which he gave in March 1897 to the Association of Russian Jewish Students, Lazare explicitly dissociated nationality from territory: The Jew who says today:

'I am a nationalist', will not say in any special, specific or clear way that he is a man who wants to reconstruct a Jewish State in Palestine and dreams of conquering Jerusalem. He will say: 'I want to be a completely free man, I want to enjoy the sun, I want to have the right to human dignity. . .' At certain times in history, nationalism, for groups of human beings, is the manifestation of the spirit of freedom.[41]

Lazare did, however, correspond with Herzl, and actively participated in the initiatives of the Zionist movement. In 1888, he seemed to rally to the idea of a return to Palestine: at the Second Zionist Congress held in Basle in August 1888 – the first and last he would attend – he was acclaimed as a hero of the Jewish people and elected to the Presiding Council and the Action Committee. But the euphoria did not last long, and he soon clashed with Herzl. The break took place when Herzl, who was negotiating with the Sultan of Turkey, refused to take a stand on the massacre of Armenians. In his letter of resignation from the Zionist Action Committee, Lazare wrote to Herzl in February 1899:

You are bourgeois, because your thoughts are bourgeois, your feelings are bourgeois, your ideas are bourgeois and your social views are bourgeois. And yet you want to lead a nation, our nation, the nation of the poor, the oppressed, the proletarians.[42]

Lazare remained linked to the movement, but from an increasingly critical point of view. Thus, in a letter to Chaim Weizmann in 1901 (who also opposed Herzl at the time), Lazare wrote: 'I understood that Herzl's Zionism would not yet give Jews their basic freedoms. Leading a herd of slaves into Palestine is not a solution to the problem.' What was important was to organize the people into Jewish centres in Galicia and Russia, and to develop the Jewish culture, not in the sense of 'narrow nationalistic sentiment', but by starting from 'Jewish tendencies that are human tendencies in the highest sense of the word'. Such a task could be achieved only by 'breaking with the political-diplomatic and bourgeois Zionism that is currently on stage'.[43]

Around 1902, Lazare seemed to abandon a Zionist perspective and advocated that Jews should participate in social libertarian movements within their respective countries. At least, that was what he proposed in his article on Jews in Romania, published in 1902 by the *Cahiers de la Quinzaine*. If, he argued, the fiercely anti-Semitic bourgeoisie of the Romanian landowners and officials

> drives the Jew to desperation and pushes him to his limits, the Jew, in spite of his passivity, in spite of the counsel given him by the fearful rich of his own people, will join the worker in the fields and help him shake off the yoke. But even if he does not join with him, it is the rebellious Romanian peasant who, directly or indirectly, will one day resolve the present Jewish question in Romania, by freeing himself and by freeing the Jews.[44]

Lazare returned to these questions in the collection of aphorisms he wrote shortly before his death, which make up a unique document in French Jewish literature. As a pariah conscious of his exclusion, Lazare declared in this cultural-nationalist and libertarian-socialist testament his pride in being Jewish, his revolt against Christian anti-Semitism and his scorn for the rich, assimilated and parvenu Jews. Only a portion of the aphorisms have been published (as *Job's Dungheap*, in 1928), but the unpublished notes are no less important. In these notes, Lazare explicitly questions the bourgeois variant of Zionism:

> Is there any difference between going to Zion in order to be exploited by the rich Jew, and our current situation? This is what you are proposing to us: the patriotic joy of no longer being oppressed except by those of our own race; we want nothing to do with it.

In another unpublished note, 'Contre le nationalisme du sol' [Against Nationalism of the Soil], he seems to criticize the very principle of Zionism:

> You want to send us to Zion? We do not want to go. . . We do not want to go there to vegetate like a dormant little tribe. Our action and our spirit lies in the wider world; it is where we want to stay, without abdicating or losing anything.[45]

This is a position similar to the one that Gustav Landauer defended a few years later before his Zionist friends. Lazare's idea of 'Jewish nationalism' was to 'participate in the human enterprise while remaining oneself';[46] his was a messianic nationalism, in which dispersion was a part of Israel's mission.[47] In the name of that universal mission, he categorically rejected assimilation: 'If the Jew becomes Christian, there is a ferment of revolution and emancipation for the world that disappears; by becoming Christian, the Jew hallows and legitimates the slavery he has endured.'[48]

The Jewish national culture proposed by Lazare could, in his view, integrate the religion of Israel only in so far as it was a 'religion without priests and dogma', for which 'the hypothesis of One God can always lead to the original cause'. His unpublished notes insist on the eminently rational nature of Judaism:

> For Maimonides . . . the revelation promulgated by God on Mount Sinai and the truth discovered by man with the help of his reason must be identical. The two truths must coincide. The flame of rationalism is never for a moment extinguished in Israel; in every century it has had its representatives, the greatest being Spinoza.

In the final analysis, what Lazare wanted was to free Judaism from 'rabbinism' – implicitly identified with the Christian clergy – and to develop it as 'a rule of life independent of any religious idea'; in other words, like 'a Jewish ethic, a Jewish eudemonism'.[49] We are a long way here from the mystical messianism that fascinated Bloch, Scholem or Benjamin.

Never the less, the idea of the Messiah continued to interest Lazare. In one of the unpublished notes, he insisted on the revolutionary potential of Old Testament messianism (and its superiority over Christianity):

> The Jew, who does not believe in an after-life, who does not believe in a settling of accounts after death, who limits all retribution to this life, who is consumed by more than the instinct for justice, must place on earth the reign of a Messiah that will bring about justice and happiness on earth. He placed Paradise in the future, denied mystical cosmogony: as a result, he came naturally to socialism.[50]

Lazare considered – rightly or wrongly is of little concern – that this aspiration to an earthly paradise was found in Sabbatai Sevi,

a person who attracted him, and about whom he apparently
intended to write an essay, because among his papers is a large
collection of excerpts from works and notes on the subject.
Unlike in the case of Gershom Scholem (a quarter of a century
later), what seemed important to Lazare was less the mystical
dimension than the profane message of emancipation:

> Two movements in Sabbatianism. A messianic and a national
> movement, with the aim of emancipation. A mystical and
> religious movement, that of the trinitarian and Christian
> cabbala. Sometimes, the two movements merge. Show all
> that, but especially the aspiration for freedom, happiness. A
> joy with which all Jews in the world would quiver.[51]

Apparently Lazare also had plans to work on Messianic texts
from the Bible, the Talmud and other traditional sources; in
another folder left among his papers (curiously entitled 'Jesus'),
he had collected numerous excerpts and summaries of texts
under the title 'Messianism', with the following sub-titles: 'I
Messianic Hope'; 'II The Time Preceding the Arrival of the
Messiah'; 'III The Messiah'; 'IV Messiah, Son of Joseph and
Messiah, Son of David'; 'V The Resurrection'; 'VI The Action of
the Messiah'; 'VII The Messianic Reign'.[52]

It seems therefore that a religious, prophetic messianic dimension formed part of Bernard Lazare's spiritual universe and moral
personality. No one understood him better than Charles Péguy,
who described him as 'one of the greatest among the prophets
of Israel', a martyr, a mystic who had 'aspects of a saint'. The
portrait Péguy painted of his friend highlighted this hidden
religious aspect: 'Naturally he was very sincerely an atheist', but
within that atheist, 'that professional atheist, that official atheist',
resounded 'the eternal word'; he was an 'atheist streaming with
the Word of God'.[53] A careful reading of *Job's Dungheap* reveals
that if Lazare did not believe, he at least had the desire to be able
to believe, the nostalgia for faith:

> As night falls ever more over my soul, as the fearsome anguish
> of the Beyond wrings and tortures my soul, what would I
> not give to be lit up by a sudden brightness; and quivering
> with both joy and fear, to say in a whisper: 'The Messiah is
> coming'.[54]

But such confessions were not the norm: rationalism and mistrust of any form of religion dominated the tone of his final work.

Unlike the messianic/ libertarian Jews of *Mitteleuropa*, the Bernard Lazare who penned *Job's Dungheap* remained a materialist, a rationalist and a convinced atheist. The Dreyfus Affair abruptly ended his youthful enchantment with mysticism and Catholicism; in the face of a terrifying wave of anti-Semitic irrationalism – fostered by religious obscurantism – he returned to the rationalism of the Enlightenment. Whereas Buber or Landauer went from Meister Eckhart to Hasidism, from Christian to Jewish mysticism, Bernard Lazare, once the Catholic temptation had passed, removed himself from all religious temptation. He had initially rejected Judaism (between 1890 and 1891) as too rationalist and materialist, but he then returned to Judaism for exactly the same reasons (which in his eyes had become precious qualities). It was not his image of the Jewish tradition that had changed, but rather his attitude towards mysticism, mystery, irrationality, and religiosity. In his writings, Jewish messianism was more a historical and a cultural reference than a transcendental religious promise. His thinking was inspired less by religious atheism (*à la* Benjamin or Bloch) than by the secularization pure and simple of certain religious traditions, like messianic hope or biblical prophecy.

Be that as it may, Bernard Lazare was the only 'Western' Jewish intellectual whose ideas were somewhat analogous to the dreams and concerns of the romantic/ revolutionary Jewish generation of German cultural origins. At least one representative of that generation was sensitive to this spiritual kinship: Martin Buber's young disciple Hans Kohn. In an article published in *Der Jude* in 1924, he hailed Lazare as a man in whom 'the old spirit of the prophets has awakened once more', and as an 'anarchist similar to Gustav Landauer', in other words, someone who shared 'the anarchism of the prophets and Jesus'. With remarkable intuition, Kohn grasped the point of convergence between Lazare and the German messianic libertarians – namely, anarchist theocracy. Lazare was one of those 'who gave nothing to Caesar and everything to God', a messenger of 'the anarchism of the Kingdom of God, in which there was no authority other than the voice of God', and a contemptuous negator of 'the other authority, the temporal'.[55]

Conclusion: 'Historical Messianism': A Romantic/ Messianic Conception of History

The purpose of this study has been not only to examine a number of Jewish thinkers of German cultural origins from a new angle, but also to explore the possibilities that the concept of elective affinity opens up within the sociology of culture, particularly with regard to the ways in which the religious and the political universe are associated with each other. The authors studied in this book represent so many distinct figures of this association, ranging from a simple correspondence between disparate elements, to a harmonious and 'organic' fusion between messianism and romantic utopia – rarely achieved outside specific historical conjunctures charged with chiliastic *Jetztzeit*. It emerges also that activation of the structural homology between cultural configurations depends on concrete social conditions: in this case, the situation of the Jews – and especially of the Jewish intelligentsia as a particular social category – in Central Europe (distinct from both Western and Eastern Europe) at the turn of the century. However, the limitations of this sociological analysis are just as clear: if social factors define the conditions that make the cultural phenomenon in question possible – that is, the 'chance' (to use Max Weber's expression) that a romantic/messianic spiritual movement with a libertarian tendency would emerge in Central Europe at the beginning of the century – they cannot in any way account for the personal itinerary of each author, or for the unique and singular *Gestalt* of his work.

The conceptual grid of elective affinity as a socio-cultural dynamic enables us to have a better understanding of how certain religious forms can take on a political meaning and how certain forms of social utopia can be permeated with religious spirituality – while a new spark shoots out from their

200

union: that of libertarian prophecy, the profane illumination of a
revolutionary *restitutio in integrum*.

In its higher forms, the elective affinity between two cultural
figures reaches – under pressure of a raised social temperature –
the degree necessary for fusion. It is at that precise moment that
a new form emerges, a structure of meaning that is irreducible to
the sum of its parts.

In several of the authors we have discussed, the dynamic
of *Wahlverwandtschaft* tends towards this uppermost point, and
sometimes, here and there, it appears to reach it. The original
form being created here, the novel product of this complex spiritual alchemy, is a new conception of history and temporality.

A new term would be needed to describe this conception, but
if we are unable to find (or to invent) one, we have to make do
with a hybrid, a compound noun built out of old terms: historical
messianism, or a romantic/messianic conception of history. It is,
none the less, as distinct from traditional Jewish messianism as
it is from classical German Romanticism, and cannot be broken
down into a simple aggregate of the two. Uniting the *Tikkun*
and social utopia, this configuration reinterprets the messianic
tradition in the light of romanticism, and charges romanticism
with a revolutionary tension – the result being a new modality
of 'philosophy of history', a new vision of the link between past,
present and future.

The relationship between historical messianism and Marxist
historical materialism varies in accordance with the authors,
from complete incompatibility (Gershom Scholem and Gustav
Landauer) to the narrowest of complementarities (Ernst Bloch
and Walter Benjamin). It goes without saying that an articulation
of the two presupposes that the traditional antinomies between
atheism and religion, materialism and spiritualism and most
notably between romanticism and rationalism, are overcome.

It cannot be denied that romanticism frequently leads to an
idealization of the past, and that its critique of modern rationality often slides towards irrationalism; on the other hand, the
confusion between the religious and the political sphere, between
messianism and social movement, is not without considerable
risks. Historical messianism – the revolutionary/romantic conception of the Central European Jewish intellectuals – does not
always escape these dangers. But its great merit is in avoiding –

or rather, explicitly rejecting – the two most catastrophic forms of combination between messianism and politics: first, the religious and totalitarian worship of the State; and second, the cult of the Supreme Guide.

Taking advantage of the most modern technological means, the 'political religion' of the nation-state has left its mark on twentieth-century history: two world wars and a spreading of totalitarian 'states of emergency'. The messianic/libertarian philosophy of the German-Jewish writers, in its hostility to the State, was the polar opposite of triumphant 'State messianism'. (Only in so far as their thinking lost its libertarian quality did some of them – Lukács and Bloch, to name but two – compromise with Stalinism for a whole period.)

The messianic/libertarian philosophy also radically contradicts all worship of an infallible Leader, of an autocratic Messiah responsible for administering the millennial Kingdom. Its messianism is distinguished by its strictly impersonal nature: it is concerned with the messianic era of the future, the accomplishment of the *Tikkun*, and hardly at all with the Messiah. Nothing is further from their spiritual approach than religious worship of a charismatic saviour, prophet or millennarian hero. Paradoxically, the Messiah himself – as an individual and a person – is a virtually non-existent figure in their writings.

One reason why the majority of these Jewish thinkers could escape the most perverse forms of twentieth-century 'political religion' may have been the integration into their world-view of certain values and principles inherited from the Enlightenment: liberty, equality, tolerance, humanism, *Vernunft* (reason). Their spirituality, though born of the romantic cultural universe, contains a decisive dimension inspired by the *Aufklärung*. Like romantic/revolutionary thought in general, it is not dominated by the irrational, authoritarian, obscurantist or intolerant tendencies of 'reactionary' romanticism; it tends (without always succeeding) towards a higher synthesis, a dialectical *Aufhebung* of the two great poles of German thought: classical (rationalist) idealism and romantic sensibility. Works by Rosenzweig, Benjamin, Lukács or Bloch, for example, cannot be understood without taking into consideration their reference – critical as well as positive – to the French Revolution, Kant or Hegel. An illuminating and provocative formula used by Theodor Adorno in *Minima Moralia* is applicable here: 'Not least among the tasks now confronting thought is that of placing all the reactionary arguments against Western culture in the service of progressive enlightenment'[1] – provided the following phrase is added: 'and of the revolutionary redemption of humanity'.

For this very reason, their romantic critique of industrial civilization does not seek the restoration pure and simple of the pre-capitalist past – which, in their eyes, is impossible and undesirable – but rather, the advent of a new world (seen by most of them as a classless and stateless society), yet one which would contain certain social, cultural and human qualities of the former *Gemeinschaft*.

Moreover, the main questions addressed in their critique (notably in the writings of Walter Benjamin), such as the destruction of nature by the modern means of production and the danger of new technologies used in the service of war, are at the heart of two of the major social movements at the end of the twentieth century: the ecology movement and the anti-nuclear peace movement. They are also very similar to the concerns of an important current of socialist criticique of modernity; the writings of Herbert Marcuse, E.P. Thompson or Jean Chesnaux are examples of its different approaches.

The central characteristic of this new vision of history is that it questions the philosophy of progress which, for two centuries, formed the common foundation of Western thought. Born in its present form with the Enlightenment, it became, implicitly or explicitly, the premise, the a priori category for the most varied interpretations of historical reality. It crossed the borders of political doctrines and social *Weltanschauungen*; its colour tinted conservatism as well as liberalism, social democracy and communism, authoritarianism and democracy, reaction and revolution, colonialism and anti-colonialism.

Based on a strictly quantitative conception of temporality, it perceived the movement of history as a continuum of constant improvement, irreversible evolution, growing accumulation and beneficial modernization, for which the driving force was scientific, technological and industrial progress. This paradigm of progress was so attractive that it even shaped the thought of its traditionalist adversaries, who tended increasingly to accept it as an inevitable fate and merely placed a minus sign where the dominant ideology marked a plus. All attempts at restoring the past (for example, through fundamentalist political-religious movements) proved to be bloody impasses; and the virtues and exigencies of the modern industrial civilization based on technological progress appeared as an inescapable fact.

In the progressive conception of history, the catastrophes of modernity – such as the two world wars, Auschwitz and Hiroshima, the colonial and imperialist wars, the destruction of the natural environment, the danger of a nuclear holocaust that would put an end to the human species – appeared as chance mishaps, regrettable but marginal incidents within the permanent Great Movement of Amelioration.

Historical messianism, or the romantic/millenarian conception of history, constitutes a break with the philosophy of progress and with the positivist worship of scientific and technological development. It brings a qualitative, non-evolutionary perception of historical time, in which the detour through the past becomes the necessary point of departure for the leap towards the future, as opposed to the linear, unidimensional and purely quantitative vision of temporality as cumulative progress. It offers a critical vision of modernity, of industrial civilization and its Golems, in the name of certain pre-capitalist social, cultural or religious values, at the same time as an aspiration to a future that will no longer be the artificial 'novelty' of goods – eternal repetition of the Ever-the-same – but a qualitatively distinct utopian world, an *écart absolu* (Fourier's 'absolute divergence') with regard to the existing state of things.

It incorporates messianism as a millenarian expression of the hopes, dreams and aspirations of the pariahs and those excluded from history, as a utopian and subversive 'tradition of the oppressed' (Benjamin) and as the source of a discontinuous vision of temporality.

Finally, this conception is romantic in so far as it seeks to re-enchant the world, to rediscover the spirit of *Gemeinschaft*, to re-establish the broken harmony between man and nature, to restore *Kultur* as a universe of qualitative, non-market, non-quantifiable values. Unlike conservative romanticism, however, it seeks to achieve these goals through a revolutionary (in the broadest sense) overturn of the established social and political order and through the abolition of all coercive and authoritarian systems ('the State'). Actually, the past at issue here is illuminated by the utopia of the future, and the desires and ideals crushed by the reality of the present world are projected onto the two.

The most daring and radical expression of historical messianism and of the romantic/revolutionary philosophy are the works of Walter Benjamin, in particular his final text, the *Theses on the Philosophy of History* (1940). However, scattered elements can be found in most of the authors of this rebellious German-Jewish generation.

In 'Thesis VIII' of *Theses on the Philosophy of History*, Benjamin warned against the illusions of progress which were apparent in the surprise that phenomena like Nazism were 'still' possible in the twentieth century. He ardently wished for a new conception of history that would make it possible to understand Fascism – in other words, the emergence of forms worse than anything that humanity had known in the past, at the very moment when knowledge, science and technology were taking an incredible leap forward. Beyond Fascism itself, Benjamin was also indicating the contradictions of modern civilization: his principal reproach against the doctrines of progress – notably social democracy, although the same held true for liberalism and Stalinist Communism, among others – was that they wanted to recognize only 'progress in the mastery of nature, not the regression of society' ('Thesis XI')[2].

Theodor Adorno uses a striking expression in *Minima Moralia* to account for this antinomy at the heart of modernity: regressive progress. But it has to be asked whether the concept of 'regression', traditionally used by Marxists to characterize phenomena such as Fascism, is really adequate. Were Nazi extermination camps – or, in another register, the Soviet camps and Hiroshima – a matter of mere regression? Regression towards what? The Middle Ages? Primitive Germanic communities? The Stone Age? Are we not talking, rather, of a completely new and perfectly modern phenomenon, instrumentally rational and scientific, and structurally industrial?

Be that as it may, Benjamin regarded the catastrophic manifestations of modernity, such as Fascism and the new technologies of war – which at that time (1940) were still far from having unveiled their full potential for barbarism and destruction – as tangible proof of the vanity of progressive ideologies. The dogma that progress was boundless, infinite, linear and automatic ('Thesis XIII') did not correspond in any way to the experience of the oppressed in history. For them, the past was not a progressive evolution, nor an accumulation of knowledge, but rather a succession of defeats: a 'great triumphal procession in which the present rulers step over those who are lying prostrate' ('Thesis VII'); a permanent 'state of emergency'; a perpetual renewal of oppression. It was in these defeats, and in the image of the enslaved ancestors, that Benjamin saw the source of inspiration and the 'greatest strength' of redemptive revolution ('Thesis XII') – as well as in privileged moments of revolt that contained a spark of messianic hope: the Spartakist rebellion, the French Revolution, June 1848, the Paris Commune, the 1919 German Spartakist insurrection.

But Benjamin's thought was more radical. Beyond the various doctrines of progress, he wanted to question their common epistemological foundation: the idea of quantitative accumulation in homogeneous, empty time ('Thesis XIII').[3]

Benjamin's critique refers us back to the Jewish/messianic conception of temporality. In a classic work on Jewish messianism, Sigmund Mowinckel emphasizes that for the Jews, eternity does not denote 'an infinite, empty, abstract, linear prolongation of time', but rather, a different concept of time – not a Kantian category, an empty formal notion, but one that is inseparable from its entire content.[4]

According to Karl Mannheim, millenarianism (Jewish or Christian) raises against the principle of evolution the absolute-chiliastic experience of the present (*Jetzerlebnis*) based on a '*qualitative* differentiation of time (*qualitative Differenzierung der Zeit*)'.[5]

This rejection of the abstract quantification of time is found in romanticism as well as in Marxism. After quoting several passages from *Das Kapital* on the mechanical character of workers' labour, Lukács commented:

> Thus time sheds its qualitative, variable, flowing nature; it freezes into an exactly delimited, quantifiable continuum filled with quantifiable 'things' (the reified, mechanically objectified 'performance' of the worker, wholly separated from his total human personality): in short, it becomes a space.[6]

Benjamin draws from all these sources when he attempts to go beyond the homogeneous, empty and purely quantitative conception of time. His first effort, the article '*Trauerspiel* and Tragedy' from 1916, contrasts historical time with the mechanical and empty time of clocks (manifested in the regularity of spatial change). According to Benjamin, when historical time is 'filled', it becomes messianic time.[7] The passage from his 1919 thesis on German Romanticism, mentioned in Chapter 7, has exactly the same import: it contrasts the 'qualitative temporal infinity' of romantic messianism with the 'empty temporal infinity' of the ideologies of progress. In the *Theses on the Philosophy of History*, he once again counterposes the time of calendars – 'monuments of a historical consciousness of which not the slightest trace has been apparent in Europe in the past hundred years' – to the time of clocks ('Thesis xv').

In this way, Benjamin gradually draws the outline of a qualitative conception of temporality, based on the discontinuity of historical time. For the tradition of the oppressed classes and for the revolutionary class at the moment of action, time is not homogeneous like that of clocks, but rather heterogeneous, qualitatively differentiated and discontinuous; it is not empty but filled (*erfüllt*) with 'present time' or 'Now-time' (*Jetztzeit*), which causes the continuity of history to explode, 'shot through with chips of "Messianic time"' ('Thesis A').[8] The Jewish messianic perception of temporality serves as the primary reference here: 'We know that the Jews were prohibited from investigating the future. . . This does not imply, however, that for the Jews the future turned into homogeneous, empty time. For every second of time was the straight gate through which the Messiah might enter' ('Thesis B').

It goes without saying that this standpoint might lead to a passive and resigned expectation of the advent of the Messiah. However, Benjamin did not attach himself to the (dominant) quietist tendency of Orthodox Jewish religion. He belonged instead to the tradition of the *dochakei ha-ketz* or 'accelerators of the end' – the tradition (of which Franz Rosenzweig spoke) of those who wanted to force the advent of the Kingdom. In Benjamin's mind, it was not a question of waiting, but rather of seizing the revolutionary opportunity that each historic moment offered.[9] Benjamin summarized his active revolutionary messian-

ism remarkably well when he quoted a statement by Focillon –
removing it, as usual, from its (aesthetic) context and endowing
it with millenarian explosiveness: 'To "mark a time" does not
mean intervening passively in chronology, it means hastening
the moment.'[10]

This qualitative/active conception of time provides the framework that makes it possible to open the historical field for
utopian novelty which is not reducible to mechanical, repetitive
and quantitative accumulation.

Notes

1   On the Concept of Elective Affinity

1. Cf. Johannes Conradus Barchusen, *Pyrosophia* (Lugduni Batavorum: Impensis Cornelii Bautestein, 1698), Book I, ch. 3.
2. Hermannus Boerhave, *Elementa Chemiae* (Lugduni Batavorum: Apud Isaacum Severinum, 1732), part II: 'De Menstruis'. Cf. also the article, 'Affinité, I. Chimie' in *La Grande Encyclopédie* (Paris: Laminault); and de Morveau, *La Chimie, Encyclopédie méthodique* (Paris: Chez Panckoucke, 1786), vol. I, p. 535.
3. De Morveau, *La Chimie*, vol. I, p. 570; and T.O. Bergman, *Traité des affinités chimiques ou attractions électives* (Paris: Chez Buisson, 1788), p. 5.
4. J. W. Goethe, *Elective Affinities*, trans. James Anthony Froude and R. Dillon Boylan (New York: Frederick Unger, 1962), pp. 32, 37. Translation slightly modified.
5. Max Weber, *Gesammelte Aufsätze zur Religionssoziologie* (Tübingen: J.C.B. Mohr, 1922), p. 153.
6. Max Weber, *Gesammelte Aufsätze zur Wissenschaftslehre* (Tübingen: J.C.B. Mohr, 1922), p. 153.
7. Max Weber, *The Protestant Ethic and the Spirit of Capitalism*, trans. Talcott Parsons (New York: Charles Scribner's Sons, 1958), pp. 91–2.
8. Ibid.
9. Karl Mannheim, *Wissenssoziologie* (Neuwied: Luchterhand, 1964), p. 458. The term also appears in Troeltsch: cf. Jean Séguy, *Christianisme et société. Introduction à la sociologie de Ernst Troeltsch* (Paris: Cerf, 1980), pp. 247–51. The expression was studied by Werner Stark, a sociologist from the Weberian school, but only in reference to the second kind of elective affinity (between world visions and social classes), which Max Weber spoke of. See Werner Stark, *Die Wissenssoziologie* (Stuttgart: Ferdinand Enke Verlag, 1960), pp. 215–48.
10. See, for instance, Alfred von Martin's essay, 'Soziologie der Kultur

des Mittelalters' in *Geist und Gesellschaft, Soziologische Skizzen zur europäischen Kulturgeschichte.* (Spirit and Society. Sociological Sketches of the European History of Civilization. Frankfurt am Main: J. Knecht, 1948)

11. Charles Baudelaire, *Oeuvres complètes* (Paris: Seuil, 1968), pp. 471, 350.

12. Danièle Hervieu-Léger, 'Apocalyptique écologique et "retour" de la religion', *Archives de Sciences sociales des Religions*, vol. 53, no. 1, (January–March 1982), p. 66.

13. For more on this subject, see my essay 'Weber against Marx? The polemic with historical materialism', in *The Protestant Ethic, Science and Society*, vol. 53, no. 1 (Spring 1989).

2   Jewish Messianism and Libertarian Utopia:
From 'Correspondences' to '*Attractio Electiva*'

1. Max Weber, *Ancient Judaism*, trans. and ed. Hans H. Gerth and Don Martindale (Glencoe, Ill.: The Free Press, 1952), p. 4.

2. Karl Mannheim, *Ideology and Utopia* (New York: Harcourt, Brace & Co., Inc. 1954), pp. 175–6, 202–3.

3. Paul Honigsheim, 'Soziologie der Mystik', in *Versuche zu einer Soziologie des Wissens*, ed. Max Scheler (Leipzig: Duncker & Humblot, 1924), p. 343.

4. Gershom Scholem, 'Toward an understanding of the messianic idea in Judaism', in *The Messianic Idea in Judaism*, trans. Michael A. Meyer (New York: Schocken Books, 1971), p. 19.

5. Gershom Scholem, ibid., p. 4. The utopian element in messianism dates back to the Old Testament itself; for example, see Isaiah 65:17: 'For, behold, I create new heavens and a new earth; and the former things shall not be remembered, nor come into mind.' On the messianic age as a recovery of Paradise lost (including in rabbinical literature), see Herman L. Strack and Paul Billerbeck, *Kommentar zum Neuen Testament, aus Talmud und Midrash* (Oscar Beck, 1924), vol. IV, pp. 886, 893; Hugo Gressmann, *Der Messias* (Göttingen: Vandenhoeck & Ruprecht, 1929), Book 3, vol. I, pp. 150–63.

6. Sigmund Mowinckel, *He that Cometh*, trans. G. W. Anderson (Oxford: Basil Blackwell, 1956), p. 143. Cf. also p. 144: 'The restoration is a return to the original perfection, the last things become like the first.'

7. See Gershom Scholem, *Major Trends in Jewish Mysticism* (London: Thames and Hudson, 3rd ed., 1968), pp. 268–286. The concept of

Tikkun appears in the writings of several German-Jewish thinkers: Gershom Scholem, Martin Buber, Ernst Bloch and (indirectly) Walter Benjamin.

8. Cf. Karl Mannheim, *Ideology and Utopia*, pp. 203–4.

9. Cf. G. Darien, 'Anarchistes', in *L'Ennemi du peuple* (Paris: Champ Libre, 1972), p. 166.

10. Cf. Max Weber, *Economy and Society*, ed. Guenther Ross and Claus Wittick (New York: Bedminster Press, 1968), vol. II, p. 515.

11. Cf. Gershom Scholem, 'Toward an understanding of the messianic idea in Judaism', p. 7. Cf. also Gershom Scholem, *Sabbatai Sevi. The Mystical Messiah* (Princeton University Press, 1973), p. 9: 'There is no continuity between the present and the messianic era . . . Redemption meant a revolution in history.'

12. Cf. Gershom Scholem, 'Toward an understanding of the messianic idea in Judaism', p. 10; and *Judaica*, vol. I, pp. 12–13, 20, 24–5, 29–30. In criticizing the evacuation of the catastrophic dimension from Jewish messianism and its reduction to an idea of the 'eternal progress' of humanity Scholem refers explicitly to Hermann Cohen. But it seems to me that he is also implicitly polemicizing with Joseph Klausner, the nationalist historian of messianism (at the Hebrew University, Jerusalem), for whom 'the quintessence of Jewish Messianism' was precisely 'the ideal of unceasing progress, of continuing spiritual increase' (Joseph Klausner, *The Messianic Idea in Israel from its Beginning to the Completion of the Mishnah* (London: Allen & Unwin, 1955), pp. 70–1).

13. Cf. Max Weber, *Economy and Society*, pp. 619–20.

14. Cf. Gershom Scholem, *On Jews and Judaism in Crisis* (New York: Schocken Books, 1976), pp. 285, 287.

15. Cf. Karl Mannheim, *Ideology and Utopia*, p. 203. For a discussion of the messianic, utopian and apocalyptic nature of anarchism, see Eric Hobsbawm's study on the agrarian libertarian Communist movement in Spain, 'the most impressive example of a modern mass millenarian or quasi-millenarian movement' (Eric Hobsbawm, *Primitive Rebels* (New York: Norton, 1965), p. 90).

16. Cf. Sigmund Mowinckel, *He that Cometh*, pp. 261–3, 265.

17. The references in Hebrew were taken from the British and Foreign Bible Society edition of the Old Testament (London, 1963). Those in English were taken from *The Holy Scriptures* (Philadelphia: The Jewish Publication Society of America, 1955).

18. For other biblical and post-biblical sources on this set of themes, see Sigmund Mowinckel, *He that Cometh*, p. 154.

19. Cf. Sigmund Mowinckel, *He that Cometh*, p. 172 and pp. 140–8.

20. Cf. Jakob Taubes, *Studien zu Geschichte und System der abendländischen*

Eschatologie (Bern: Buchdruckerei Rösch, Vogt & Co., 1947), p. 24.

21. Cf. Gershom Scholem, 'Toward an understanding of the messianic idea', pp. 22-4; and 'The crisis of tradition in Jewish messianism', p. 55, in *The Messianic Idea in Judaism*. In referring to the doctrine of the Sabbatians, Scholem spoke of a 'Messianic-anarchic' Judaism. Cf. *The Messianic Idea in Judaism*, p. 77.

22. Karl Mannheim, *Ideology and Utopia*, p. 196.

23. For more on this subject, see my article, co-authored with Robert Sayre, 'Figures of romantic anti-capitalism', *New German Critique*, no. 32 (Spring 1984).

3   Pariahs, Rebels and Romantics: A Sociological Analysis of the Central European Jewish Intelligentsia

1.   Pierre Guillen, *L'Allemagne de 1848 à nos jours* (Paris: Nathan, 1970), pp. 58–60.

2.   For more information on the sociological significance and various expressions of this concept, see two of my books, *Marxisme et romantisme révolutionnaire* (Paris: Edition du Sycomore, 1980); and *Georg Lukács: From Romanticism to Bolshevism* (London: New Left Books, 1979).

3.   Fritz K. Ringer, *The Decline of the German Mandarins. The German Academic Community 1890–1933* (Cambridge, Mass.: Harvard University Press, 1969), pp. 12–13.

4.   Gershom Scholem, 'On the social psychology of the Jews in Germany 1900-1933', in *Jews and Germans from 1860 to 1933. The Problematic Symbiosis*, ed. David Bronsen (Heidelberg: Carl Winter Universitätsverlag, 1979), p. 11.

5.   Walther Rathenau, *Ein preussischer Europäer, Briefe*, ed. M. V. Eynern (Berlin, 1955), p. 145.

6.   Gershom Scholem, 'On the social psychology of the Jews in Germany', pp. 16–17.

7.   Franz Rosenzweig, *Briefe* (Berlin: Schocken Verlag, 1935), p. 474.

8.   Moritz Goldstein, 'Deutsch-Jüdischer Parnass', *Kunstwart*, 11 March 1912.

9.   Max Weber, *Economy and Society*, p. 493.

10. Hannah Arendt, *The Jew as Pariah. Jewish Identity and Politics in the Modern Age* (New York: Grove Press, 1978), p. 68.

11. Friedrich Paulsen, *Die deutschen Universitäten und das Universitätsstudium* (Berlin, 1902), pp. 149–50.

12. Ismar Elbogen, *Geschichte der Juden in Deutschland* (Berlin: E. Lichtenstein Verlag, 1935), p. 303.
13. Ibid.; and Erich Rosenthal, 'Trends of the Jewish population in Germany (1910–1939)', *Jewish Social Studies*, vol. VI, no.3 (July 1944), p. 257.
14. Cf. the unpublished manuscript of the Hungarian researcher Zador Tordai, 'Wie kann man in Europa Jude sein? Walter Benjamin' (Budapest, 1979), fols. 35, 48.
15. For more information, see the analysis of this phenomenon in Frederic Grunefeld's recent work on German-Jewish culture, *Prophets without Honour. A Background to Freud, Kafka, Einstein and their World* (New York: McGraw-Hill, 1980) pp. 19, 28–9.
16. Mathias Greffrath (coll.), *Die Zerstörung einer Zukunft* (Reinbek bei Hamburg: Rowohlt, 1979), p. 199.
17. Karl Mannheim, 'Das Problem der Generationen', in *Wissenssoziologie*, p. 542.
18. The neologism 're-culturalization' is used here to denote a reversal of the process of cultural integration and the return of a group or an individual to its original culture.
19. Martin Buber, 'Über Jakob Böhme', *Wiener Rundschau*, vol. V, no. 12 (1901).
20. Hans Helmuth Knutter, *Die Juden und die deutsche Linke in der Weimarer Republik (1918–1933)* (Düsseldorf: Droste Verlag, 1971), p. 37. 'A large part of the Left intellectuals are Jewish, and nearly all left-wing Jews are intellectuals.'
21. Hannah Arendt, *The Jew as Pariah*, p. 144. For a contrast between a *'parvenu'* and a 'rebel' within the pariah nation, see Hannah Arendt, *Rahel Varnhagen, The Life of a Jewish Woman*, trans. Richard and Clara Winston (New York: Harcourt Brace Jovanovich, 1974), pp. 199–215.
22. Elisabeth Lenk, 'Indiscretions of the Literary Beast: Pariah Consciousness of Women Writers since Romanticism', *New German Critique*, no. 27 (Fall 1982), pp. 106–7, 113–14.
23. Robert Michels, *Zur Soziologie des Parteiwesens in der modernen Demokratie* (Leipzig: Alfred Kröner Verlag, 2nd ed., 1925), p. 336. This sentence was not included in the English edition, *Political Parties*.
24. Victor Karady and Istvan Kemény, 'Les Juifs dans la structure des classes en Hongrie', *Actes de la recherche en sciences sociales*, no. 22 (June 1978), p. 59.
25. Walter Laqueur, *Weimar: A Cultural History 1918–1933* (New York: G.P. Putnam's Sons, 1974), p. 73.
26. There were, of course, Jewish (atheist) Marxists within the ranks of

the French Communist Party, and a generation later within the far left movements of the 1960s. They were nearly always Eastern or Central European Jews, or their descendants.

27. L.H. Haimson, *The Russian Marxists and the Origins of Bolchevism* (Boston: Beacon Press, 1955), p. 60.

28. Cf. Rachel Ertel's introduction to Moishe Kulback's book *Lundi* (Lausanne: Edition L'Age d'Homme, 1982). This attitude resurfaced, much later, in Isaac Bashevis Singer's book *Satan in Goray* (1958), which describes the horrors resulting from the fanatical delirium of disciples of Sabbatai Sevi in a Polish *shtetl*.

29. Vladimir Medem, 'The youth of a bundist', in *The Golden Tradition. The Jewish Life and Thought in Eastern Europe*, ed. Lucy S. Dawidowicz (Boston: Beacon Press, 1967), p. 432.

30. Ezra Mendelsohn, 'Worker opposition in the Russian Jewish socialist movement from the 1890s to 1903', *International Review of Social History*, vol. x, part 2 (1965), p. 270.

31. Rachel Ertel, *Le Shtetl, la bourgade juive de Pologne* (Paris: Payot, 1982), pp. 148, 151.

32. Lucy S. Dawidowicz, 'Introduction: the world of East European Jewry', in *The Golden Tradition*, p. 81.

33. Rachel Ertel, *Le Shtetl*, pp. 292–3.

34. Isaac Deutscher, *The Non-Jewish Jew and other Essays* (London: Oxford University Press, 1968), pp. 46–7.

35. For more on this subject, see Jutta Scherrer's remarkable work *Die Petersburger religiös-philosophischen Vereinigungen* (Wiesbaden: Otto Harrassowitz, 1973), pp. 44, 272.

36. Eugen Leviné could be considered an exception, but he was too immersed in German culture – he received a German education at home, he studied in Heidelberg – to be considered a true representative of the Russian Jewish intelligentsia.

4   Religious Jews tending to Anarchism:
Martin Buber, Franz Rosenzweig, Gershom Scholem, Leo Löwenthal

1. Martin Buber, 'Alte und neue Gemeinschaft' in *AJS Review* (1976), pp. 50–6.

2. Martin Buber, 'Gemeinschaft' (Munich-Vienna-Zurich: Dreiländerverlag, 1919), p. 12; and 'Aussprache über den Staat', unpublished lecture given in Zurich on 29 November 1923 (Buber Archives of the Hebrew University of Jerusalem, MS. Var. 350, 47d/*Beth*).

3. Martin Buber, 'Aussprache über den Staat'.

4. Martin Buber, *Werke* (Heidelberg: Lambert Schneider Verlag, 1963), vol. III, p. 758.

5. Gershom Scholem, *The Messianic Idea in Judaism*, p. 245.

6. Martin Buber, *Die chassidischen Bücher* (Berlin: Schocken Verlag, 1927), p. 661.

7. W. Sombart, *Les Juifs et la vie économique* (Paris: Payot, 1923), p. 344. For more information on the subject, see the excellent book by Freddy Raphaël, *Judaïsme et capitalisme* (Paris: Presses Universitaires de France, 1982).

8. Martin Buber, *On Judaism*, trans. Eva Jospe (New York: Schocken Books, 1967), pp. 33, 50. In a letter to Hugo Bergmann, dated 4 December 1917, Buber wrote: 'My concept of the Messiah, my belief in the Messiah, is the ancient Jewish one, as expressed in the words of Ezra 13:26: "God shall bring redemption to creation", and 6:27: "Evil shall be destroyed and lies shall be abolished"' (Martin Buber, *Briefwechsel aus sieben Jahrzehnten*, (Heidelberg: Lambert Schneider Verlag, 1972), vol. I, p. 516).

9. Martin Buber, 'Das messianische Mysterium (Jesaja 53)', unpublished lecture given in Berlin on 6 April 1925 (Buber Archives at the Hebrew University in Jerusalem, MS. Var. 350, 64 Zayim), fol. 7.

10. Martin Buber, *On Judaism*, p. 35. Cf. *Drei Reden über das Judentum* (Frankfurt: Rutten & Loenig, 1920), pp. 60–1.

11. Martin Buber, 'Das messianische Mysterium', p. 9.

12. Martin Buber, *The Legend of the Baal-Shem*, trans. Maurice Friedman (New York: Harper & Brothers, 1955), p. 38.

13. Martin Buber, *Die chassidischen Bücher*, pp. xxiii, xxvi, xxvii.

14. The distinction goes back to Buber's first works on prophecy. See, for example, the 1930 lecture on 'The Two Centres of the Jewish Soul', in *Kampf um Israel* (Berlin: Schocken Verlag, 1933), pp. 50–67. A concise summary can be found in *Pfade in Utopia* (Heidelberg, 1950), ch. 2.

15. Martin Buber, Letter of 16 July 1926 to an Association for Judeo-Christian Reconciliation, quoted in Franz Freiherr von Hammerstein, *Das Messias-Problem bei Martin Buber* (Stuttgart: Kohlhammer Verlag, 1958), p. 49.

16. Martin Buber, 'Zion, der Staat und die Menschheit. Bemerkungen zu Hermann Cohens "Antwort"', *Der Jude*, vol. I (1916–17), pp. 427–8.

17. Martin Buber, 'Die Revolution und wir', *Der Jude*, vol. III (1918–19, pp. 346–7.

18. Martin Buber, 'Gemeinschaft', pp. 16–17.

19. Martin Buber, 'Landauer und die Revolution', *Masken*, no. 14 (1918–19), p. 282.

20. Martin Buber, 'In später Stunde', *Der Jude*, vol. v (1920–1), p. 4.
21. Martin Buber, *On Judaism*, pp. 111, 120–3. Translation modified.
22. Martin Buber, 'Staat und Gemeinschaft', unpublished lecture given in February 1924 (Buber Archives, MS Var. 350, 47).
23. Martin Buber, *Königtum Gottes* (Berlin: Schocken Verlag, 1932), p. 142.
24. Avraham Yassour, 'Utopia and anarchism in Buber and Landauer's social thought', in *Buber Ha-Kibbuts Ve-Harayon Ha-Shitufi* [Buber, the Kibbutz and the Communal Index] (Haifa University, 1979), p. 29.
25. Martin Buber, *Pfade in Utopia*, chs 2, 10.
26. Martin Buber, *Pfade in Utopia*, chs 8, 9.
27. Emmanuel Levinas, 'Preface', in Martin Buber, *Utopie et socialisme* (Paris: Ambier, 1977), p. 11.
28. Martin Buber, *Utopie et socialisme*, pp. 26–8.
29. Martin Buber, *On Judaism*, pp. 83, 92.
30. Martin Buber, 'Das messianische Mysterium', p. 8. In a lecture he gave in Jerusalem in 1939, Buber criticized the nationalist movements within the Jewish community in Palestine (Martin Buber, *On Judaism*, p. 185).
31. Cf. Günther Henning, *Walter Benjamin zwischen Marxismus und Theologie* (Olten Wolter Verlag, 1974), p. 45.
32. Cf. Paul Honigsheim, *On Max Weber* (New York: Free Press, 1968), p. 79.
33. 'In Rosenzweig's mind, the First World War made the core idea of all Western philosophy crumble: namely, that of a reasonable universe ruled by Logos, structured according to laws . . . which assigned man to his place harmoniously in the general order of things' (Stephane Mosès, *Systeme et Révélation. La Philosophie de Franz Rosenzweig* (Paris: Seuil, 1982), p. 18).
34. Franz Rosenzweig, *The Star of Redemption*, trans. William W. Hallo (New York: Holt, Rinehart and Winston, 1971), pp. 227–9. Translation slightly modified. It seems to me that Stephane Mosès is wrong when, in his otherwise remarkable book on Rosenzweig's philosophy, he writes that in *The Star of Redemption*, the coming of eternity 'soon and within our lifetime', means 'the anticipation of redemption through rituals, as opposed to any attempt to hasten the coming of messianic time' (Stephane Mosès, *Système et Révélation*, p. 217). The passage from *The Star of Redemption* quoted above suggests that in Rosenzweig's mind, the aspiration to 'hasten the coming of the Messiah' is an integral element of the Jewish concept of time. Prayer does have precisely this role: 'If there is no such force, no such prayer as can accelerate the

coming of the kingdom, then it does not come in eternity; rather
– it eternally does not come' *The Star of Redemption*, p. 288).

35. Franz Rosenzweig, *Briefe*, p. 292.
36. Franz Rosenzweig, *Jehuda Halevi, Zweiundneunzig Hymnen und Gedichte* (Berlin, 1927), pp. 239, 242.
37. Franz Rosenzweig, *Briefe*, p. 291. As Guy Petitdemange notes in a fine essay, in the religious thinking of Rosenzweig, the Revelation 'has, as a historical correlate, the idea of messianic eruption' ('La Provocation de Franz Rosenzweig', *Recherches de science réligieuse* (October–December 1982), p. 503).
38. Franz Rosenzweig, *Kleinere Schriften* (Berlin: Schocken Verlag, 1937), p. 470.
39. Franz Rosenzweig, *The Star of Redemption*, pp. 333, 334.
40. Günther Henning, *Walter Benjamin*, p. 51.
41. Franz Rosenzweig, *Star of Redemption*, p. 287.
42. Günther Henning, *Walter Benjamin*, p. 51.
43. Franz Rosenzweig, *The Star of Redemption*, p. 285.
44. David Joseph Biale, 'The Demonic in History: Gershom Scholem and the Revision of Jewish Historiography' (Ph.D. thesis, University of California, 1977), p. 171. For Scholem's favourable view of German Romanticism ('emotionally attached to the living peoplehood', 'the active comprehension of the organism of their own history'), see *The Messianic Idea in Judaism*, pp. 305, 307. However, Scholem does not agree with Biale's theory that German Romanticism was an important source in his thinking (Memorandum of a Conversation with Gershom Scholem, December 1979).
45. In an autobiographical letter that Scholem wrote in 1937 to the editor Zalman Schocken, he referred to Molitor's 'deep insight' and mentioned how he had been greatly 'fascinated' by Molitor's book. See David Biale, *Gershom Scholem. Kabbalah and Counter-History* (Cambridge, Mass.: Harvard University Press, 1979), pp. 216, 75. This book is a revised and corrected version of the Ph.D. thesis mentioned in the preceding note.
46. Gershom Scholem, *From Berlin to Jerusalem. Memories of my Youth*, trans. Harry Zohn (New York: Schocken Books, 1980), p. 50; *On Jews and Judaism in Crisis* (New York: Schocken Books, 1976), pp. 7–9, 17–18; and Memorandum of a conversation between Michael Löwy and Gershom Scholem, December 1979. Scholem's interest in Romanticism was evident once again during the 1920s, when he studied the work of the Romantic Nature Philosopher Johann Wilhelm Ritter, which had been enthusiastically recommended to him by Walter Benjamin. (See the letter from Walter Benjamin to Gershom Scholem dated 5 March 1924, in Walter Benjamin, *Briefe*

(Frankfurt-am-Main: Suhrkamp Verlag, 1966), vol. I, p. 342.) Fifty years later, Scholem recalled that it was an 'impressive' work. (Memorandum of a conversation with Scholem, December 1979.)

47. David Biale, *Gershom Scholem. Kabbalah and Counter-History*, p. 182. In an essay written in 1969, Scholem referred to Zionism as a 'movement of youth in which strong romantic motives necessarily played a role' (David Biale, *Gershom Scholem*, p. 182).

48. Gershom Scholem, *On Jews and Judaism in Crisis*, p. 21.

49. Gershom Scholem, 'Ha-Matarah ha-Sofit' [The Final Goal], *Sheifotenu*, no. 2 (August 1931), p. 156. See also 'Zur Frage des Parlaments', *Jüdische Rundschau*, no. 34 (1929), p. 65. The word 'revisionist' refers to the nationalist movement led by Jabotinsky (and later by Menachem Begin).

50. Gershom Scholem, 'Lyrik der Kabbala?', *Der Jude*, vol. VI, 1921–2, p. 55. Cf. David Biale, *Gershom Scholem*, p. 73.

51. In another context, cf. David Biale, *The Demonic in History*, p. 181: 'History is Scholem's alternative to Maimonidean rationalist theology and Buberian irrational existentialism.'

52. Gershom Scholem, *From Berlin to Jerusalem*, p. 166.

53. Memorandum of a conversation between Michael Löwy and Gershom Scholem, December 1979.

54. Gershom Scholem, 'Lyrik der Kabbala?', pp. 61–2.

55. Gershom Scholem, *From Berlin to Jerusalem*, p. 155.

56. Gershom Scholem, 'Ha-Mekubal Abraham Ben Eliezer Halevi', *Kiriat Sefer*, pamphlet 'A', 2nd year (1925), p. 111.

57. *Encyclopaedia judaica*, vol. I (Berlin: Eschkol Verlag, 1928), pp. 637–9.

58. Gershom Scholem, 'Über die Theologie des Sabbatianismus im Lichte Abraham Cardozos', *Der Jude*, vol. IX (1928); re-printed in *Judaica*, vol. I (1963).

59. *Encyclopaedia judaica*, vol. 9 (1932), pp. 659, 663, 697–8, 703. The religious/messianic meaning of the concept of *apokatastasis* (Greek for re-establishment of the previous situation) also appears in Benjamin's works of the 1930s.

60. Gershom Scholem, 'Al Shlosha Pishei Brit Shalom' [On the Three Sins of the Brit Shalom], *Davar* (12 December 1929), p. 2.

61. Gershom Scholem, *Walter Benjamin. The Story of a Friendship*, trans. Harry Zohn (Philadelphia: The Jewish Publication Society of America, 1981), pp. 11, 15.

62. Gershom Scholem, *From Berlin to Jerusalem*, p. 53; and Memorandum of a conversation with Gershom Scholem, December 1979. David Biale suggests that there was a link between Landauer's anarchism and the Zionism in Scholem's nascent world-view

during the First World War (David Biale, *The Demonic in History*, p. 110). According to Scholem himself, the fact that the theme of a 'Jewish State' was missing in the Zionist writings of his youth may have had something to do with the anarchist problematic (Memorandum of a conversation, December 1979).

63. Gershom Scholem, *Mi-Berlin le-Yerushalayim, Zichronot Neurim* (Tel-Aviv: Hotzaat Am-Oved, 1982), p. 115. This is an enlarged version in Hebrew of *From Berlin to Jerusalem*.

64. Gershom Scholem, *Mi-Berlin le-Yerushalayim*, pp. 178–9. Several years later, the *Hashomer Hatzair* claimed allegiance to Marx and Lenin and so abandoned its anarchist references.

65. Gershom Scholem, *On Jews and Judaism in Crisis*, pp. 35–6.

66. Gershom Scholem, 'Une éducation au judaisme', *Dispersion et unité*, no. 11 (1971), pp. 153–4, 159.

67. Gershom Scholem, *On Jews and Judaism in Crisis*, p. 33.

68. For example, in the article 'Reflections on Jewish Theology' (1973), there is a passage which mentions Bloch, Benjamin, Adorno and Marcuse (*On Jews and Judaism in Crisis*, pp. 286–7).

69. Gershom Scholem, 'Die Metamorphose des häretischen Messianismus der Sabbatianer im religiösen Nihilismus im 18. Jahrhundert', *Judaica*, vol. III (1963), p. 207. See also the Frankists' 'anarchist utopia of the land' (p. 217).

70. David Biale, *The Demonic in History*, p. 3.

71. David Biale, *Gershom Scholem*, p. 174. See also page 154.

72. Leo Löwenthal, *Mitmachen wollte ich nie. Ein autobiographisches Gespräch mit Helmut Dubiel* (Frankfurt-am-Main: Suhrkamp Verlag, 1980), pp. 16–19.

73. Leo Löwenthal, 'Wir haben nie im Leben diesen Ruhm erwartet', in *Die Zerstörung einer Zukunft*, ed. Mathias Greffrath (Reinbek bei Hamburg: Rowohlt, 1979), pp. 200–1.

74. Excerpts from Löwenthal's unpublished thesis were published much later as, 'Franz von Baader: Ein religiöser Soziologe der Soziologie' in *Internationales Jahrbuch für Religionssoziologie* (Cologne: Westdeutscher Verlag, 1966–7). Cf. vol. II (1966), pp. 235–9 and vol. III (1967), pp. 202–3.

75. Leo Löwenthal, *Mitmachen wollte ich nie*, pp. 153–60.

76. Leo Löwenthal, *Mitmachen wollte ich nie*, pp. 40–7, 55–8.

77. Conversation held between Leo Löwenthal and Michael Löwy, October 1984. See Leo Löwenthal, *Schriften* (Frankfurt-am-Main: Suhrkamp Verlag, 1984), vol. 4, p. 9.

78. Leo Löwenthal, 'Das Dämonische. Entwurf einer negativen Religionsphilosophie', in *Gabe Herrn Rabbiner Dr. Nobel zum 50. Geburtstag* (Frankfurt: J. Kaufmann Verlag, 1921), pp. 51–62.

5 'Theologia negativa' and 'Utopia negativa': Franz Kafka

1. Quoted by Klaus Wagenbach, *Franz Kafka* (Reinbek bei Hamburg: Rowohlt, 1964), p. 143.
2. In a recent work, Ritchie Robertson refers to Kafka's social vison as 'romantic anti-capitalism', and uses my own definition of the concept. However, he interprets it in a somewhat one-sided manner, as if it were synonymous with 'anti-industrialism' (cf. Ritchie Robertson, *Kafka. Judaism, Politics and Literature* (Oxford: Clarendon Press, 1985), p. 141).
3. Franz Kafka, *America*, trans. Willa and Edwin Muir (London: Secker & Warburg, 1967), pp. 58, 64, 153–4.
4. Wilhelm Emrich, *Franz Kafka* (Frankfurt: Athenäum Verlag, 1961), pp. 227–8.
5. Klaus Hermsdorf, *Kafka. Weltbild und Roman* (Berlin: Rütten & Loening, 1961), p. 52.
6. Arthur Holitscher, *Amerika heute und morgen* (Berlin: Fischer Verlag, 1912), p. 316. He also complains of the metallic din of the Chicago factories, a noise that was as 'cold and inconsolable as the entire modern world, with its civilization–the most sinister (*grimmigsten*) enemy of the human species' (p. 321).
7. Franz Kafka, *Letters to Felice*, trans. James Stern and Elizabeth Duckworth (London: Penguin Books, 1978), p. 264. Translation slightly modified.
8. Gustav Janouch, *Conversations with Kafka*, trans. Goronwy Rees, 2nd ed. (London: Quartet Books, 1985), p. 115.
9. Franz Kafka, 1917 'Diary' entry, quoted in Max Brod, *Franz Kafka: A Biography*, trans. G. Humphrey Roberts and Robert Winston (New York: Schocken Books, 1960), p. 178.
10. Franz Kafka, *America*, p. 28.
11. Franz Kafka, *Wedding Preparations in the Country*, Penguin Books, 1978), pp. 56, 58.
12. Klaus Wagenbach, *Franz Kafka. Eine Biographie seiner Jugend 1883-1912* (Berne: A. Francke Verlag, 1958), p. 180.
13. Werner Kraft, *Gespräche mit Martin Buber* (Munich: Kosel Verlag, 1966), pp. 111, 124. In a letter to Buber in 1915, Kafka referred to their meeting as 'the best souvenir' of his stay in Berlin. In 1917, Kafka wrote to thank Buber for having published two of his stories – 'Jackals and Arabs' and 'A Report to an Academy' – in the magazine *Der Jude*, 'something that never seemed possible to me' (cf. Martin Buber, *Briefwechsel*, volume I, pp. 409, 494). The Buber

Archives in Jerusalem contain seven letters from Kafka to Buber, written between 1914 and 1917; three have been published in the *Briefwechsel*.

14. *Das Kafka-Buch* ed. Heinz Politzer (Frankfurt: Fischer Bücherei, 1965), p. 250. For more on Kafka's ambiguous attitude towards Judaism and Zionism, see Helen Milfull, 'Franz Kafka. The Jewish Context', in *Year Book of the Leo Baeck Institute*, vol. XXIII (London: Secker & Warburg, 1978).

15. Franz Kafka, *Shorter Works*, trans. Malcolm Pasley (London: Secker & Warburg, 1973), vol. I, p. 92.

16. Max Brod, *Über Franz Kafka* (Frankfurt: S. Fischer Verlag, 1966), p. 213. According to Brod, Kafka's belief in divine promise and redemption – absent in his novels – is particularly evident in the aphorisms; however, the analysis he outlines is far from convincing.

17. *The Diaries of Franz Kafka, 1914–1923* (New York: Schocken Books, 1974 [4th printing]), p. 132. Cf. Max Brod, *Über Franz Kafka*, p. 326. Quoting from the two sources, Brod tried to interpret them in a non-contradictory and positive manner by suggesting that once Rossmann was executed, he would find his place in paradise. Of course, such an interpretation could also lead one to decipher the conclusion of *The Trial* (K.'s assassination 'like a dog') as a prologue to the ascension of his blessed soul to the Garden of Eden.

18. Alfred Wirkner, *Kafka und die Aussenwelt. Quellenstudien zum 'Amerika'-Fragment* (Stuttgart, 1976), p. 81.

19. Walter Sokel, *Franz Kafka – Tragik und Ironie* (Vienna: Albert Langen, 1964), p. 215; and Ernst Fischer, 'Kafka Conference', in *Franz Kafka. An Anthology of Marxist Criticism*, ed. and trans. Kenneth Hughes (London: University Press of New England, 1981), p. 91.

20. Hannah Arendt, 'Franz Kafka', in *Franz Kafka. An Anthology of Marxist Criticism*, p. 8.

21. Marthe Robert, *As Lonely as Franz Kafka*, trans. Ralph Manheim (New York: Harcourt Brace Jovanovich, 1982), p. 119. Translation slightly modified. Noting Kafka's admiration for certain people who had served as spiritual models–for example, the socialist Lily Braun, the pietist Erdmuthe von Zinzendorf, Prince Kropotkin–Marthe Robert defines the common element of that heterogeneous group as follows: 'all incarnated to an exceptional degree the perfect harmony between an individual and his spiritual choice, and in this harmony all found the strength to act in the world against the established order, undeterred by

doubts and conflicts.' (Marthe Robert, *As Lonely as Franz Kafka*, p. 86). In an article on the legend of the doorkeeper, Ingeborg Henel also draws the conclusion that 'obedience to the external law, prevents entry into the true law' . . . which is 'the law of each individual'. (Ingeborg Henel, 'The legend of the doorkeeper and its significance for Kafka's *Trial*', in *Twentieth Century Interpretations of 'The Trial'*, ed. James Rolleston (Englewood Cliffs: Prentice Hall, 1976), pp. 41, 48).

22. Franz Kafka, *The Trial*, trans. Willa and Edwin Muir (New York: Schocken Books, 1984), p. 7.

23. Franz Kafka, *Hochzeitsvorbereitungen auf dem Lande und andere Prosa aus dem Nachlass* (New York: S. Fischer Verlag and Schocken Books, 1953), pp. 88, 90.

24. See the different but analogous hypothesis put forward by Ritchie Robertson: 'when everyone has achieved such [individualistic] faith, the Messiah will be superfluous, for the Kingdom of God will already exist' (Ritchie Robertson, *Kafka. Judaism, Politics and Literature*, p. 192).

25. Ritchie Robertson, *Kafka*, p. 164. See also Jens Tismar, 'Kafka's "Schakale und Araber" im zionistischen Kontext betrachtet', *Jahrbuch der Deutschen Schiller-Gesellschaft*, no. 19 (1975). A similar point of view is suggested by Robert Kauf ('Kafka's "A Report to the Academy"', *Modern Language Quarterly*, XV (1954), p. 365).

26. Gershom Scholem, 'Mit einem Exemplar von Kafkas *Prozess*', in *Benjamin über Kafka*, ed. Hermann Schweppenhauser (Frankfurt-am-Main: Suhrkamp Verlag, 1981), p. 73.

27. Walter Benjamin, *Briefe*, (Frankfurt-am-Main: Suhrkamp Verlag, 1966), vol. II, p. 614. In his 1934 essay on Kafka, Benjamin compared *The Castle* to a talmudic legend on the expectation of the Messiah (Walter Benjamin, 'Franz Kafka', in *Illuminations*, ed. Hannah Arendt, trans. Harry Zohn (New York: Schocken Books, 1969), p. 126).

28. Gershom Scholem, *On Jews and Judaism in Crisis*, p. 196.

29. Theodor Adorno, in a letter to Benjamin dated 17 December 1934, in *Benjamin über Kafka*, p. 101.

30. Moreover, in his letters to Scholem, Benjamin made explicit reference to what he called 'the messianic aspect' and the 'messianic category' of these writings (Walter Benjamin, Letter to Scholem dated 11 August 1934, in *The Correspondence of Walter Benjamin and Gershom Scholem (1932–1940)*, trans. Gary Smith and Andre Lefevre (New York: Schocken Books, 1989), p. 135.

31. Max Brod, Postscript to the first edition of Kafka's *Das Schloss* (*The Castle*) in Franz Kafka, *Gesammelte Schriften*, (Berlin: Schocken

Verlag 1946), vol. IV, pp. 417–21. [Translator's Note: Mr Brod's postcript is not included in the English edition.]

32. Nevertheless, there are those who subscribe to this interpretation: see, for example, Ritchie Robertson, *Kafka. Judaism, Politics and Literature*, p. 260. For negative criticism, see, for example, Marthe Robert, *L'Ancien et le nouveau, de Don Quichotte à Kafka* (Paris: Payot, 1967), pp. 176–86; and Erich Heller, 'The World of Franz Kafka', in *Kafka. A Collection of Critical Essays*, ed. Ronald Gray (Englewood Cliff: Prentice Hall, 1965), pp. 117–18.

33. Hannah Arendt, 'Franz Kafka', p. 5.

34. Erich Heller, *Franz Kafka* (Princeton: Princeton University Press, 1982), pp. 105, 123.

35. This is the position that Alfred Döblin defends in 'Die Romane von Franz Kafka', *Die literarische Welt* (4 March 1927).

36. Martin Buber, *Werke*, vol. I (Heidelberg: Lambert Schneider Verlag, 1962), p. 778. Hans Joachim Schoeps also defined Kafka's religion as a theology on the absence of salvation (*Heillosigkeit*), and he adds this comment: 'Only Jewish theology has known the phenomenon of a true history-of-non-salvation (*Unheilsgeschichte*) in which the history of salvation changes into its direct opposite' (Hans Joachim Schoeps, 'Theologische Motive in der Dichtung Franz Kafkas', in *Die Neue Rundschau* (1951), p. 21).

37. Kafka, *Hochzeitsvorbereitungen auf dem Lande*, p. 52.

38. Theodor Adorno, *Prisms* (Cambridge Mass.: MIT Press, 1982), p. 269. See also Hans Joachim Schoeps, 'Theologische Motive', p. 37: 'Only an absolutely desperate existence can allow an *insane* (*irrsinnige*) messianic hope–that was what he himself once called it.'

39. Kafka, *Hochzeitsvorbereitungen auf dem Lande*, p. 108.

40. Maurice Blanchot, *De Kafka à Kafka* (Paris: Gallimard, 1981), p. 69. For more on the aphorisms, see Ingeborg Henel, *Franz Kafka. Themen und Probleme* (Göttingen: Vandenhoeck & Ruprecht, 1980) pp. 60–1. See also the excellent work by Rosemarie Ferenczi, *Kafka, subjectivité, histoire et structures* (Paris: Klincksieck, 1975) p. 101.

41. Heinz Politzer, ed., *Das Kafka-Buch*, p. 151.

42. Michal Mares, 'Erinnerungen an Kafka', in Klaus Wagenbach, ed., *Franz Kafka. Eine Biographie seiner Jugend 1883–1912*, pp. 163–4; and Max Brod, 'Franz Kafka. Eine Biographie' in *Über Franz Kafka*, p. 79.

43. Michal Mares, 'Erinnerungen an Kafka', p. 162; and Michal Mares, 'Setkanis Franzem Kafkou', *Literarni Noviny*, vol. 15 (1946).

44. Michal Mares, 'Erinnerungen an Kafka', p. 166. Franz Kafka, *The Diaries of Franz Kafka (1910–1913)* (London: Penguin Books,

1964), pp. 233, 333; Gustav Janouch, *Conversations with Kafka* 2nd ed., p. 90.

45. Gustav Janouch, *Conversations with Kafka*, trans. Goronwy Rees, 1st ed. (London: Derek Verschoyle, 1953), p. 98.

46. Max Brod, *Über Franz Kafka*, p. 76: 'Statt die Anstalt zu stürmen und alles kurz und klein zu schlagen, kommen sie bitten.'

47. Gustav Janouch, *Conversations with Kafka*, 1st ed., p. 53, 71, 86. Translation slightly modified.

48. Marthe Robert is correct to write that reserve is an essential component of his art, 'the *stylistic principle* that saved his novels from the flatness of the *roman à idées*.' (Marthe Robert, *As Lonely as Franz Kafka*, p. 47).

49. Franz Kafka, *Wedding Preparations in the Country*, pp. 35, 48.

50. Franz Kafka, *Letters to Friends, Family, and Editors*, trans. Richard and Clara Winston (New York: Schocken Books, 1977) p. 167: 'If any journal seemed tempting to me for any length of time . . . it was Dr Gross's.' See also G. Baioni, *Kafka, Letteratura ed ebraismo* (Turin: Einaudi, 1979), pp. 203-5. For more information on Otto Gross, see Arthur Mitzman, 'Anarchism, Expressionism and Psycho-analysis', *New German Critique*, no. 1 (Winter 1977).

51. Milan Kundera, 'Quelque part là-derrière', *Le Débat*, No. 8, June 1981, p. 58.

52. Franz Kafka, *America*, p. 241, 188.

53. Franz Kafka, *America*, p. 13, 28, 229. The Manageress, a maternal figure, is an exception.

54. Franz Kafka, 'Letter to His Father', in *Wedding Preparations in the Country*, p. 48.

55. Arthur Holitscher, *Amerika heute und morgen*, pp. 102–3.

56. Franz Kafka, *Letters to Felice*, p. 681.

57. Walter Benjamin, Letter to Gershom Scholem dated 12 June 1938, *The Correspondence of Walter Benjamin and Gershom Scholem 1932–1940*, p. 223.

58. Walter Benjamin, *Understanding Brecht* (London: Verso Editions, 1984), p. 108. In an essay published in 1974, J. P. Stern drew a detailed (but somewhat forced) parallel between Kafka's *The Trial* and Nazi legislation or the court practices during the Third Reich (J.P. Stern, 'The Law of the Trial', in *On Kafka: Semi-centenary Perspectives*, ed. F. Kuna (New York: Harper & Row, 1976).

59. Franz Kafka, *The Trial*, p. 3.

60. R. Ferenczi, *Kafka, subjectivité, histoire et structures*, p. 62.

61. Gustav Janouch, *Kafka und seine Welt* (Vienna: Verlag Hans Deutsch, 1965), p. 55.

62. Max Brod, 'Franz Kafka: eine Biographie', in *Über Franz Kafka*, p.

177. Brod cites Dora Dymant's testimony: 'According to Dora, among the burned papers, there was also a story by Kafka about a ritual-murder trial filed against Beiliss in Odessa.' [Translator's Note: This passage was excluded from the English version, *Franz Kafka: A Biography*.] For more on this subject, see Arnold J. Band, 'Kafka and the Beiliss Affair', *Comparative Literature*, vol. 32, no. 2 (Spring 1980).

63. Franz Kafka, 'The Problem of our Laws', in *The Great Wall of China: Stories and Reflections*, trans. Willa and Edwin Muir (New York: Schocken Books, 1948), p. 257. True, he added: 'yet, no such party can come into existence, for nobody would dare to repudiate the nobility'. But this negative assessment is rather a call for revolt. A similar theme shows up in the parable 'The Refusal', in which the old colonel, the traditional holder of power, always denies the simple requests of the people, who submit with resignation. However, added Kafka,

'so far as my observations go, there is a certain age group that is not content – these are the young people roughly between seventeen and twenty. Quite the young fellows, in fact, who are utterly incapable of foreseeing the consequences of even the least significant, far less a revolutionary, idea. And it is among just them that discontent creeps in.' (Kafka, *Shorter Works*, vol. I, p. 130)

As a matter of fact, such suggestions of a future revolt are rather rare in Kafka's works.

64. Franz Kafka, *The Trial*, pp. 45–6.
65. Michel Carrouges, 'Dans le rire et les larmes de la vie', *Cahiers de la compagnie M. Renaud et J.-L. Barrault* (October 1957), p. 19.
66. Hannah Arendt, 'Franz Kafka', p. 4.
67. Franz Kafka, *Letters to Milena*, trans. Tania and James Stern (New York: Schocken Books, 1953), p. 225.
68. Franz Kafka, *The Castle*, trans. Willa and Edwin Muir (New York: Alfred A. Knopf, 1968), p. 84.
69. Franz Kafka, *The Castle*, pp. 88–9.
70. Marthe Robert, *As Lonely as Franz Kafka*, p. 175.

6 Outside all Currents, at the Crossing of the Ways: Walter Benjamin

1. Walter Benjamin, ed. Rolf Tiedemann and Hermann Schweppenhauser, *Gesammelte Schriften*, (5 volumes, Frankfurt-am-Main: Suhrkamp Verlag, 1977), vol. II, p. 46. Around the same time,

Benjamin wrote a manuscript (which remained unpublished) entitled 'Dialog über die Religiosität der Gegenwart' (Dialogue on the Religiosity of the Present), which contrasted the 'heroic-revolutionary efforts' with the pitiful pace ('nearly that of a crab') of evolution and progress (*Fortschritt*). Cf. *Gesammelte Schriften*, vol. II, 1, pp. 25–6, 34.

2. Walter Benjamin, *Der Begriff der Kunstkritik in der deutschen Romantik* (Frankfurt-am-Main: Suhrkamp Verlag, 1973), pp. 65–6, 70.

3. Walter Benjamin, Letter to Gershom Scholem dated June 1917, *Briefe*, vol. I, p. 138.

4. Walter Benjamin, *Gesammelte Schriften*, vol. II, pp. 75–87.

5. Walter Benjamin, *Gesammelte Schriften*, vol. III, p. 308. The attempt to link Romanticism and the Enlightenment also emerged in other works by Benjamin; for example, see the 1936 anthology *Deutsche Menschen* (*Gesammelte Schriften*, vol. IV, 1, pp. 149–233), which gives evidence of this orientation, both in the choice of authors and in the manner in which they are presented.

6. Walter Benjamin, *Der Begriff der Kunstkritik*, pp. 8–9. In a letter that Benjamin wrote to Ernst Schoen in April 1919, Benjamin explained that he could not place messianism as the 'heart of romanticism' at the centre of his thesis, because that would have kept him from maintaining the conventional ('in my eyes, separate from true') scientific attitude demanded by the University (Letter to Ernst Schoen dated 7 April 1919, *Briefe*, vol. I, p. 208).

7. Walter Benjamin, *Der Begriff der Kunstkritik*, pp. 86–7. See also the 1916 essay 'Trauerspiel and Tragedy', which contrasts fulfilled (*erfüllt*) messianic time with the empty time of mechanical objects and clocks (*Gesammelte Schriften*, vol. II, 1 pp. 133–7).

8. Gershom Scholem, *Walter Benjamin. The Story of a Friendship*, p. 38.

9. Winfried Menninghaus, *Walter Benjamins Theorie der Sprachmagie* (Frankfurt-am-Main: Suhrkamp Verlag, 1980), pp. 189–92.

10. Walter Benjamin, 'On Language as Such and on the Language of Man', in *Reflections: Essays, Aphorisms, Autobiographical Writings*, trans. Edmund Jephcott (New York: Harcourt Brace Jovanovich, 1978), pp. 327–9.

11. Hannah Arendt, ed. *Illuminations* pp. 75, 80.

12. Unpublished letter from Gershom Scholem to Hannah Arendt, 28 November 1960, Arendt Papers, Container 12, Library of Congress, Washington, D.C.

13. Gershom Scholem, 'The Meaning of the Torah in Jewish Mysticism', *Diogenes*, no. 15 (Fall 1956), pp. 89–90.

14. Franz Joseph Molitor, *Philosophie der Geschichte oder über die Tradi-*

tion (Munster: Theissingsche Buchhandlung, Part Three, 1834), p. 598.

15. Walter Benjamin, Letter to Gershom Scholem dated 30 March 1918, *Briefe*, vol. I, p. 181.

16. In the previously mentioned essay, 'Dialog über die Religiosität der Gegenwart' (1913), Benjamin refers to Tolstoy, Nietzsche and Strindberg as prophets of a new religion and a new socialism (*Gesammelte Schriften*, vol. II, 1, pp. 22–34).

17. Gershom Scholem, *Walter Benjamin. The Story of a Friendship*, p. 84; and notes from a conversation between Gershom Scholem and Michael Löwy in December 1979. Cf. also Walter Benjamin, *Reflections*, p. 312: 'theocracy has no political, but only a religious meaning. To have repudiated with utmost vehemence the political significance of theocracy is the cardinal merit of Bloch's *Spirit of Utopia*.'

18. Notes from an interview with Werner Kraft, January 1980.

19. Walter Benjamin, *Briefe*, vol. I, p. 355; and Gershom Scholem, *Walter Benjamin. Story of a Friendship*, p. 123.

20. Gershom Scholem, *Walter Benjamin. Story of a Friendship*, pp. 11–13. Benjamin had obtained a copy of Sorel's book–unavailable in Germany–through Bernd Kampffmeyer, an anarchist intellectual and secretary of Max Nettlau; the book had been recommended by a mutual friend, Adolf Otto, the anarchist architect. In a letter to Kampffmeyer which Benjamin wrote in 1920, Benjamin sought a bibliographic opinion on anarchist literature that referred to violence: 'writings that are negative to State violence as well as those that are apologetic to the revolutionary'. (This document was discovered by Chryssoula Kambas in the Nettlau Archive in Amsterdam. Cf. Chryssoula Kambas, 'Walter Benjamin und Gottfried Salomon. Bericht über eine unveröffentlichte Korrespondenz', *Deutsche Vierteljahrschrift für Literaturwissenschaft und Geistesgeschichte*, vol. 56 (December 1982), p. 617.

21. Walter Benjamin, *Reflections*, pp. 287–8, 291–2, 296–300.

22. Walter Benjamin, *Reflections*, p. 312; and Franz Rosenzweig, *The Star of Redemption*, p. 287. Adorno estimated the date of this text to be 1937 (the year in which Benjamin apparently showed it to him as a 'recent' work), but Scholem demonstrated convincingly that this was a 'mystico-anarchist' writing from 1920 or 1921 (see his letter to Maurice de Gandillac in *Poesie et révolution* (Paris: Denoël, 1971) p. 149. If my hypothesis concerning the relationship of this work to that of Rosenzweig is correct, it would be more accurate to date it 1921 to 1922.

23. Walter Benjamin, *Reflections*, p. 313.

24. Walter Benjamin, *The Origin of German Tragic Drama*, trans. John Osborne (London: New Left Books, 1977), pp. 65–8.

25. Norbert Bolz, 'Charisma und Souveränität. Carl Schmitt und Walter Benjamin im Schatten Max Webers', in *Religionstheorie und politische Theologie*, ed. Jacob Taubes (Munich: Wilhelm Fink Verlag, 1983), vol. I, pp. 254–7. Christine Buci-Glucksmann detected very clearly the implicitly anti-statist conclusions that Benjamin drew from Schmitt's ideas on sovereignty (Christine Buci-Glucksmann, 'Walter Benjamin et l'ange de l'histoire: une archéologie de la modernité', *L'Ecrit du Temps*, no. 2, (1983), p. 67).

26. Walter Benjamin, Letter to Scholem dated 16 September 1924, *Briefe*, vol. I, p. 355. Even in 1929, Benjamin considered *History and Class Consciousness* (along with Rosenzweig's *The Star of Redemption!*) as one of the few books that remained alive and relevant. He called it 'the most accomplished philosophical work of Marxist literature', whose singular merit was to have grasped, in the critical situation of the class struggle and the revolution, 'the final word in theoretical knowledge'. (Walter Benjamin, *Gesammelte Schriften*, vol. III, p. 169).

27. Walter Benjamin, Letter to Gershom Scholem dated 29 May 1926, *Briefe*, vol. I, p. 426.

28. Richard Wolin, *Walter Benjamin, An Aesthetic of Redemption* (New York: Columbia University Press, 1982), p. 117.

29. English translation taken from Richard Wolin, *Walter Benjamin, An Aesthetic of Redemption*, pp. 115–17.

30. Walter Benjamin, *One Way Street*, trans. Edmund Jephcott and Kingsley Shorter (London: New Left Books, 1979), p. 56.

31. Walter Benjamin, *One Way Street*, p. 80.

32. Walter Benjamin, *One Way Street*, p. 104.

33. Walter Benjamin, *One Way Street*, p. 53.

34. Walter Benjamin, *Reflections*, pp. 180–2, 187, 189.

35. Walter Benjamin, *Reflections*, pp. 189-92.

36. Walter Benjamin, *Briefe*, vol. II, pp. 529–36.

37. Walter Benjamin, *Gesammelte Schriften*, vol. III, p. 250. Benjamin attached great importance to this idea, which had been censured in a previous publication. In an article he wrote in 1929 about an anti-militarist play, he stated that 'armed insurrection' (*bewaffneter Aufstand*) was the only response to war. *Die literarische Welt* published the article in May 1929–without this incendiary passage. Cf. *Gesammelte Schriften*, vol. IV, 1, p. 463; and *Gesammelte Schriften*, vol. IV, 2, p. 1031.

38. Walter Benjamin, Letter to Fritz Lieb dated 9 July 1937, *Briefe*, vol. II, p. 732.

39. Walter Benjamin, Letter to Alfred Cohn dated 6 February 1935, *Briefe*, vol. II, p. 648.

40. Drieu La Rochelle, *La Comédie de Charleroi* (Paris: Gallimard, 1960), pp. 217–27. In Drieu's short-story, there is a moving passage that one cannot read without thinking immediately of Port-Bou in September 1940: 'In 1914, I was one of the few of whom there will be thousands during the next war. There will be thousands of men who will defend themselves against the quaking earth, by fleeing–or who, faced with two types of death, will choose to be the protester before the firing squad rather than the resigned, bombarded or gassed subject.'

41. Walter Benjamin, *Moscow Diary*, trans. Richard Sieburth (Cambridge, Mass.: Harvard University Press, 1986), p. 53.

42. Walter Benjamin, Letter to Gretel Adorno, *Briefe*, vol. II, p. 553. In an article published in 1932, he quoted Trotsky's statement that only the 'armed masses' would know how to put an end to the war (Walter Benjamin, *Gesammelte Schriften*, vol. III, p. 351).

43. Irving Wohlfarth, 'On the messianic structure of Benjamin's last reflections', *Glyph*, no. 3, (Baltimore, 1978), p. 168.

44. Gershom Scholem, *On Jews and Judaism in Crisis*, p. 188.

45. Nathalie Heinrich, 'L'Aura de Walter Benjamin. Notes sur l'œuvre d'art à l'ère de sa reproductibilité technique', *Actes de la recherche en sciences sociales*, no. 49 (September 1983).

46. In a letter to Horkheimer from August 1936, shortly after the execution of Zinoviev and Kamenev, Benjamin writes 'Naturally I am following the events in Russia very closely. And it seems to me I am not the only one who has run out of answers.' (English translation from Rolf Tiedemann, 'Historical materialism or political messianism? An interpretation of the thesis "On the concept of history" ', in *Benjamin. Philosophy, History, Aesthetics*, ed. Gary Smith, trans. Barton Byg, Jeremy Gaines, and Doris L. Jones (Chicago: The University of Chicago Press, 1989), p. 193. Cf. Walter Benjamin, Letter to Max Horkheimer dated 31 August 1936, *Briefe*, vol. II, p. 722.

47. Untitled folder, *Fonds Walter Benjamin*, Envelope no. 2, Bibliothèque Nationale de Paris. In 'Historical Materialism', Rolf Tiedemann suggests the date 1937. (Rolf Tiedemann, 'Historical Materialism or Political Messianism?' in *Benjamin. Philosophy, History, Aesthetics*, p. 194). I might add that Benjamin also regarded the foreign policy of the Soviet Union with distrust; in a letter he wrote in March 1938, he complained of the 'Machiavellianism of the Russian leaders' in Spain (Letter to Karl Thieme dated 27 March 1938, *Briefe*, vol. II, p. 747).

48. Walter Benjamin, *Understanding Brecht*, pp. 117, 121. Mr Pierre
     Missac was so kind as to share with me memories of his
     conversations with Benjamin in 1937.
49. Hannah Arendt, ed. *Illuminations*, p. 258.
50. Walter Benjamin, *Gesammelte Schriften*, vol. I, 2, p. 683. The contra-
     diction between progress in the control of nature and regression
     (*Rückschritt*) in social life is the central theme of "Thesis XI" of
     Theses On the Philosophy of History.
51. Hannah Arendt, ed. *Illuminations*, pp. 92, 97.
52. Walter Benjamin, *Gesammelte Schriften*, vol. II, 2, pp. 474–88.
53. Walter Benjamin, *Gesammelte Schriften*, vol. V, 1, p. 592.
54. J. Habermas, 'L'Actualité de Walter Benjamin. La critique: prise de
     conscience ou préservation', *Revue d'Esthétique*, no. 1 (Paris: Privat,
     1981), p. 121.
55. Miguel Abensour, *Walter Benjamin et Paris* (Paris: Cerf, 1986), p.
     239.
56. Walter Benjamin, *Gesammelte Schriften*, vol. V, 1, pp. 378, 428, 437.
     Cf. also *Gesammelte Schriften*, vol. I, 2, p. 687. For Baudelaire's text,
     see *Œuvres complètes* (Paris: Seuil, 1968), p. 363.
57. Walter Benjamin, *Gesammelte Schriften*, vol. I, 3, pp. 1151–2.
58. Walter Benjamin, *Charles Baudelaire: A Lyric Poet in the Era of High
     Capitalism*, trans. Harry Zohn and Quintin Hoare (London: Verso
     Editions, 1985), pp. 109–154.
59. Walter Benjamin, 'Program of the Coming Philosophy', trans. Mark
     Ritter, *The Philosophical Forum*, vol. XV, nos. 1–2 (Fall–Winter
     1983–4), p. 42.
60. Hannah Arendt, ed. *Illuminations*, pp. 83–4, 102.
61. Walter Benjamin, *Charles Baudelaire* pp. 121, 131–4; and *Gesammelte
     Schriften*, vol. V, 2, p. 966.
62. Walter Benjamin, *Gesammelte Schriften*, vol. II, 2, pp. 664–7.
63. Edgar Allen Poe, *The Works of Edgar Allen Poe*, (New York: P. F.
     Collier & Son, 1904), vol. 4, pp. 293–5, 302, 310. Benjamin was
     familiar with this work by Poe, which Baudelaire translated; he
     quoted it in *Charles Baudelaire: A Lyric Poet in the Era of High
     Capitalism*. Quotations from the *Theses* are taken from *Theses on
     the Philosophy of History*, in *Illuminations*, p. 253.
64. Walter Benjamin, *Gesammelte Schriften*, vol. II, 2, p. 644.
65. E.T.A. Hoffmann, 'The Sandman', in *Selected Writings of E.T.A.
     Hoffmann*, trans. Leonard J. Kent and Elizabeth C. Knight (Chicago:
     The University of Chicago Press, 1969), vol. I, p. 161.
66. Walter Benjamin, *Gesammelte Schriften*, vol. V, 2, pp. 850–1. The char-
     acter of Olympia is also mentioned in 'Passagenwerk' (*Gesammelte
     Schriften*, vol. V, I, p. 269), although in another context, as it is

included in the section on the collector.

67. Walter Benjamin, *Gesammelte Schriften*, vol. V, 2, p. 847.

68. Walter Benjamin, *Gesammelte Schriften*, vol. I, 2, p. 681.

69. Walter Benjamin, *Gesammelte Schriften*, vol. V, 1, p 589.

70. Walter Benjamin, *Gesammelte Schriften*, vol. I, 3. As Irving Wohlfarth showed so well, for Benjamin, the Jewish religion and revolutionary action shared a reference to remembrance–as opposed to the empty temporality of 'progress'–as a means to redeem the past. Cf. Irving Wohlfarth, 'On the messianic structure of Benjamin's last reflections', p. 153.

71. Walter Benjamin, *Charles Baudelaire: A Lyric Poet in the Era of High Capitalism*, p. 159.

72. Walter Benjamin, *Gesammelte Schriften*, vol. II, 1, pp. 220–30. In this article (written for the *Nouvelle Revue française*, which refused it), Benjamin contested Klages' conservative interpretation and appealed to Erich Fromm's Freudian-Marxist reading of Bachofen.

73. It seems to me that Irving Wohlfarth's analysis of the relationship between anarchism and Marxism in Benjamin's thought is the most pertinent: 'He did not feel the need to choose between these fronts. He regularly stressed his anarchist sympathies just when he was drawing closer to Communism, in order to preserve them both within their common space/ boundary' (Irving Wohlfarth, 'Der destruktive Charakter–Benjamin zwischen den Fronten', in *Links hatte noch alles sich zu enträtseln . . . Walter Benjamin im Kontext*, ed. B. Lindner (Frankfurt: Syndikat, 1978), p. 78).

74. Walter Benjamin, *Gesammelte Schriften*, vol. II, 2, p. 582; and *Gesammelte Schriften*, vol. V, 1, p. 47. In Benjamin's opinion, Marx and Fourier did not conflict with each other; he sought out their points of convergence and several times mentioned the text in which Marx defended Fourier from Karl Grün, hailing his 'gigantic vision of mankind' (*Gesammelte Schriften*, vol. V, p. 47).

75. Walter Benjamin, *Gesammelte Schriften*, vol. V, 1, pp. 456–7.

76. Hannah Arendt, ed. *Illuminations*, p. 259. Cf. *Gesammelte Schriften*, vol. V, 1, p. 64: 'One of the most remarkable traits of the Fourierist utopia is that the idea of mankind's exploitation of nature, so widespread later, is alien to him.'

77. Walter Benjamin, *Gesammelte Schriften*, vol. V, 1, p. 456.

78. *Marx–Engels Selected Correspondence* (Moscow: Progress Publishers, 1975), p. 189.

79. Theodor Adorno, *Über Walter Benjamin* (Frankfurt-am-Main: Suhrkamp Verlag, 1970), pp. 115–20.

80. Walter Benjamin, *Gesammelte Schriften*, vol. V, 1, pp. 61, 71, 75, 77. On Baudelaire's 'seven old men', see Marc Sagnol's essay,

'Théorie de l'histoire et de la modernité chez Benjamin', *L'Homme et la Société, no. 69–70, (December 1983)*.

81. Walter Benjamin, *Gesammelte Schriften*, vol. v, 1, pp. 162–78; and *Gesammelte Schriften*, vol. v, 2, p. 813. On the myth and power of the *Immergleichen*, see the interesting talks given by Rolf Janz and Burkhardt Lindner at the Benjamin Colloquium held in Paris in June 1983, published in the collection *Walter Benjamin et Paris*.

82. Walter Benjamin, *Charles Baudelaire*, p. 113.

83. Walter Benjamin, *Charles Baudelaire*, pp. 139, 141.

84. Rolf Tiedemann, 'Epilogue' to Walter Benjamin, *Charles Baudelaire. Ein Lyriker im Zeitalter des Hochkapitalismus* (Frankfurt-am-Main: Suhrkamp verlag, 1980), pp. 205-6.

85. Richard Wolin's commentary on this subject strikes me as pertinent: 'The *correspondences* hark back to an *un*historical state of reconciliation . . . and thus recapture a relation to nature whose last traces are being extirpated with the ruthless advance of rationalization' (Richard Wolin, *Walter Benjamin, An Aesthetic of Redemption*, p. 236).

86. Walter Benjamin, Letter to Gretel Adorno dated 17 January 1940, in *Briefe*, vol. II, p. 843.

87. R. Caillois, 'La Fête', in *Le Collège de sociologie*, ed. Denis Hollier, (Paris: Gallimard, 1979), pp. 486–90.

88. Walter Benjamin, *Charles Baudelaire*, pp. 142–3.

89. Walter Benjamin, *Gesammelte Schriften*, vol. I, 2, p. 667.

90. Walter Benjamin, *Gesammelte Schriften*, vol. v, 1, p. 600.

91. Walter Benjamin, *Gesammelte Schriften*, vol. I, 3, p. 1232.

92. Hannah Arendt, ed. *Illuminations*, p. 260. Cf. the original text in *Gesammelte Schriften*, vol. I, 3, p. 700; and 'Zentralpark', in *Gesammelte Schriften*, vol. I, 2, p. 687.

93. See Miguel Abensour and V. Pelosse, 'Libérer l'Enfermé', in 'Postface' to Blanqui, *Instructions pour une prise d'armes et autres textes* (Paris: La Tête des Feuilles, 1973), p. 208. Curiously, Adorno considered certain ideas in Benjamin's article on the work of art as being 'on the verge of anarchism' (Letter from Adorno to Benjamin dated 13 March 1936, in Theodor Adorno, *Über Walter Benjamin*, p. 129); in particular, he criticized as 'anarchist romanticism', the 'blind confidence in the proletariat's mastery of itself throughout the course of history' (Adorno, *Über Walter Benjamin*, p. 130).

94. Rolf Tiedemann, 'Epilogue' to Walter Benjamin, *Charles Baudelaire. Ein Lyriker im Zeitalter des Hochkapitalismus*, p. 207.

95. Rolf Tiedemann, 'Historical Materialism or Political Messianism? An Interpretation of the Thesis "On the Concept of History"', in *Benjamin. Philosophy, History, Aesthetics*, p. 200. Cf. also p. 202, in

which he asserts that 'theoretical elements of anarchism' can be
identified in the *Theses*.

96. J. Habermas, 'L'Actualité de W. Benjamin', p. 121.
97. Walter Benjamin, *Gesammelte Schriften*, vol. I, 3, pp. 1240–1.
98. Gershom Scholem, *On Jews and Judaism in Crisis*, pp. 194–5.
99. Hannah Arendt, ed. *Illuminations*, p. 255. In an article of 1938
   about a novel by Anna Seghers, Benjamin wrote that the Third
   Reich mimicked socialism in the same way that the Antichrist
   mimicked the Messiah (*Gesammelte Schriften*, vol. III, p. 539). In
   an article published in 1934, Fritz Lieb, the Protestant theologist
   (and revolutionary socialist) who was a close friend of Benjamin's,
   had already defined Nazism as the modern Antichrist; in a lecture
   published in 1938, he wrote that the Antichrist would perish
   during a final battle against the Jews and that Christ would
   then appear to establish his millennial Kingdom (see Chryssoula
   Kambas, 'Wider den "Geist der Zeit". Die antifaschistische Politik
   Fritz Liebs und Walter Benjamin', in *Religionstheorie und politische
   Theologie*, ed. Jacob Taubes (Munich: Wilhelm Fink Verlag, 1983),
   vol. I, pp. 582–3.
100. Walter Benjamin, *Gesammelte Schriften*, vol. I, 2, p. 697. Scholem's
   remark is found in 'Walter Benjamin and His Angel' in *On Walter
   Benjamin: Critical Essays and Recollections*, ed. Gary Smith, trans.
   Wener Dannhauser (Cambridge, Mass.: The MIT Press, 1988),
   p. 84. The word *Tikkun* does not appear directly in Benjamin's
   writings, but there is no doubt that he was very familiar with
   this Jewish doctrine, notably through Scholem's 'Kabbala' article
   for the *Encyclopaedia judaica* in 1932. In his letter of 15 January
   1933, he thanked Scholem for this article (*The Correspondence of
   Walter Benjamin and Gershom Scholem*, pp. 25–6).
101. Walter Benjamin, *Gesammelte Schriften*, vol. I, 3, p. 1243. The
   analogy between Benjamin's messianic conception of history in
   the *Theses* and certain ideas advanced by Franz Rosenzweig in
   The Star of Redemption is surprising. See Stephane Mosès', 'Walter
   Benjamin und Franz Rosenzweig', *Deutsche Vierteljahrschrift für
   Literaturwissenschaft und Geistesgeschichte*, no. 4 (1982).
102. Among the preparatory notes for the *Theses* there was a passage
   associating the messianic era with the advent of a universal
   language, capable of replacing the confusion of the Tower of
   Babel, a language that everyone would understand, 'as children
   on Sunday understand the language of the birds'. There can be
   no denying that there is a link between this idea and Benjamin's
   theological reflections of 1914 on the 'blissful, Adamite language'.
103. Gerhard Kaiser, 'Walter Benjamin, "Geschichtsphilosophische The-

sen"', in *Materialien zu Benjamins Thesen 'Über den Begriff der Geschichte'*, ed. P. Bulthaup, (Frankfurt-am-Main: Suhrkamp Verlag, 1975), p. 74.

104. Walter Benjamin, *Gesammelte Schriften*, vol. I, 3, pp. 1231–2. According to the manuscript of the *Theses*, recently discovered by Giorgio Agamben and presented at the Benjamin Colloquium in Paris in June 1983, this note should really be 'Thesis XVIII'.

105. Rolf Tiedemann, 'Historical materialism or political messianism?', p. 200. Translation modified.

106. Miguel Abensour, 'L'utopie socialiste: une nouvelle alliance de la politique et de la religion', in *Le Temps de la réflexion* (Paris: Gallimard, 1981), vol. II, pp. 64–5.

7   The Religious-Atheist and Libertarian Assimilated Jews: Gustav Landauer, Ernst Bloch, Georg Lukács, Erich Fromm

1.   Ulrich Linse, *Gustav Landauer und die Revolutionszeit (1918-1919)* (Berlin: Karin Kramer Verlag, 1974), p. 28.

2.   For more information on Landauer's romanticism, see Eugen Lunn, *Prophet of Community. The Romantic Socialism of Gustav Landauer* (Berkeley: University of California Press, 1973).

3.   Gustav Landauer, 'Vor fünfundzwanzig Jahren', *Rechenschaft*, 2nd ed. (Cologne, 1924), p. 135.

4.   'Die deutsche Romantik in der Literatur', Library of the Hebrew University of Jerusalem, Gustav Landauer Archives, MS. Var. 432, File 14. To support his argument, Landauer quotes the following passage from the Romantic Friedrich Schlegel: 'The French Revolution, Fichte's theory of science, and Goethe's *Wilhelm Meister* are the spiritual trends of the times.'

5.   Gustav Landauer, *Der werdende Mensch. Aufsätze über Leben und Schriften* (Potsdam: Gustav Kiepenhauer Verlag, 1921), pp. 136–7.

6.   Gustav Landauer, *Aufruf zum Sozialismus* (Berlin: Paul Cassirer, 1919), pp. 9, 20, 43. Landauer seemed to be unaware that Marx and Engels saw precisely the German *Mark* and Russian *Mir* communities as a possible foundation for development towards socialism. For more on this subject, see my book *Marxisme et romantisme révolutionnaire*.

7.   Gustav Landauer, 'Die Revolution' (Berlin: Kromer Verlag, 1977), pp. 29–118.

8.   Gustav Landauer, *Aufruf zum Sozialismus*, pp. 11, 44, 108; and 'Preface' to the 1919 reissue, p. X.

9.   Karl Mannheim, *Ideology and Utopia* (New York: Harcourt, Brace &

Co., Inc., 1954), pp. 202–3.

10. Gustav Landauer, 'Die Revolution', p. 96.
11. Gustav Landauer, *Aufruf zum Sozialismus*, pp. 6, 100, 102.
12. Gustav Landauer, *Aufruf zum Sozialismus*, pp. 46–7, 87, 145–6, 149.
13. Gustav Landauer, *Der werdende Mensch*, p. 190.
14. Martin Buber, *Pfade in Utopia*, ch. 6.
15. Gustav Landauer, 'Die Revolution', pp. 55–6, 63.
16. Gustav Landauer, *Unsere Sprache übertragen von G. Landauer* (Berlin: Verlag Karl Schnabel, 1903), p. 5.
17. See Hans Kohn, *Martin Buber, sein Werk und seine Zeit* (Hellerau: Verlag von Jakob Hegner, 1930), p. 30.
18. Gustav Landauer, 'Durch Absonderung zur Gemeinschaft', *Die Neue Gemeinschaft*, no. 2 (Leipzig: Eugen Diederichs, 1901), pp. 55–6. See also Ruth Link-Salinger, *Gustav Landauer, Philosopher of Utopia* (Indianapolis: Hackett, 1977), p. 31.
19. Gustav Landauer, Letter to Ida Wolf dated 15 June 1891, Landauer *Archives* (International Institute of Social History, Amsterdam), File x.
20. Notes on Romanticism, Gustav Landauer Archives (Hebrew University of Jerusalem), MS Var. 432, File 14.
21. Gustav Landauer, 'Die religiose Jugenderziehung', *Die Freie Bühne* (February 1891).
22. Commentary on the Gospel according to Saint John, Gustav Landauer Archives (Hebrew University of Jerusalem), MS Var. 432, File 12. Undated manuscript of approximately 20 pages.
23. Gustav Landauer, *Der werdende Mensch*, p. 200; and Gustav Landauer Archives (Hebrew University of Jerusalem), MS. Var. 432, Files 31 and 26.
24. Cf. his letter to Rafael Seligmann dated 17 September 1910, in *Briefe*, vol. I, p. 324: 'If you take Moses, Jesus, Spinoza out of Judaism, there will in effect not be a Jewish people.'
25. Gustav Landauer Archives (Hebrew University of Jerusalem), MS. Var. 432, File 23.
26. Gustav Landauer, *Beginnen. Aufsätze über Sozialismus* (Cologne: Marcan-Block Verlag, 1924), p. 7.
27. Gustav Landauer, Letter to Margarete Faas-Hardegger dated 20 October 1908, *Briefe*, vol. I, p. 218.
28. Gustav Landauer, 'Die Legende des Baalschem', *Das literarische Echo*, vol. 13, no. 2 (1 October 1910), p. 149.
29. Gustav Landauer, 'Die Legende des Baalschem', p. 148.
30. This unpublished document is found in the Gustav Landauer Archives (Hebrew University of Jerusalem), MS Var. 432, File 162. Although the document is not dated, it can certainly be established

as having been written prior to 1908.

31. Gustav Landauer, *Der werdende Mensch*, p. 244.

32. For more on this subject, see the excellent article by Norbert Altenhofer, 'Tradition als Revolution: Gustav Landauer, "geworden-werdendes" Judentum', in *Jews and Germans from 1860 to 1933*, ed. David Bronsen (Heidelberg: Carl Winter Universitätsverlag, 1979).

33. Heinz Joachin Heydorn, 'Preface' to Gustav Landauer, *Zwang und Befreiung* (Cologne: Hegner Bücherei, 1968), p. 15.

34. Gustav Landauer, *Der Werdende Mensch*, pp. 30, 35.

35. Gustav Landauer, *Der Werdende Mensch*, p. 125.

36. Gustav Landauer, *Aufruf zum Sozialismus*, pp. 136–7.

37. Landauer Archives (Hebrew University of Jerusalem), MS Var. 432, File 23.

38. Gustav Landauer, *Der werdende Mensch*, p. 125.

39. Gustav Landauer, *Der werdende Mensch*, p. 284.

40. Norbert Altenhofer, 'Tradition als Revolution', pp. 194–5.

41. Letter to Max Nettlau dated 28 January 1913, *Briefe*, vol. I, p. 430.

42. Gustav Landauer, *Der werdende Mensch*, pp. 126–8. In polemic with the Zionists, Landauer criticized what he called the doctrinaire concept of a 'Hebraic Judaism' which would deny the German or Russian dimension of the Jews (p. 127).

43. Gustav Landauer, 'Judentum und Sozialismus', *Die Arbeit* (organ for the Zionist People's Socialist Party *Hapoel Hatzair*), vol. 2 (June 1920), p. 51. As Paul Breines underscores, in Landauer's opinion, 'the Diaspora became the social base so to speak of the idea of the Jews as redeemers of humanity . . . The dispersion, in fact, freed the Jews; it allowed them to remain a nation, and at the same time, to transcend that nation and all nations, and to perceive the future unity of mankind as being made up of a variety of true nations' (Paul Breines, 'The Jew as Revolutionary, The Case of Gustav Landauer', *Year Book of the Leo Baeck Institute*, no. XII (1967), p. 82.)

44. This letter was not included in the collection that Buber published in 1928. It can be found in the correspondence published posthumously in 1972 (Martin Buber, *Briefwechsel aus sieben Jahrzehnten*, vol. I p. 258). Nevertheless, Landauer was interested in the outcome of the rural Jewish communes in Palestine and agreed to participate in a meeting with Zionists socialists (which Buber organized) in order to debate the topic; the meeting was to have taken place in April 1919. On this subject, there is some correspondence between Landauer and Nahum Goldmann, dated March 1919, in the Landauer Archives in Jerusalem MS Var. 432,

Files 167–8). It has been published in Hebrew with an introduction by Avraham Yassour, 'Al Hitiashvut Shitufit va-Tiuss' [Communal Industrialization in the Settlements], *Kibbutz*, no. 2, (1975), pp. 165–75.

45. Ulrich Linse, *Gustav Landauer und die Revolutionszeit*, p. 63.

46. Gustav Landauer, *Aufruf zum Sozialismus*, pp. vii, viii, x, xvii; and Letter to Hans Cornelius dated 20 March 1919, *Briefe*, vol. II, p. 403. Cf. also Heinz Joachin Heydorn, 'Preface' Gustav Landauer, *Zwang und Befreiung*, p. 30.

47. Martin Buber, 'Landauer und die Revolution', *Masken*, no. 19 (1919), pp. 290–1. Buber compared Landauer to his ancestors, the Jewish prophets and martyrs of the past and to Christ crucified by the Romans.

48. The term 'revolutionary romantic' refers in particular to the works he wrote between 1918 and 1923. See Ernst Bloch, *Geist der Utopie*, 2nd ed. (Frankfurt-am-Main: Suhrkamp Verlag, 1973), p. 347.

49. Arno Münster, ed., *Tagträume vom aufrechten Gang. Sechs Interviews mit Ernst Bloch* (Frankfurt-am-Main: Suhrkamp Verlag, 1978), p. 21.

50. Paul Honigsheim, 'Der Max-Weber-Kreis in Heidelberg', *Kölner Vierteljahrschrift für Soziologie*, no. 3 (1926), No. 3, p. 284; and Marianne Weber, *Max Weber. A Biography*, trans. and ed. Harry Zohn (New York: John Wiley & Sons, 1975), p. 468.

51. See 'Interview with Ernst Bloch' by M. Löwy, *New German Critique*, no. 9 (1976), pp. 36–7.

52. Ernst Bloch, *Geist der Utopie* 2nd ed., pp. 20–1, 38–9.

53. Ernst Bloch, *Geist der Utopie* 1st ed., (Munich-Leipzig: Duncker & Humblot, 1918), p. 410.

54. Michael Löwy, 'Interview with Ernst Bloch', pp. 42–3.

55. Ernst Bloch, *Geist der Utopie* 2nd ed., pp. 294–5.

56. Ibid., pp. 303, 307.

57. Ibid., pp. 297–9, 335.

58. Ibid., p. 302.

59. Ernst Bloch, 'Über einige politische Programme und Utopien in der Schweiz', *Archiv für Sozialwissenschaft und Sozialpolitik*, vol. 46 (1918–19), pp. 159–62. The version of this article that was published in 1970 in Bloch's collection, *Politische Messungen, Pestzeit, Vormärz* (Frankfurt-am-Main: Suhrkamp Verlag) was greatly revised.

60. Scholem recalled a conversation with Bloch in 1919, when he saw lying on his work table a book containing chapters on the Jewish messianic tradition (Memorandum of a conversation between Michael Löwy and Gershom Scholem, December 1979). Cf. also Gershom Scholem, *Walter Benjamin. The Story of a Friendship*, pp.

79–80, in which he refers to it as the most scholarly anti-Semitic work published in the eighteenth century (Andreas Eisenmenger, *Entdecktes Judentum* [Judaism unmasked], 1701), containing translations of major Jewish religious sources. In the Buber Archives in Jerusalem, there is a letter from Bloch dated 2 July 1920, which testifies to the personal ties between the two thinkers (Buber Archives of the Hebrew University of Jerusalem, MS Var. 350, 123/ Chet 2). In the first edition of *Geist der Utopie* (1918, p. 320), Buber is presented in a favourable light; however, this presentation was not included in 'Symbol: die Juden', reissued in 1923 in the collection *Durch die Wüste*.

61. Arno Münster, ed., *Tagträume vom aufrechten Gang*, p. 110.

62. E. Levinas, 'Sur la mort dans la pensée de Ernst Bloch', in *Utopie, marxisme selon Ernst Bloch*, ed. G. Raulet (Paris: Payot, 1976), p. 326.

63. In his remarkable book on Bloch's early writings, Arno Münster mentions several of these sources. Cf. Arno Münster, *Utopie, Messianismus und Apokalypse im Frühwerk von Ernst Bloch* (Frankfurt-am-Main: Suhrkamp Verlag, 1982), pp. 131–41. See also his article, 'Messianisme juif et pensée utopique dans l'œuvre d'Ernst Bloch', *Archives de Sciences Sociales des Religions*, no. 57/1, (1984).

64. Ernst Bloch, *Geist der Utopie*, 1st ed., pp. 320, 332.

65. Theodor Adorno, 'Henkel, Krug und frühe Erfahrung', in *Noten zur Literatur*, vol. IV (Frankfurt-am-Main: Suhrkamp Verlag, 1974), p. 92.

66. Ernst Bloch, *Geist der Utopie*, 1st ed., pp. 323, 331–2. Bloch also suggests another theory: Jesus as the suffering Messiah, the 'son of Joseph', distinct from the triumphant Messiah, the 'son of David'–a distinction that goes back to Deuteronomy.

67. Ernst Bloch, *Geist der Utopie*, 1st ed., This passage was not included in the 1923 edition.

68. Arno Münster, *Utopie, Messianismus und Apokalypse*, p. 199.

69. For more on the striking resemblances between Bloch's work and that of Landauer, see Anton Christen, *Ernst Blochs Metaphysik der Materie* (Bône: Bouvier, 1979), pp. 36–8; D. Eisenbarth, 'Ernst Bloch–Empiriker der Mystischen', *Schwarze Protokolle*, no. 16 (1978); and Arno Münster, *Utopie, Messianismus und Apokalypse*, p. 125.

70. This expression was taken from Anton Christen, *Ernst Blochs Metaphysik der Materie*, p. 36-7.

71. Ernst Bloch, *Thomas Münzer als Theologen der Revolution* (Frankfurt-am-Main: Suhrkamp Verlag, 1972), pp. 94–174, 228 . In Bloch's eyes, the libertarian reference did not conflict with Bolshevism. Münzer was perceived as a forerunner not only of Bakunin but

also of Karl Liebknecht and Lenin (Ernst Bloch, *Thomas Münzer*, pp. 94, 110).

72. Ernst Bloch, *Thomas Münzer*, pp. 51–64.
73. Ibid., pp. 114, 127. Cf. *Geist der Utopie*, 2nd ed., p. 40.
74. Ernst Bloch, *Thomas Münzer*, pp. 228–9.
75. Ernst Bloch, *The Principle Of Hope*, trans. Neville Plaice, Stephen Plaice and Paul Knight (Cambridge, Mass.: The MIT Press, 1986), vol. II, pp. 572–4.
76. For a detailed analysis of the various aspects of Lukács's thought to which I make reference here, see my book *Georg Lukács: From Romanticism to Bolshevism*.
77. Lee Congdon, *The Young Lukács* (London, New England: The University of North Carolina Press, 1983), p. 158.
78. This letter is found in the Buber Archives of the Hebrew University of Jerusalem, MS Var. 350.
79. Georg Lukács, 'Zsido miszticizmus', *Szellem*, No. 2, (1911), pp. 256–7.
80. *Notizbuch* (1911), C, p. 29. Lukács Archives, Budapest.
81. Georg Lukács, *Dostojevsky, Notizen und Entwurfe* (Budapest: Akademiai Kiado, 1985), pp. 164–8. Cf. Martin Buber, *The Legend of the Baal-Schem*, p. 148: 'The Sabbath is, in fact, the source of the world to come.' It was probably Lukács who suggested to Bloch that he read Buber's writings, since in a letter dated July 1911, Bloch wrote to his friend: 'I am not yet familiar with the Baal-Schem' (Ernst Bloch, *Briefe, vol. I: 1903–1975*, (Frankfurt-am-Main: Suhrkamp Verlag, 1985), pp. 57–9.
82. Marianne Weber, *Max Weber, A Biography*, p. 466. Cf. the original text, *Max Weber. Ein Lebensbild*, p. 474.
83. Paul Honigsheim, 'Der Max-Weber-Kreis in Heidelberg', p. 284.
84. Quoted by Lee Congdon, in *The Young Lukács*, pp. 135–6. Lukács did not recognize himself in the character of Donath, whom he considered to be a mixture between Bloch and the Hungarian philosopher, Béla Zalai.
85. Béla Balász, 'Notes from a Diary (1911–1921)', *New Hungarian Quarterly*, no. 47 (1972), pp. 124–6.
86. Georg Lukács, *Dostojevsky, Notizen*, pp. 156–8, 172. Two nineteenth-century works were Lukács's principal sources for heretical messianism: Peter Beer, *Geschichte, Lehren und Meinungen aller bestandenen und noch bestehender religiösen Sekten der Juden und der Geheimlehre oder Kabbalah* (Brünn: Joseph Georg Frassler, 1823) vol. 2; and Adolphe Franck, *La Kabbale ou la philosophie religieuse des Hébreux* (Paris, 1843).
87. For example, see Georg Lukács, *Gelebtes Denken. Eine Autobiographie*

im Dialog (Frankfurt-am-Main: Suhrkamp Verlag, 1980), p. 45: 'I always knew I was Jewish, but that ever had a major impact on my development.'

88. Letter from Max Weber to Georg Lukács dated 6 March 1913, in Georg Lukács, *Correspondance de jeunesse (1908–1917)* (Budapest: Ed. Corvina, 1981), p. 234.

89. Letter from Georg Lukács to Felix Bertaux dated March 1913, *Correspondance de jeunesse*, p. 239.

90. Georg Lukács, *Die Theorie des Romans* (Darmstadt and Neuwied: Luchterhand, 1971), p. 137. See also Georg Lukács, *Dostojevsky, Notizen*, p. 60.

91. Georg Lukács, 'Ariadne auf Naxos', in Paul Ernst and Georg Lukács, *Dokumente einer Freundschaft* (Emsdetten: Verlag Lechte, 1974), p. 56.

92. Georg Lukács, *Dostojevsky, Notizen*, p. 62. Lukács discovered Kaliaev through the novels and autobiographical books of the Narodnik writer, Boris Savinkov. See my article, 'Idéologie révolutionnaire et messianisme mystique chez le jeune Lukács 1910–1919', *Archives de Sciences sociales des Religions*, No. 43/1,(1978).

93. Georg Lukács, *Dostojevsky, Notizen*, pp. 179–80.

94. Letters from Georg Lukács to Paul Ernst dated 14 April 1915 and 4 May 1915, *Correspondance de jeunesse*, pp. 254–5, 258.

95. Georg Lukács, *Dostojevsky, Notizen*, p. 185.

96. Ferenc Feher, *Die Seele und das Leben. Studien zum frühen Lukács* (Frankfurt-am-Main: Suhrkamp Verlag, 1977), p. 290. Feher acutely observes that Lukács's notes on Dostoevsky show 'an apocalyptic experience, a nostalgia for Christ's return at the end of time and the demand for the State's immediate abolition' (p. 319).

97. Georg Lukács, *Dostojevsky, Notizen*, p. 116.

98. Georg Lukács, 'Bibliography', vol. I, Lukács Archives, Budapest. The texts quoted were written between 1902 and 1910.

99. Georg Lukács, *Dostojevsky, Notizen*, p. 92. The quotation from Sorel is in French, and the reference is to the Bulletin published by the French Philosophical Society in 1907.

100. In *La Décomposition du marxisme*, Sorel emphasized that the apocalypse corresponded perfectly with the general strike, which, in the eyes of revolutionary syndicalists meant the advent of a new world.

101. Georg Lukács, *Magyar irodálom, magyar kultura* (Budapest: Gondolat, 1970), pp. 8–9. (French translation in *L'Homme et la société*, no. 43–44 (1977), pp. 13–14.

102. Georg Lukács, 'Idéalisme conservateur et idéalisme progressiste' (1918). The French translation is published in the Annex to my

book *Pour une sociologie des intellectuels révolutionnaires*, p. 304.

103. Georg Lukács, 'Der Bolschewismus als moralisches Problem', in *Taktik und Ethik* (Neuwied: Luchterhand, 1975), pp. 27–34.

104. Georg Lukács, 'Unpublished Autobiography', in *Littérature, philosophie, marxisme (1922–1923)*, a collection of Lukács's essays assembled by Michael Löwy (Paris: PUF, 1978), p. 144.

105. See the remark in Lukács's late autobiographical interview, *Gelebtes Denken*, p. 95.

106. Ibid., p. 95.

107. Georg Lukács, *Frühschriften II (Geschichte und Klassenbewusstsein)* (Neuwied: Luchterhand, 1968), p. 16.

108. Herbert Marcuse, *Eros and Civilisation* (Boston: Beacon Press, 1955).

109. Erich Fromm, *You shall be as Gods. A Radical Interpretation of the Old Testament and its Tradition* (New York: Holt, Rinehart and Winston, 1966), pp. 12–13.

110. Erich Fromm, *Beyond the Chains of Illusion. My Encounters with Marx and Freud* (New York, 1962), p. 5.

111. Erich Fromm, *Marx's Concept of Man* (New York: F. Unger, 1961), pp. 3, 5.

112. Gershom Scholem, *From Berlin to Jerusalem*, p. 155.

113. See Reiner Funk, *Mut zum Menschen. Erich Fromms Denken und Werk, seine humanistische Religion und Ethik* (Deutsche Verlagsanstalt, 1978), p. 19.

114. Gershom Scholem, *Mi-Berlin le-Yerushalayim*, (Jerusalem: Hotzaat Am Oved, 1982), p. 186. This is an enlarged version in Hebrew of *From Berlin to Jerusalem*.

115. Gershom Scholem, *Mi-Berlin le-Yerushalayim*, pp. 186–7.

116. Erich Fromm, 'Der Sabbath', *Imago*, vol. XIII, (Vienna: Internationaler Psychoanalytischer Verlag, 1927), pp. 226, 228, 233.

117. Erich Fromm, *The Forgotten Language. An Introduction to the Understanding of Dreams, Fairy Tales and Myths* (New York: Holt, Rinehart and Winston, 1951), pp. 246–7.

118. Erich Fromm, 'Zur Psychologie des Verbrechers und der strafenden Gesellschaft', *Imago*, vol. XVII, (1931), pp. 247–9.

119. Erich Fromm, *The Dogma of Christ and Other Essays on Religion, Psychology and Culture* (New York: Holt, Rinehart and Winston, 1963), pp. 35–49.

120. Ibid., pp. 56–65.

121. Franz Borkenau wrote the article. Cf. Martin Jay, *The Dialectical Imagination. A History of the Frankfurt School and the Institute of Social Research* (Boston, Mass.: Little, Brown and Company, 1973), p. 91.

122. Erich Fromm, *The Crisis of Psychoanalysis* (New York: Holt, Rinehart, and Winston, 1970), p. 151.

242   *Redemption and Utopia*

1

23. Erich Fromm, *The Crisis of Psychoanalysis*, pp. 84–5, 92–6, 104–9.
124. Walter Benjamin, *Gesammelte Schriften*, vol. II, 1, pp. 220–31.
125. Erich Fromm, Max Horkheimer, Herbert Marcuse, et al., *Autorität und Familie* (Paris: Felix Alcan, 1936), vol. 1, pp. 131–3.
126. Erich Fromm, *You shall be as Gods*, pp. 194–9.

8   Crossroads, Circles and Figures: A Few Examples

1. Hans Kohn, *Martin Buber*, pp. 61, 65.
2. Hans Kohn, *Living in a World Revolution. My Encounters with History* (New York: Trident Press, 1964), p. 67.
3. Ibid., pp. 63–4, 68.
4. Hans Kohn, 'Perspektiven', *Der Jude*, vol. IV (1919–1920), pp. 490–3.
5. Hans Kohn, *Nationalismus* (Vienna/ Leipzig: R. Löwith Verlag, 1922), pp. 124-6.
6. Hans Kohn, *Die politische Idee des Judentums* (Munich: Meyer & Jessen, 1924), pp. 18, 60, 61.
7. Hans Kohn, *Martin Buber*, pp. 194–5.
8. What is found is a (reversed) echo of his previous concerns. For example, in a work from 1949, Kohn criticized Marxism as a doctrine that was 'extremist in methods and goals', whose messianic vision of a 'total revolution bringing a total salvation' is the same as a 'secularized Kingdom of God' (Hans Kohn, *Political Ideologies of the Twentieth Century* (New York: Harper & Row, 1966), pp. 9–10).
9. Rudolf Kayser, 'Franz Werfel', in *Juden in der deutschen Literatur*, ed. Gustav Krojanker (Berlin: Welt Verlag, 1922).
10. Rudolf Kayser, 'Der neue Bund', *Der Jude*, vol. III (1918–1919), pp. 524–6.
11. Rudolf Kayser, 'Der jüdische Revolutionär', *Neue jüdische Monatshefte. Zeitschrift für Politik, Wirtschaft und Literatur in Ost und West*, vol. IV, (1919), pp. 96–8.
12. Gershom Scholem, *Walter Benjamin. The Story of a Friendship*, p. 100. It seems that Kayser presided over the meeting of the Free Student Association, where Benjamin presented his talk in 1914 on the life of students. Cf. Werner Kraft, 'Über Benjamin', in *Zur Aktualität Walter Benjamins*, ed. Siegfried Unseld (Frankfurt-am-Main: Suhrkamp Verlag, 1972), p. 59.
13. Rudolf Kayser, *Die Zeit ohne Mythos* (Berlin: Verlag Die Schmiede, 1923), pp. 24, 54. Rudolf Kayser emigrated to the United States and died in New York in 1964.
14. Manes Sperber, *God's Water Carriers*, trans. Joachim Neugroschel

(New York: Holmes & Meier, 1987), p. 12; and 'My Jewishness', *New German Critique*, no. 20 (Summer 1980), p. 10.

15. Manes Sperber, *God's Water Carriers*, pp. 11, 23, 56, 95. Translation slightly modified.

16. Manes Sperber, *God's Water Carriers*, p. 120; and *Le Pont inachevé* (Paris: Calmann-Levy, 1977), pp. 37, 69, 71.

17. Manes Sperber, *Le pont inachevé*, p. 38.

18. Manes Sperber, *God's Water Carriers*, pp. 16-17. Emphasis added.

19. See Elkana Margalit, 'Social and intellectual origins of the Hashomer Hatzair Youth Movement (1913–1920)', *Journal of Contemporary History*, vol. 4, no. 2, (1969). See also Manes Sperber, *God's Water Carriers*, p. 130. Sperber left the Zionist movement around 1923; it was not until later, around 1926–7, that the *Hashomer Hatzair* rallied to Marxism.

20. Manes Sperber, *God's Water Carriers*, p. 100. Scholem's and Benjamin's attitudes at the time were completely analagous.

21. Manes Sperber, *Le Pont inachevé*, pp. 12–15, 19, 57–60. As we have seen Lukács, too, was also fascinated by sacrificial individuals with a religious aura, notably Kaliaev.

22. Manes Sperber, *Alfred Adler. Der Mensch und seine Lehre* (Munich: J.F. Berhmann Verlag, 1926), pp. 37–8.

23. Manes Sperber, *Le Pont inachevé*, pp. 155–6. The remainder of the work does not provide an answer to the question. But it is clear that he was attracted by the libertarian, anti-authoritarian and anti-power aspects of anarchism.

24. Manes Sperber, *Le Pont inachevé*, pp. 168–206.

25. Manes Sperber, *Individuum und Gemeinschaft. Versuch einer sozialen Charakterologie* (Stuttgart: Klett-Cotta, 1978), pp. 221–2.

26. Manes Sperber, *Zur Analyse der Tyrannis* (Paris: Ed. Science et Littérature, 1938), p. 80. Cf. Sperber's essay, also in the same volume, 'Das Unglück begabt zu sein', p. 158.

27. Manes Sperber, *The Achilles Heel*, trans. Constantine FitzGibbon (London: Andre Deutsch Ltd., 1959), pp. 26, 28. Translation modified.

28. Manes Sperber, *The Achilles Heel*, pp. 81, 120. Shortly after Manes Sperber's death, one of his friends wrote: 'Sperber never turned away from the God in Whom he could no longer believe, and in his works as in his life, one often had the impression that it was to Him that Sperber was calling out, above the heads of his contemporaries.' (Jean Blot, 'Un optimisme désespéré', *Le Monde*, (7 February 1984).

29. Manes Sperber, *Au-delà de l'oubli* (Paris: Calmann-Levy, 1979), p. 133.

30. Manes Sperber, 'My Jewishness', p. 13.
31. Albert Ehrenstein, *Gedichte und Prosa* (Neuwied: Luchterhand, 1961), p. 207.
32. Historians of modern German literature refer to him by this term. Cf. Walter Sokel and Ernst Toller, *Deutsche Literatur im 20. Jahrhundert* (Heidelberg: Wolfgang Rothe, 1961), vol. II, pp. 284–5. In a letter written from prison in 1922, Toller mentioned among his favourite authors: Dostoevsky, Schopenhauer, Novalis, Hölderlin, Byron, Kleist, Goethe, Hebbel, Tolstoy, Hamsun, Rilke, Landauer. (Ernst Toller, *Prosa, Briefe, Dramen, Gedichte* (Reinbek bei Hamburg: Rowohlt, 1979), p. 51.)
33. Ernst Toller, *I was a German*, trans. Edward Crankshaw (New York: William Morrow and Co., 1934), p. 105.
34. Ernst Toller, *Quer durch, Reisebilder und Reden* (Berlin: Kiepenheuer Verlag, 1930), p. 191. At that time he formed a group of pacifist/socialist students in Heidelberg, known as the Kulturpolitischer Bund der Jugend in Deutschland. See Margarete Turnowski-Pinter, 'A student's friendship with Ernst Toller', *Year Book of the Leo Baeck Institute*, XV (1970), pp. 211–22.
35. Ernst Toller, *I was a German*, pp. 102, 108.
36. Ernst Toller, *Prosa, Briefe, Dramen, Gedichte*, pp. 284–5.
37. Ernst Toller, *Man and the Masses*, trans. Louis Untermeyer (Garden City, New York: Doubleday, Page & Co., 1924), p. 94.
38. H. W. G. Randall, 'The German Drama', *The Contemporary Review* (December 1925), p. 760.
39. Ernst Toller, *Man and the Masses*, p. 103.
40. Ernst Toller, *Prosa, Briefe, Dramen, Gedichte*, pp. 229–30.
41. Ernst Toller, *I was a German*, pp. 12, 20–3.
42. Ernst Toller, *Prosa, Briefe, Dramen, Gedichte*, pp. 245–6. Incidentally, although Toller explicitly rejected Zionism, he was interested in the fate of the Jewish community in Palestine; in 1925, he visited the country and the *kibbutzim* in particular. He subsequently stated that the Jews should ally themselves with the Arabs rather than with the Europeans (cf. 'Ernst Toller discusses Palestine', *American Hebrew* (2 June 1927); and Margaret Green, 'Communism in Munich and Palestine. What Ernst Toller saw', *The New Leader*, vol. II (December 1925).
43. Ernst Toller, *I was a German*, pp. 284–7.
44. Ernst Toller, *Prosa, Briefe, Dramen, Gedichte*, pp. 272, 277, 285. In this play, there is also an echo of Landauer's vision of the messianic role that Jews play in the universal human revolution.
45. Ernst Toller, *Man and the Masses*, p. 101.
46. Marianne Weber, *Max Weber. A Biography*, p. 661. According to

Thomas Mann, who also came to testify at Toller's trial, 'his writings are a type of prayer; in his own way, this poet is a believer'.

47. Kurt Hiller, '*Vorwort*' (1961) in Ernst Toller, *Prosa, Briefe, Dramen, Gedichte*, p. 19.

48. Ernst Toller, *Quer durch*, p. 82.

49. Gershom Scholem, *Walter Benjamin. The Story of a Friendship*, pp. 95–7.

50. Erich Unger, *Politik und Metaphysik* (Berlin: Verlag David, 1921), pp. 4, 5, 51.

51. Walter Benjamin, *Briefe*, vol. I, pp. 252–3.

52. Erich Unger, *Die staatenlose Bildung eines jüdischen Volkes* (Berlin: Verlag David, 1922), pp. 26, 28. Scholem had promised Benjamin that he would write a criticism of this book, but in the end he did not do so.

53. Julius Braunthal, *In Search of Millennium*, (London: Victor Gollancz, 1945), pp. 39, 79. Some historians also refer to Kurt Eisner's messianism and his 'libertarian socialism', despite his Kantian formation. Cf. Heinz Sproll, 'Messianisches Denken und pazifistische Utopie im Werk Kurt Eisners', in *Gegenseitige Einflüsse deutscher und jüdischer Kultur*, ed. Walter Grab, (University of Tel-Aviv: Institute of German History, 1983).

54. Eugen Leviné, 'Ahasver', *Emuna, Blätter für christliche-jüdische Zusammenarbeit*, vol. IV, no. 2, April 1969, pp. 338–9.

55. Gerhard Schmolze, 'Eugen Leviné-Nissen. Israelit unter den jüdischen Dissidenten der bayerischen Revolution', *Emuna*, vol. IV, no. 2, April 1969.

56. Rosa Meyer-Leviné, *Vie et mort d'un révolutionnaire. Eugen Leviné et les conseils ouvriers de Bavière* (Paris: Maspero, 1980).

57. Theodor Adorno, *Minima Moralia. Reflections from Damaged Life*, trans. E.F.N. Jephcott (Frankfurt: Verso Editions, 1985), p. 247. (Very similar thoughts were expressed in the previously mentioned article on Kafka). As for Hannah Arendt, her political ideas are too often reduced to an insipid rationalist liberalism; this does not take into consideration her sympathies for revolutionary spontaneity, direct democracy and Rosa Luxemburg's socialism. Nevertheless, despite her ties of friendship with Benjamin and Scholem, she did not in any way share their messianic/libertarian *Weltanschauung*.

58. Arthur Koestler, *Arrow in the Blue. An Autobiography* (New York: The Macmillan Company, 1952), p. 279.

59. For more on this subject, see Jutta Scherrer's remarkable work, *Die Petersburger religiös-philosophischen Vereinigungen*.

9   A French Exception: Bernard Lazare

1.   Jean Thorel, 'Les Romantiques allemands et les Symbolistes français' *Entretiens politiques et littéraires*, vol. III, no. 18 (September 1891).
2.   Thomas Carlyle, 'Symbols', in *Sartor Resartus: The Life and Opinions of Herr Teufelsdrockh* (London: Chapman & Hall, Ltd., 1988), Book III, ch. III, pp. 153, 155.
3.   Phoebus Jouve, 'Sur Bernard Lazare', *La chronique mondaine* (3 October 1908). Quoted by Nelly Wilson in *Bernard Lazare. Antisemitism and the problem of Jewish Identity in Late Nineteenth-century France* (Cambridge: Cambridge University Press, 1978), p. 9. My interpretation of Bernard Lazare owes much to this excellent book.
4.   For more information on this period, see Nelly Wilson, *Bernard Lazare*, pp. 9–29.
5.   Bernard Lazare, *Antisemitism. Its History and Causes* (New York: The International Library Publishing Co., 1903), p. 370.
6.   Bernard Lazare, 'Juifs et Israelites' [Jews and Israelites], *Entretiens politiques et littéraires*, vol. I, no. 6 (September 1890), p. 176.
7.   Bernard Lazare, *Le Fumier de Job* (Paris: Ed. Rieder, 1928), pp. 58–9.
8.   Bernard Lazare, Review of E. Picard, *Synthèse de l'antisémitisme*, in *Entretiens politiques et littéraires*, vol. IV, no. 27 (June 1892), pp. 265.
9.   Bernard Lazare, *Antisemitism*, pp. 17, 49–51.
10. Bernard Lazare, 'L'Eternel fugitif', *Entretiens politiques et littéraires*, vol. I, no. 4 (July 1890), p. 127.
11. Bernard Lazare, 'Les Incarnations', *Entretiens politiques et littéraires*, vol. II, no. 12 (March 1891), p. 77.
12. George Woodcock, *Anarchism* (Penguin Books, 1963), p. 286.
13. Bernard Lazare, Review of Kropotkin, *La Conquête du pain* in *Entretiens politiques et littéraires*, vol. IV, no. 25 (April 1892), p. 183.
14. Bernard Lazare, review of Mallarmé, *Villiers de l'Isle-Adam*, in *Entretiens politiques et littéraires*, vol. V, no. 32 (November 1892), pp. 234–5.
15. Bernard Lazare, Review of J. Peladan, *Tiphonia*, in *Entretiens politiques et littéraires*, vol. VI, no. 34 (January 1893), p. 43.
16. Nelly Wilson, *Bernard Lazare*, p. 34.
17. Ibid., p. 64.
18. Ibid., p. 52.
19. Charles Péguy, 'A Portrait of Bernard Lazare' in *Job's Dungheap. Essays on Jewish Nationalism and Social Revolution*, ed. Hannah

Arendt, trans. Harry Lorin Binsse (New York: Schocken Books, 1948), p. 25.

20. Bernard Lazare, 'Du népotisme', *Entretiens politiques et littéraires*, vol. III, no. 17 (August 1891), pp. 41–2.
21. Charles Peguy, 'A Portrait of Bernard Lazare', p. 29. There is also a striking elegy on page 30:

> For authority, for those in command, for the government, for force, for the state, for the reason of state, for gentlemen vested with authority, vested with reasons of state, he had such a hatred, such an aversion, such a constant revulsion that the hatred wiped them out, that they did not enter, did not have the honor of entering into his comprehension.

22. Bernard Lazare, *Antisemitism*, p. 134.
23. Bernard Lazare, 'Une école de liberté', *Le Magazine international* (December 1894).
24. Bernard Lazare, 'Du marxisme', *Le Paris* (21 August 1896), quoted by Nelly Wilson in *Bernard Lazare*, p. 56.
25. Bernard Lazare, 'Juifs et Israélites', *Entretiens politiques et littéraires*, vol. I, no. 6 (September 1890), p. 179.
26. Bernard Lazare, 'La solidarité juive', *Entretiens politiques et littéraires*, vol. I, no. 7 (October 1890), pp. 230–1.
27. Nelly Wilson, *Bernard Lazare*, p. 97.
28. Bernard Lazare, *Antisemitism*, p. 360.
29. Ibid., pp. 285–90.
30. Ibid., p. 294.
31. Ibid., pp. 310, 317.
32. Ibid., pp. 370–5.
33. Quoted by Nelly Wilson in *Bernard Lazare*, p. 144.
34. According to Charles Péguy, when some Dreyfusards wanted to create a great new daily newspaper and requested money from certain Jewish circles 'the Jewish capitalists and partners imposed only one condition: that Bernard Lazare should not contribute to it ('A Portrait of Bernard Lazare', p. 26). See Michael R. Marrus, *Les Juifs de France à l'époque de l'Affaire Dreyfus* (Paris: Calmann-Levy, 1972), pp. 216–18.
35. Charles Péguy, 'L'Epreuve', *Cahiers de la Quinzaine*, no. 7 (undated).
36. Bernard Lazare, 'Antisémitisme et revolution', *Les Lettres prolétariennes*, no. 1 (March 1895), pp. 13–14.
37. Bernard Lazare Papers (Alliance Israélite Universelle), MS 422, Box 3, Note no. 470. Of course, Lazare could not have predicted at the time that the genocide against the Jews would be perpetrated by 'pagan' barbarians, coming from a nation with a Protestant majority.
38. Charles Péguy, 'A Portrait of Bernard Lazare' in *Job's Dungheap*,

p. 34. Translation slightly modified. He also used the following
(typically romantic) beautiful words to describe Lazare's libertarian integrity:

> He had freedom in his skin, in his marrow and in his blood; in his spine. And
> not at all an intellectual and conceptual freedom, a bookish freedom, a ready-
> made freedom, a library freedom. A trade-marked freedom. But a freedom,
> rather, of the wellspring, a wholly organic and living freedom. (p. 39)

39. Quoted by Nelly Wilson, (*Bernard Lazare*, p. 231), who argues that
Lazare's anarchist conception of nationality 'made his Zionism
a revolutionary, Messianic Zionism reminiscent of Moses Hess'
(p. 230).
40. Bernard Lazare, 'Nécessité d'être soi-même', *Zion*, (1897), p. 3.
41. Quoted in Nelly Wilson, *Bernard Lazare*, pp. 232-3.
42. Quoted in Michael R. Marrus, *Les Juifs de France à l'époque de l'Affaire
Dreyfus*, p. 307. For more on the correspondence between Herzl and
Lazare, see the article (written in Hebrew) by Edmund Silberner,
'Bernar Lazar ve Ha-Zionut' [Bernard Lazare and Zionism], *Shivat
Zion*, II–III (1953). For additional information about the break in
relations between Lazare and Herzl, see Robert Wistrich, *Revolutionary Jews from Marx to Trotsky* (London: Harrap, 1976), p. 148.
According to Hannah Arendt, the two men's attitudes to anti-
Semitism were also diametrically opposed: Herzl thought it was
important to take advantage of the anti-Semites' encouragement
of a Jewish exodus from Europe. What Lazare sought, on the other
hand, 'was not an escape from antisemitism but a mobilization
of the people against its foes.' (Hannah Arendt, *The Jew as Pariah*
pp. 127–8).
43. Cf. Nelly Wilson, *Bernard Lazare* p. 232.
44. Bernard Lazare, *L'Oppression des Juifs dans l'Europe orientale. Les Juifs
en Roumanie* (Paris: Editions des Cahiers, 1902), p. 103. A curious
detail: the pages of the copy of this brochure I consulted at the
Bibliothèque de la Sorbonne, had not yet been cut. From 1902
until January 1987, no one, among the successive generations of
students and teachers at the Sorbonne had been curious enough to
open it. Just one example, among others, of the oblivion that fell
on Lazare–an oblivion already denounced by Péguy in 1910.
45. Bernard Lazare Papers, MS 522, Box 4, Notes 253 and 62. In some
notes, references can still be found that advocate a return to the
ancestral country; several notes include a dialogue between a
'patriotic' (Zionist) Jew and a 'cosmopolitan' (international) Jew,
although the exact stance of the author is not disclosed. In other
notes, the impression is given that Lazare was expressing his own
feelings. For example, in the note entitled, 'Zionism', he explains

the movement as a reaction against the old anti-Semitic grievance that 'Jews have no homeland'. In response, they tried 'to show that they wanted to create, on rocks and in sand, a small, wretched State that would become their homeland, – one that the best of Jews used to scorn enough, and which they gave up well before it was destroyed by Roman authorities' (Box 4, Note 61).

46. Bernard Lazare, *Le Fumier de Job*, p. 166.
47. Nelly Wilson, *Bernard Lazare*, p. 268.
48. Bernard Lazare, *Le Fumier de Job*, pp. 166–7.
49. Bernard Lazare, *Le Fumier de Job*, p. 118; Bernard Lazare papers, Box 3, Notes 529, 530; and Box 4, Note 631.
50. Bernard Lazare Papers, Box 3, Note 458.
51. Bernard Lazare Papers, Box 5, Folder 'Sabbatai Sevi'.
52. Bernard Lazare Papers, Box 5, Folder 'Jesus'.
53. Charles Péguy, 'A Portrait of Bernard Lazare', in *Job's Dungheap*, pp. 22, 27, 36.
54. Bernard Lazare, *Le Fumier de Job*, p. 84.
55. Hans Kohn, 'Bernard Lazare und die Dreyfus-Affaire', in *Der Jude* (Berlin: Jüdischer Verlag, 1924), p. 291.

Conclusion: 'Historical Messianism': A Romantic/Messianic Concept of History

1. Theodor Adorno, *Minima Moralia. Reflections from Damaged Life*, p. 192.
2. The English translation of the *Theses* is taken from *Illuminations*, pp. 253–64.
3. *Illuminations*, pp. 256, 260–1. See also Walter Benjamin, *Gesammelte Schriften*, vol. I, 3, p. 1232: 'Confidence in quantitative accumulation is at the root both of the narrow doctrine of progress and of confidence in the "backing of the masses".'
4. Sigmund Mowinckel, *He that Cometh*, pp. 105–6.
5. Karl Mannheim, *Ideology and Utopia*, p. 203.
6. Georg Lukács, *History and Class Consciousness*, trans. Rodney Livingstone (London: Merlin Press 1971), p. 117. This problematic has been developed further by some of the most insightful critics of modernity today, such as Jean Chesnaux (Cf. Jean Chesnaux, *De la modernité* (Paris: La Découverte, 1983), p. 36.
7. Walter Benjamin, *Gesammelte Schriften*, vol. II, 1, pp. 133–137.
8. Walter Benjamin, *Illuminations*, pp. 262, 263, 264.
9. Walter Benjamin, *Gesammelte Schriften*, vol. I, 3, p. 1231.
10. Walter Benjamin, *Gesammelte Schriften*, vol. I, 3, pp. 1229–30.

Bibliography

Abensour, Miguel, 'L'utopie socialiste: une nouvelle alliance de la politique et de la religion', *Le Temps de la réflexion*, Paris, Gallimard, 1981.
— *Walter Benjamin et Paris*, Paris, Cerf, 1986.
— and Pelosse, V, 'Libérer l'Enfermé', 'Postface' to Blanqui, *Instructions pour une prise d'armes et autres textes*, Paris, La Tête des Feuilles, 1973.
Adorno, Theodor, *Über Walter Benjamin*, Frankfurt-am-Main, Suhrkamp Verlag, 1970.
— 'Henkel, Krug und frühe Erfahrung', in *Noten zur Literatur*, Frankfurt-am-Main, Suhrkamp Verlag, 1974, vol. IV.
— *Prisms*, Cambridge, Mass., MIT Press, 1982.
— *Minima Moralia. Reflections from Damaged Life*, trans. E.F.N. Jephcott, Frankfurt, Verso Editions, 1985.
Altenhofer, Norbert, 'Tradition als Revolution: Gustav Landauer "geworden-werdendes" Judentum', in *Jews and Germans from 1860–1933. The Problematic Symbiosis*, ed. David Bronsen, Heidelberg, Carl Winter Universitätsverlag, 1979.
Arendt, Hannah, *Rahel Varnhagen. The Life of a Jewish Woman*, trans. Richard and Clara Winston, New York, Harcourt Brace Jovanovich, 1974.
— *The Jew as Pariah. Jewish Identity and Politics in the Modern Age*, New York, Grove Press, 1978.
— 'Franz Kafka', in *Franz Kafka. An Anthology of Marxist Criticism*, ed. and trans. Kenneth Hughes, London, University Press of New England, 1981.
— ed., *Illuminations*, trans. Harry Zohn, New York, Schocken Books, 1969.
Baioni, G., *Kafka. Letteratura ed ebraismo*, Turin, Einaudi, 1979.
Balázs, Béla, 'Notes from a Diary (1911–1921)', *New Hungarian Quarterly*, no. 47, 1972.
Band, Arnold J., 'Kafka and the Beiliss Affair', *Comparative Literature*, vol. 32, no. 2, Spring 1980.
Barchusen, Johannes Conradus, *Pyrosophia*, Batavorum, Impensis Cornelii Bautestein, 1698.
Baudelaire, Charles, *Œuvres complètes*, Paris, Seuil, 1968.
Beer, Peter, *Geschichte, Lehren und Meinungen aller bestandenen und noch*

bestehender religiösen Sekten der Juden und der Geheimlehre oder Kabbalah, Brünn, Joseph Georg Frassler, 1823.

Benjamin, Walter, *Briefe*, 2 vols, Frankfurt-am-Main, Suhrkamp Verlag, 1966.

— *Poésie et Révolution*, Paris, Denoël, 1971.

— *Der Begriff der Kunstkritik in der deutschen Romantik*, Frankfurt-am-Main, Suhrkamp Verlag, 1973.

— *The Origin of German Tragic Drama*, trans. John Osborne, London, New Left Books, 1977.

— *Gesammelte Schriften*, ed. Rolf Tiedemann and Hermann Schweppenhauser, 5 vols, Frankfurt-am-Main, Suhrkamp Verlag, 1977.

— *Reflections: Essays, Aphorisms, Autobiographical Writings*, trans. Edmund Jephcott, New York, Harcourt Brace Jovanovich, 1978.

— *One Way Street*, trans. Edmund Jephcott and Kingsley Shorter, London, New Left Books, 1979.

— *Understanding Brecht*, London, Verso Editions, 1984.

— *Charles Baudelaire: A Lyric Poet in the Era of High Capitalism*, trans. Harry Zohn and Quintin Hoare, London, Verso Editions, 1985.

— *Moscow Diary*, trans. Richard Sieburth, Cambridge, Mass., Harvard University Press, 1986.

Bergman, T.O., *Traité des affinités chimiques, ou attractions électives*, Paris, Chez Buisson, 1788.

Biale, David Joseph, 'The Demonic in History. Gershom Scholem and the Revision of Jewish Historiography', Ph.D. Thesis, University of California, 1977.

— *Gershom Scholem. Kabbalah and Counter-History*, Cambridge, Mass., Harvard University Press, 1979.

Blanchot, Maurice, *De Kafka à Kafka*, Paris, Gallimard, 1981.

Bloch, Ernst, *Geist der Utopie*, 1st ed., Munich-Leipzig, Duncker & Humblot, 1918.

— 'Über einige politische Programme und Utopien in der Schweiz', *Archiv für Sozialwissenschaft und Sozialpolitik*, vol. 46, 1918–19.

— *Geist der Utopie*, 2nd ed., Frankfurt-am-Main, Suhrkamp Verlag, 1973.

— *Durch die Wuste, 1923.*

— *Politische Messungen, Pestzeit, Vormärz*, Frankfurt-am-Main, Suhrkamp Verlag, 1970.

— *The Principle of Hope*, trans. Neville Plaice, Stephen Plaice and Paul Knight, Cambridge, Mass., The MIT Press, 1986.

— *Thomas Münzer, als Theologe der Revolution*, Frankfurt-am-Main, Suhrkamp Verlag, 1972.

— *Briefe, Vol. I: 1903–1975*, Frankfurt-am-Main, Suhrkamp Verlag, 1985.

Blot, Jean, 'Un optimisme désespéré', *Le Monde*, 7 February 1984.

Boerhave, Hermannus, *Elementa Chemiae*, Lugduni Batavorum, Apud Isaacum Severinum, 1732.

Bolz, Norbert, 'Charisma und Souveränität. Carl Schmitt und Walter Benjamin im Schatten Max Webers', in *Religionstheorie und politische Theologie*, ed. Jacob Taubes, Munich, Wilhelm Fink Verlag, 1983, vol. I.

Braunthal, Julius, *In Search of Millenium*, London, Victor Gollancz, 1945.

Breines, Paul, 'The Jew as Revolutionary. The Case of Gustav Landauer', *Year Book of the Leo Baeck Institute*, no. XII, London, 1967.

Brod, Max, *Franz Kafka: A Biography*, trans. G. Humphrey Roberts and Robert Winston, New York, Schocken Books, 1960.

— *Über Franz Kafka*, Frankfurt, S. Fischer Verlag, 1966.

— Postscript to the first edition of Kafka's *Das Schloss*, in Franz Kafka, *Gesammelte Schriften*, Berlin, Schocken Verlag, 1946, vol. IV.

Buber, Martin, 'Über Jakob Böhme', *Wiener Rundschau*, vol. V, no. 12, 1901.

— 'Kultur und Zivilisation', *Kunstwart*, vol. XIV, 1901.

— 'Zion, der Staat und die Menschheit. Bemerkungen zu Hermann Cohens "Antwort"', *Der Jude*, vol. I, 1916–17.

— 'Die Revolution und wir', *Der Jude*, vol. III, 1918–19.

— 'Landauer und die Revolution', *Masken*, no. 14, 1918–19; no. 19, 1919.

— 'Gemeinschaft', 1919.

— *Drei Reden über das Judentum*, Frankfurt, Rutten & Loenig, 1920.

— 'In später Stunde', *Der Jude*, vol. V, 1920–21.

— 'Aussprache über den Staat', unpublished lecture given in Zurich, 29 November 1923.

— 'Staat und Gemeinschaft', unpublished lecture given in February 1924.

— 'Das messianische Mysterium (Jesaja 53)', unpublished lecture given in Berlin, 6 April 1925.

— *Die chassidischen Bücher*, Berlin, Schocken Verlag, 1927.

— *Königtum Gottes*, Berlin, Schocken Verlag, 1932.

— *Kampf um Israel*, Berlin, Schocken Verlag, 1933.

— *Pfade in Utopia*, Heidelberg, 1950.

— *The Legend of the Baal-Schem*, trans. Maurice Friedman, New York, Harper & Brothers, 1955.

— *Werke*, vol. I, Heidelberg, Lambert Schneider Verlag, 1962.

— *Werke*, vol. III, Heidelberg, Lambert Schneider Verlag, 1963.

— *On Judaism*, trans. Eva Jospe, New York, Schocken Books, 1967.

— *Briefwechsel aus sieben Jahrzehnten*, Heidelberg, Lambert Schneider Verlag, 1972.

— 'Alte und neue Gemeinschaft', *AJS Review*, 1976.

— *Utopie et socialisme*, Paris, Aubier, 1977.

Buci-Glucksmann, Christine, 'Walter Benjamin et l'ange de l'histoire: une archéologie de la modernité', *L'Écrit du Temps*, no. 2, 1983.

Caillois, R. 'La Fête', *Le Collège de sociologie*, Ed. Denis Hollier, Paris, Gallimard, 1979.

Carlyle, Thomas, 'Symbols', in *Sartor Resartus: The Life and Opinions of Herr Teufelsdrockh*, London, Chapman & Hall, Ltd., 1988, Book III, ch. III.

Carrouges, Michel, 'Dans le rire et les larmes de la vie', *Cahiers de la compagnie M. Renaud et J.-L. Barrault*, October 1957.

Chesnaux, Jean, *De la modernité*, Paris, La Découverte, 1983.

Christen, Anton, *Ernst Blochs Metaphysik der Materie*, Bône, Bouvier, 1979.

Cohn, Norman, *The Pursuit of the Millenium. Revolutionary Millenarians and Mystical Anarchists of the Middle Ages*, London, Secker & Warburg, 1957.

Congdon, Lee, *The Young Lukács*, London, New England, The University of North Carolina Press, 1983.

Darien, G., 'Anarchistes', *L'Ennemi du Peuple*, Paris, Champ Libre, 1972.

Dawidowicz, Lucy S., ed., *The Golden Tradition. Jewish Life and Thought in Eastern Europe*, Boston, Beacon Press, 1967.

Deutscher, Isaac, *The Non-Jewish Jew and Other Essays*, London, Oxford University Press, 1968.

Döblin, Alfred, 'Die Romane von Franz Kafka', *Die literarische Welt*, 4 March 1927.

Ehrenstein, Albert, *Gedichte und Prosa*, Neuwied, Luchterhand, 1961.

Eisenbarth, D., 'Ernst Bloch – Empiriker der Mystischen', *Schwarze Protokolle*, no. 16, 1978.

Eisenmenger, Andreas, *Entdecktes Judentum*, 1701.

Elbogen, Ismar, *Geschichte der Juden in Deutschland*, Berlin, E. Lichtenstein Verlag, 1935.

Emrich, Wilhelm, *Franz Kafka*, Frankfurt, Athenäum Verlag, 1961.

Ertel, Rachel, *Le Shtetl, la bourgade juive de Pologne*, Paris, Payot, 1982.

Feher, Ferenc, *Die Seele und das Leben. Studien zum frühen Lukács*, Frankfurt-am-Main, Suhrkamp Verlag, 1977.

Ferenczi, Rosemarie, *Kafka, subjectivité, histoire et structures*, Paris, Klincksieck, 1975.

Fischer, Ernst, 'Kafka Conference', in *Franz Kafka. An Anthology of Marxist Criticism*, ed. and trans. Kenneth Hughes, London, University Press of New England, 1981.

Franck, Adolphe, *La Kabbale ou la philosophie religieuse des Hébreux*, Paris, 1843.

Fromm, Erich, 'Der Sabbath', *Imago*, vol. XIII, Vienna, Internationaler Psychoanalytischer Verlag, 1927.

— 'Zur Psychologie des Verbrechers und der strafenden Gesellschaft', *Imago*, vol. XVII, 1931.

— *The Forgotten Language. An Introduction to the Understanding of Dreams, Fairy Tales and Myths*, New York, Holt, Rinehart and Winston, 1951.

— *Marx's Concept of Man*, New York, Frederick Unger, 1961.

— *Beyond the Chains of Illusion. My Encounters with Marx and Freud*, New York, 1962.

— *The Dogma of Christ and Other Essays on Religion, Psychology and Culture*, New York, Holt, Rinehart and Winston, 1963.

— *You shall be as Gods. A Radical Interpretation of the Old Testament and its Tradition*, New York, Holt, Rinehart and Winston, 1966.

— *The Crisis of Psychoanalysis*, New York, Holt, Rinehart and Winston, 1970.

Fromm, Erich, Horkheimer, Max, and Marcuse, Herbert, et al., *Autorität und Familie*, Paris, Felix Alcan, 1936.

Funk, Reiner, *Mut zum Menschen. Erich Fromms Denken und Werk, seine humanistische Religion und Ethik*, Deutsche Verlagsanstalt, 1978.

Goethe, J.W., *Elective Affinities*, trans. James Anthony Froude and R. Dillon Boylan, New York, Frederick Unger, 1962.

Goldstein, Moritz, 'Deutsch-Jüdischer Parnass', *Kunstwart*, 11 March 1912.

Green, Margaret, 'Communism in Munich and Palestine. What Ernst Toller saw', *The New Leader*, vol. II, December 1925.

Gressmann, Hugo, *Der Messias*, Göttingen, Vandenhoeck & Ruprecht, 1929.

Grunefeld, Frederic V., *Prophets without Honour. A Background to Freud, Kafka, Einstein and their World*, New York, McGraw-Hill, 1980.

Guillen, Pierre, *L'Allemagne de 1848 a nos jours*, Paris: Nathan, 1970.

Habermas,J.,'L'ActualitedeWalterBenjamin'.Lacritique:prisedeconscience ou préservation', *Revue d'Esthétique*, no. 1, Paris, Privat, 1981.

Haimson, L. H., *The Russian Marxists and the Origins of Bolchevism*, Boston, Beacon Press, 1955.

Hammerstein, Franz Freiherr von, *Das Messias-Problem bei Martin Buber*, Stuttgart, Kohlhammer Verlag, 1958.

Heinrich, Nathalie, 'L'Aura de Walter Benjamin. Notes sur l'œuvre d'art à l'ère de sa reproductibilité technique', *Actes de la recherche en sciences sociales*, no. 49, September 1983.

Heller, Erich. 'The World of Franz Kafka', in *Kafka. A Collection of Critical Essays*, ed. Ronald Gray, Englewood Cliffs, Prentice Hall, 1965.

— *Franz Kafka*, Princeton, Princeton University Press, 1982.

Henel, Ingeborg, 'The legend of the doorkeeper and its significance for Kafka's *Trial*', in *Twentieth Century Interpretations of 'The Trial'*, ed. James Rolleston, Englewood Cliffs, Prentice Hall, 1976.

— *Franz Kafka. Themen und Probleme*, Göttingen, Vandenhoeck & Ruprecht, 1980.

Henning, Günther, *Walter Benjamin zwischen Marxismus und Theologie*, Olten Wolter Verlag, 1974.

Hermsdorf, Klaus, *Kafka. Weltbild und Roman*, Berlin, Rutten & Loening, 1961.

Hervieu-Léger, Danièle, 'Apocalyptique écologique et "retour" de la religion', *Archives de Sciences Sociales des Religions*, no. 53/1,January–March 1982.

Heydorn, Heinz Joachin, 'Preface' to Gustav Landauer, *Zwang und Befreiung*, Cologne, Hegner Bücherei, 1968.

Hobsbawm, Eric, *Primitive Rebels*, New York, Norton, 1965.

Hoffmann, E.T.A., 'The Sandman', in *Selected Writings of E.T.A. Hoffmann*, trans. Leonard J. Kent and Elizabeth C. Knight, Chicago, The University of Chicago Press, 1969, vol. I.

Holitscher, Arthur, *Amerika heute und morgen*, Berlin, Fischer Verlag, 1912.

Holy Scriptures (English edition), Philadelphia, The Jewish Publication Society of America, 1955.

Honigsheim, Paul, 'Soziologie der Mystik', in *Versuche zu einer Soziologie des Wissens*, ed. Max Scheler, Leipzig, Duncker & Humblot, 1924.

— 'Der Max-Weber-Kreis in Heidelberg', *Kölner Vierteljahrschrift für Soziologie*, no. 3, 1926.

— *On Max Weber*, New York, Free Press, 1968.

Janz, Rolf, and Lindner, Burkhardt, Colloquium on Walter Benjamin held in Paris, June 1983. Published in the collection, *Walter Benjamin et Paris*.

Janouch, Gustav, *Kafka und seine Welt*, Vienna, Verlag Hans Deutsch, 1965.

— *Conversations with Kafka*, trans. Goronwy Rees, 1st ed., London, Derek Verschoyle, 1953.

— *Conversations with Kafka*, trans. Goronwy Rees, 2nd ed., London, Quartet Books, 1985.

Jay, Martin, *The Dialectical Imagination. A History of the Frankfurt School and the Institute of Social Research*, Boston, Mass., Little, Brown and Company, 1973.

Jouve, Phoebus, 'Sur Bernard Lazare', *La Chronique mondaine*, 3 October 1908.

Kafka, Franz, 'The Problem of our Laws', in *The Great Wall of China*, trans. Willa and Edwin Muir, New York, Schocken Books, 1948.

— 'In the Penal Colony', in *The Penal Colony*, trans. Willa and Edwin Muir, New York, Schocken Books, 1948.

— *Hochzeitsvorbereitungen auf dem Lande und andere Prosa aus dem Nachlass*, New York, S. Fischer Verlag and Schocken Books, 1953.

— *Letters to Milena*, trans. Tania and James Stern, New York, Schocken Books, 1953.

— *The Diaries of Franz Kafka (1910–1913)*, London, Penguin Books, 1964.

— *America*, trans. Willa and Edwin Muir, London, Secker & Warburg, 1967.

— *The Castle*, trans. Willa and Edwin Muir, New York, Alfred A. Knopf, 1968.

— *Shorter Works*, trans. Malcolm Pasley, London, Secker & Warburg, 1973.

— *The Diaries of Franz Kafka (1914-1923)*, New York, Schocken Books, 1974.

— *Letters to Friends, Family, and Editors*, trans. Richard and Clara Winston, New York, Schocken Books, 1977.

— *Letters to Felice*, trans. James Stern and Elizabeth Duckworth, London, Penguin Books, 1978.

— *Wedding Preparations in the Country*, London, Penguin Books, 1978.

— *The Trial*, trans. Willa and Edwin Muir, New York, Schocken Books, 1984.

Kaiser, Gerhard, 'Walter Benjamin, "Geschichtsphilosophische Thesen"'. in *Materialien zu Benjamins Thesen 'Über den Begriff der Geschichte'*, Ed. P. Bulthaup, Frankfurt-am-Main, Suhrkamp Verlag, 1975.

256 *Redemption and Utopia*

Kambas, Chryssoula, 'Walter Benjamin und Gottfried Salomon. Bericht über eine unveröffentliche Korrespondenz', *Deutsche Vierteljahrschrift für Literaturwissenschaft und Geistesgeschichte*, vol. 57, December 1982.
— 'Wider den "Geist der Zeit". Die antifaschistische Politik Fritz Liebs und Walter Benjamin', in *Religionstheorie und politische Theologie*, ed. Jacob Taubes, Munich, Wilhelm Fink Verlag, 1983, vol. I.
Karady, Victor, and Kemény, Istvan, 'Les Juifs dans la structure des classes en Hongrie', *Actes de la recherche en sciences sociales*, no. 22, June 1978.
Kauf, Robert. 'Kafka's "A Report to the Academy"', *Modern Language Quarterly*, XV, 1954.
Kayser, Rudolf, 'Der neue Bund', *Der Jude*, vol. III, 1918–19.
— 'Der jüdische Revolutionär', *Neue jüdische Monatshefte. Zeitschrift für Politik, Wirtschaft und Literatur in Ost und West*, vol. IV, 1919.
— 'Franz Werfel', in *Juden in der deutschen Literatur*, ed. Gustav Krojanker, Berlin, Welt Verlag, 1922.
— *Die Zeit ohne Mythos*, Berlin, Verlag Die Schmiede, 1923.
Klausner, Joseph, *The Messianic Idea in Israel from its Beginning to the Completion of the Mishnah*, New York, The Macmillan Company, 1955.
Knutter, Hans Helmuth, *Die Juden und die deutsche Linke in der Weimarer Republik (1918–1933)*, Düsseldorf, Droste Verlag, 1971.
Koestler, Arthur, *Arrow in the Blue. An Autobiography*, New York, The Macmillan Company, 1952.
Kohn, Hans, 'Perspektiven', *Der Jude*, vol. IV, 1919–20.
— *Die politische Idee des Judentums*, Munich, Meyer & Jessen, 1924.
— 'Bernard Lazare und die Dreyfus-Affaire', in *Der Jude*, Berlin, Jüdischer Verlag, 1924.
— *Nationalismus*, Vienna/Leipzig, R. Löwith Verlag, 1922.
— *Martin Buber, sein Werk und seine Zeit*, Hellerau, Verlag von Jakob Hegner, 1930.
— *Political Ideologies of the Twentieth Century*, New York, Harper & Row, 1966.
— *Living in a World Revolution. My Encounters with History*, New York, Trident Press, 1964.
Kraft, Werner, *Gespräche mit Martin Buber*, Munich, Kosel Verlag, 1966.
— 'Über Benjamin', in *Zur Aktualität Walter Benjamins*, ed. Siegfried Unseld, Frankfurt-am-Main, Suhrkamp Verlag, 1972.
Kulback, Moishe, *Lundi*, Lausanne, Edition L'Age d'Homme, 1982.
Kundera, Milan, 'Quelque part là-derrière', *Le Débat*, no. 8, June 1981.
Landauer, Gustav, 'Die religiöse Jugenderziehung', *Die Freie Bühne*, February 1891.
— Letter to Ida Wolf dated 15 June 1891, *Landauer Archives*, International Institute of Social History, Amsterdam, File X.
— 'Durch Absonderung zur Gemeinschaft', *Die Neue Gemeinschaft*, no. 2, Leipzig, Eugen Diederichs, 1901.
— *Unsere Sprache übertragen von G. Landauer*, Berlin, Verlag Karl Schnabel, 1903.

— 'Die Legende des Baalschem', *Das literarische Echo*, vol. 13, no. 2, 1 October 1910.
— *Aufruf zum Sozialismus*, Berlin, Paul Cassirer, 1919.
— 'Judentum und Sozialismus', *Die Arbeit* (organ for the Zionist People's Socialist Party *Hapoel Hatzair*) vol. 2 , June 1920.
— *Der werdende Mensch, Aufsätze über Leben und Schriften*, Potsdam, Gustav Kiepenhauer Verlag, 1921.
— 'Vor fünfundzwanzig Jahren', *Rechenschaft*, 2nd ed., Cologne, 1924.
— *Beginnen. Aufsätze über Sozialismus*, Cologne, Marcan-Block Verlag, 1924.
— 'Die deutsche Romantik in der Literatur', Library of the Hebrew University of Jerusalem, Gustav Landauer Archives, MS Var. 432, File 14.
— *Briefe*, 2 vols.
— 'Die Revolution', Berlin, Kromer Verlag, 1977.
Laqueur, Walter, *Weimar: A Cultural History 1918–1933*, New York, G.P. Putnum's Sons, 1974.
Lazare, Bernard, 'Juifs et Israelites', *Entretiens politiques et littéraires*, vol. I, no. 6, September 1890.
— 'L'Eternel Fugitif', *Entretiens politiques et littéraires*, vol. I, no. 4, July 1890.
— 'La Solidarité juive', *Entretiens politiques et littéraires*, vol. I, no. 7, October 1890.
— 'Les Incarnations', *Entretiens politiques et littéraires*, vol. II, no. 12, March 1891.
— 'Du népotisme', *Entretiens politiques et littéraires*, vol. III, no. 17, August 1891.
— Review of Kropotkin, *La Conquête du Pain*, in *Entretiens politiques et littéraires*, vol. IV, no. 25, April 1892.
— Review of E. Picard, *Synthèse de l'antisémitisme*, in *Entretiens politiques et littéraires*, vol. IV, no. 27, July 1892.
— Review of Mallarmé, *Villiers de l'Isle-Adam*, in *Entretiens politiques et littéraires*, vol. V, no. 32, November 1892.
— Review of J. Peladan, *Tiphonia*, in *Entretiens politiques et littéraires*, vol. VI, no. 34, January 1893.
— 'Une école de liberté', *Le Magazine international*, December 1894.
— 'Antisémitisme et révolution', *Les Lettres prolétariennes*, no. 1, March 1895.
— 'Nécessité d'être soi-même', *Zion*, 1897.
— *L'oppression des Juifs dans l'Europe orientale. Les Juifs en Roumanie*, Paris, Editions der Cahiers, 1902.
— *Antisemitism. Its History and Causes*, New York, The International Library Publishing Co., 1903.
— *Le Fumier de Job*, Paris, Edition Rieder, 1928.
Bernard Lazare Papers, Alliance Israélite Universelle.
Lenk, Elizabeth, 'Indiscretions of the Literary Beast: Pariah Consciousness of Women Writers since Romanticism', *New German Critique*, no. 27, Fall 1982.

Redemption and Utopia

Levinas, E., 'Sur la mort dans la pensée de Ernst Bloch', in *Utopie, marxisme selon Ernst Bloch,* ed. G. Raulet, Paris, Payot, 1976.

Leviné, Eugen, 'Ahasver', *Emuna, Blatter für christliche-jüdische Zusammenarbeit,* vol. IV, no. 2, April 1969.

Link-Salinger, Ruth, *Gustav Landauer, Philosopher of Utopia,* Indianapolis, Hackett, 1977.

Linse, Ulrich, *Gustav Landauer und die Revolutionszeit (1918–1919),* Berlin, Karin Kramer Verlag, 1974.

Löwenthal, Leo, 'Das Dämonische. Entwurf einer negativen Religionsphilosophie', in *Gabe Herrn Rabbiner Dr. Nobel zum 50. Geburtstag,* Frankfurt, J. Kaufmann Verlag, 1921.

— 'Franz von Baader: Ein religiöser Soziologe der Soziologie', *Internationales Jahrbuch für Religionssoziologie,* Cologne, Westdeutscher Verlag, 1966–7.

— 'Wir haben nie im Leben diesen Ruhm erwartet', in *Die Zerstörung einer Zukunft,* ed. Mathias Greffrath, Reinbek bei Hamburg, Rowohlt, 1979.

— *Mitmachen wollte ich nie. Ein Autobiographisches Gësprach mit Helmut Dubiel,* Frankfurt-am-Main, Suhrkamp Verlag, 1980.

— *Schriften,* Frankfurt-am-Main, Suhrkamp Verlag, 1984.

Löwy, Michael, 'Interview with Ernst Bloch', *New German Critique,* no. 9, 1976.

— 'Idéologie révolutionnaire et messianisme mystique chez le jeune Lukács 1910–1919', *Archives de Sciences sociales des Religions,* no. 43/1,1978.

— *Georg Lukács: From Romanticism to Bolshevism,* London, New Left Books, 1979.

— *Marxisme et romantisme révolutionnaire,* Paris, Edition du Sycomore, 1980.

— 'Weber against Marx. The polemic with historical materialism in *The Protestant Ethic',* *Science and Society,* vol. 53, no. 1, Spring 1989.

— and Sayre, Robert, 'Figures of Romantic Anti-Capitalism', *New German Critique,* no. 32, Spring 1984.

Lukács, Georgy, 'Zsido miszticizmus', *Szellem,* no. 2, 1911.

— 'Notizbuch', Lukács Archives, Budapest, 1911.

— 'Bibliography', vol. 1, Lukács Archives, Budapest, 1902–10.

— *Frühschriften II (Geschichte und Klassenbewusstsein),* Neuwied, Luchterhand, 1968.

— *Magyar irodalom, magyar kultura,* Budapest, Gondolat, 1970.

— *Die Theorie des Romans,* trans. Anna Bostock, Darmstadt and Neuwied, Luchterhand Verlag, 1971.

— *History and Class Consciousness,* trans. Rodney Livingstone, London, Merlin Press, 1971.

— 'Der Bolschewismus als moralisches Problem', in *Taktik und Ethik,* Neuwied, Luchterhand, 1975.

— 'Unpublished Autobiography', in *Littérature, philosophie, marxisme (1922–1923),* collected by Michael Löwy, Paris, PUF, 1978.

— *Gelebtes Denken, Eine Autobiographie im Dialog*, Frankfurt-am-Main, Suhrkamp Verlag, 1980.

— *Correspondance de jeunesse (1908–1917)*, Budapest, Ed. Corvina, 1981.

— *Dostojevsky, Notizen und Entwurfe*, Budapest, Akademiai Kiado, 1985.

— and Ernst, Paul, *Dokumente einer Freundschaft*, Emsdetten, Verlag Lechte, 1974.

Lunn, Eugen, *Prophet of Community. The Romantic Socialism of Gustav Landauer*, Berkeley, University of California Press, 1973.

Mannhein, Karl, *Ideology and Utopia*, New York, Harcourt, Brace & Co., 1954.

— *Wissenssoziologie*, Neuwied, Luchterhand, 1964.

Marcuse, Herbert, *Eros and Civilisation*, Boston, Beacon Press, 1955.

Mares, Michal, 'Setkanis Franzem Kafkou', *Literarni Noviny*, vol. 15, 1946.

— 'Erinnerungen an Kafka', in Klaus Wagenbach, ed., *Franz Kafka. Eine Biographie seiner Jugend 1883–1912*, Berne, A. Francke Verlag, 1958.

Margalit, Elkana, 'Social and intellectual origins of the Hashomer Hatzair Youth Movement (1913–1920)', *Journal of Contemporary History*, vol. 4, no. 2, 1969.

Marrus, Michael R., *Les Juifs de France à l'époque de l'Affaire Dreyfus*, Paris, Calmann-Levy, 1972.

Martin, Alfred von, 'Soziologie der Kultur des Mittelalters', in *Geist und Gesellschaft. Soziologische Skizzen zur europäischen Kulturgeschichte*, Frankfurt-am-Main, J. Knecht, 1948.

Marx-Engels Selected Correspondence, Moscow, Progress Publishers, 1975.

Mendelsohn, Ezra, 'Worker Opposition in the Russian Jewish Socialist Movement, from the 1890s to 1903', *International Review of Social History*, vol. X, part 2, 1965.

Menninghaus, Winfried, *Walter Benjamins Theorie der Sprachmagie*, Frankfurt-am-Main, Suhrkamp Verlag, 1980.

Meyer-Leviné, Rosa, *Vie et mort d'un révolutionnaire. Eugen Leviné et les conseils ouvriers de Bavière*, Paris, Maspero, 1980.

Michels, Robert, *Zur Soziologie des Parteiwesens in der modernen Demokratie* 2nd ed., Leipzig, Alfred Kröner Verlag, 1925.

Milfull, Helen, 'Franz Kafka, The Jewish Context', *Year Book of the Leo Baeck Institute*, vol. XXIII, 1978.

Mitzman, Arthur 'Anarchism, Expressionism, and Psycho-Analysis', *New German Critique*, no. 1, Winter 1977.

Molitor, Franz Joseph, *Philosophie der Geschichte oder über die Tradition*, Münster, Theissingsche Buchhandlung, 1834.

Morveau, Baron Guyton de, *La Chimie, Encyclopédie méthodique*, vol. I, 1786.

Mosès, Stephane, *Système et Révélation. La Philosophie de Franz Rosenzweig*, Paris, Seuil, 1982.

— 'Walter Benjamin und Franz Rosenzweig', *Deutsche Vierteljahrschrift für Literaturwissenschaft und Geistesgeschichte*, no. 4, 1982.

Mowinckel, Sigmund, *He that Cometh*, trans. G. W. Anderson, Oxford, Basil Blackwell, 1956.

260 *Redemption and Utopia*

Münster, Arno, *Utopie, Messianismus und Apokalypse im Frühwerk von Ernst Bloch*, Frankfurt-am-Main, Suhrkamp Verlag, 1982.
— 'Messianisme juif et pensée utopique dans l'œuvre d'Ernst Bloch', *Archives de Sciences Sociales des Religions*, no. 57/1, 1984.
— ed., *Tagträume vom aufrechten Gang. Sechs Interviews mit Ernst Bloch*, Frankfurt-am-Main, Suhrkamp Verlag, 1978.
Old Testament (Hebrew edition), London, The British and Foreign Bible Society, 1963.
Paulsen, Friedrich, *Die deutschen Universitäten und das Universitätsstudium*, Berlin, 1902.
Péguy, Charles, 'L'Épreuve', *Cahiers de la Quinzaine*, no. 7, undated.
— 'A Portrait of Bernard Lazare', in *Job's Dungheap. Essays on Jewish Nationalism and Social Revolution*, ed. Hannah Arendt, trans. Harry Lorin Binsse, New York, Schocken Books, 1948.
Petitdemange, Guy, 'La Provocation de Franz Rosenzweig', *Recherches de science religieuse*, October–December 1982.
Poe, Edgar Allen, *The Works of Edgar Allen Poe*, New York, P. F. Collier & Son, 1904.
Politzer, Heinz, ed., *Das Kafka-Buch*, Frankfurt, Fischer Bücherei, 1965.
Randall, H.W.G., 'The German Drama', *The Contemporary Review*, December 1925.
Raphaël, Freddy, *Judaïsme et capitalisme*, Paris, PUF, 1982.
Rathenau, Walther, *Ein preussischer Europäer, Briefe*, ed. M. V. Eynern, Berlin, 1955.
Ringer, Fritz K., *The Decline of the German Mandarins. The German Academic Community 1890-1933*, Cambridge, Mass. Harvard University Press, 1969.
Robert, Marthe, *L'Ancien et le nouveau, de Don Quichotte à Kafka*, Paris, Payot, 1967.
— *As Lonely as Franz Kafka*, trans. Ralph Manheim, New York, Harcourt Brace Jovanovich, 1982.
Robertson, Ritchie, *Kafka. Judaism, Politics and Literature*, Oxford, Clarendon Press, 1985.
Rochelle, Drieu La, *La Comédie de Charleroi*, Paris, Gallimard, 1960.
Rosenthal, Erich, 'Trends of the Jewish Population in Germany (1910–1939)', *Jewish Social Studies*, vol. VI, no. 3, July 1944.
Rosenzweig, Franz, *Jehuda Halevi, Zweiundneunzig Hymnen und Gedichte*, Berlin, 1927.
— *Kleinere Schriften*, Berlin, Schocken Verlag, 1937.
— *Briefe*, Berlin, Schocken Verlag, 1935.
— *The Star of Redemption*, trans. William W. Hallo, New York, Holt, Rinehart and Winston, 1971.
Sagnol, Marc, 'Théorie de l'histoire et de la modernité chez Benjamin', *L'Homme et la Société*, no. 69–70, December 1983.
Scherrer, Jutta, *Die Petersburger religiös-philosophischen Vereinigungen. Die Entwicklung des religiösen Selbstverständnisses ihrer Intelligencija-Mitglieder (1901–1917)*, Wiesbaden, Otto Harrassowitz, 1973.
Schmolze, Gerhard, 'Eugen Leviné-Nissen. Israelit unter den jüdischen

Dissidenten der bayerischen Revolution', *Emuna, Blätter für christ-liche-jüdische Zusammenarbeit*, vol. IV, no. 2, April 1969.

Schoeps, Hans Joachim, 'Theologische Motive in der Dichtung Franz Kafkas', *Die Neue Rundschau*, 1951.

Scholem, Gershom, 'Lyrik der Kabbala?' *Der Jude*, vol. VI, 1921–22.

— 'Ha-Mekubal Abraham Ben Eliezer Halevi', *Kiryat Sefer*, pamphlet 'A', 2nd year, 1925.

— 'Über die Theologie des Sabbatianismus im Lichte Abraham Cardozos', *Der Jude*, vol. IX, 1928.

— 'Al Shlosha Pishei Brit Shalom' [On the Three Sins of the Brit Shalom], *Davar*, 12 December 1929.

— 'Zur Frage des Parlaments', *Jüdische Rundshau*, no. 34, 1929.

— 'Ha-Matarah ha-Sofit' [The Final Goal], *Sheifotenu*, no. 2, August 1931.

— 'Die Metamorphose des häretischen Messianismus der Sabbatianer im religiösen Nihilismus im 18. Jahrhundert', *Judaica*, vol. III, 1963.

— *Major Trends in Jewish Mysticism*, 3rd ed., London, Thames and Hudson, 1968.

— 'Israel und die Diaspora', *Judaica*, vol. II, 1970.

— *The Messianic Idea in Judaism*, trans. Michael A. Meyer, New York, Schocken Books, 1971.

— 'Une education au judaïsme', *Dispersion et Unité*, no. 11, 1971.

— *Sabbatai Sevi. The Mystical Messiah*, Princeton, Princeton University Press, 1973.

— *On Jews and Judaism in Crisis*, New York, Schocken Books, 1976.

— 'On the social psychology of the Jews in Germany 1900–1933', in *Jews and Germans from 1860–1933. The Problematic Symbiosis*, ed. David Bronsen, Heidelberg, Carl Winter Universitätsverlag, 1979.

— *From Berlin to Jerusalem. Memories of my Youth*, trans. Harry Zohn, New York, Schocken Books, 1980.

— *Walter Benjamin. The Story of a Friendship*, trans. Harry Zohn, Philadelphia, The Jewish Publication Society of America, 1981.

— *Mi-Berlin le-Yerushalayim*, Jerusalem, Hotzaat Am-Oved, 1982.

— 'The meaning of the Torah in Jewish mysticism', *Diogenes*, no. 15, Fall 1956.

— *On Walter Benjamin: Critical Essays and Recollections*, ed. Gary Smith, trans. Werner Dannhauser, Cambridge, Mass., The MIT Press, 1988.

— *The Correspondence of Walter Benjamin and Gershom Scholem 1932–1940*, trans. Gary Smith and Andre Lefevre, New York, Schocken Books, 1989.

Schweppenhauser, Hermann, ed., *Benjamin über Kafka*, Frankfurt-am-Main, Suhrkamp Verlag, 1981.

Séguy, Jean, *Christianisme et société. Introduction à la sociologie de Ernst Troeltsch*, Paris, Cerf, 1980.

Silberner, Edmund, 'Bernar Lazar ve Ha-Zionut' [Bernard Lazare and Zionism], *Shivat Zion*, II–III, 1953.

Singer, Isaac Bashevis, *Satan in Goray*, 1958.

Sokel, Walter, *Franz Kafka – Tragik und Ironie*, Vienna, Albert Langen, 1964.

— and Toller, Ernst, *Deutsche Literatur im 20. Jahrhundert*, Heidelberg, Wolfgang Rothe, 1961.

Sombart, W., *Les Juifs et la vie économique*, Paris, Payot, 1923.

Sperber, Manes, *Alfred Adler. Der Mensch und seine Lehre*, Munich, J.F. Bergmann Verlag, 1926.

— *Zur Analyse der Tyrannis*, Paris, Ed. Science et Litterature, 1938.

— *The Achilles Heel*, trans. Constantine FitzGibbon, London, Andre Deutsch Ltd., 1959.

— *Le pont inachevé*, Paris, Calmann-Levy, 1977.

— *Individuum und Gemeinschaft. Versuch einer sozialen Charakterologie*, Stuttgart, Klett-Cotta, 1978.

— *Au-delà de l'oubli*, Paris, Calmann-Levy, 1979.

— 'My Jewishness', *New German Critique*, no. 20, Summer 1980.

— *God's Water Carriers*, trans. Joachim Neugroschel, New York, Holmes & Meier, 1987.

Sproll, Heinz, 'Messianisches Denken und pazifistische Utopie im Werk Kurt Eisners', in *Gegenseitige Einflüsse deutscher und jüdischer Kultur*, ed. Walter Grab, University of Tel Aviv, Institute of German History, 1983.

Stark, Werner, *Die Wissenssoziologie*, Stuttgart, Ferdinand Enke Verlag, 1960.

Stern, J. P., 'The Law of the Trial', in *On Kafka: Semi-centenary Perspectives*, ed. F. Kuna, New York, Harper & Row, 1976.

Strack, Herman L., and Billerbeck, Paul, *Kommentar zum Neuen Testament, aus Talmud und Midrash*, Oscar Beck, 1924.

Talmon, Jacob, *Political Messianism. The Romantic Phase*, London, Secker & Warburg, 1960.

Taubes, Jakob, *Studien zu Geschichte und System der abendländischen Eschatologie*, Bern, Buchdruckerei Rösch, Vogt & Co., 1947.

Thorel, Jean, 'Les Romantiques allemands et les Symbolistes français', *Entretiens politiques et littéraires*, vol. III, no. 18, September 1891.

Tiedemann, Rolf, 'Historical materialism or political messianism? An interpretation of the theses "On the concept of history"', in *Benjamin. Philosophy, History, Aesthetics*, ed. Gary Smith, trans. Barton Byg, Jeremy Gaines and Doris L. Jones, Chicago, The University of Chicago Press, 1989.

— 'Epilogue' to Walter Benjamin, *Charles Baudelaire. Ein Lyriker im Zeitalter des Hochkapitalismus*, Frankfurt-am-Main, Suhrkamp Verlag, 1980.

Tismar, Jens, 'Kafka's "Schakale und Araber" im zionistischen Kontext betrachtet', *Jahrbuch der Deutschen Schiller-Gesellschaft*, no. 19, 1975.

Toller, Ernst, *Man and the Masses*, trans. Louis Untermeyer, Garden City, New York, Doubleday, Page & Company, 1924.

— 'Ernst Toller discusses Palestine', *American Hebrew*, 2 June 1927.

— *Quer durch. Reisebilder und Reden*, Berlin, Kiepenheuer Verlag, 1930.

— *I was a German*, trans. Edward Crankshaw, New York, William Morrow and Co., 1934.

— *Prosa, Briefe, Dramen, Gedichte*, Reinbek bei Hamburg, Rowohlt, 1979.

Tordai, Zador, 'Wie kann man in Europa Jude sein? Walter Benjamin', unpublished MS, Budapest, 1979.

Turnowski-Pinter, Margarete, 'A Student's friendship with Ernst Toller', *Year Book of the Leo Baeck Institute*, xv, 1970.

Unger, Erich, *Politik und Metaphysik*, Berlin, Verlag David, 1921.

— *Die staatenlose Bildung eines jüdischen Volkes*, Berlin, Verlag David, 1922.

Wagenbach, Klaus, *Franz Kafka*, Reinbek bei Hamburg, Rowohlt, 1964.

— *Franz Kafka, Eine Biographie seiner Jugend 1883–1912*, Berne, A. Francke Verlag, 1958 .

— *Franz Kafka par lui-même*, Paris, Seuil, 1969.

Weber, Marianne, *Max Weber. A Biography*, trans. and ed. Harry Zohn, New York, John Wiley & Sons, 1975.

Weber, Max, *Gesammelte Aufsätze zur Religionssoziologie*, Tübingen, J.C.B. Mohr, 1922.

— *Gesammelte Aufsätze zur Wissenschaftslehre*, Tübingen, T.C.B. Mohr, 1922.

— *Ancient Judaism*, trans. and ed. Hans H. Gerth and Don Martindale, Glencoe, Ill., The Free Press, 1952.

— *The Protestant Ethic and the Spirit of Capitalism*, trans. Talcott Parsons, New York, Charles Scribner's Sons, 1958.

— *Economy and Society*, ed. Guenther Ross and Claus Wittich, New York, Bedminster Press, 1968.

Wilson, Nelly, *Bernard Lazare. Antisemitism and the Problem of Jewish Identity in Late Nineteenth-century France*, Cambridge, Cambridge University Press, 1978.

Wirkner, Alfred, *Kafka und die Aussenwelt. Quellenstudien zum 'Amerika'-Fragment*, Stuttgart, 1976.

Wistrich, Robert, *Revolutionary Jews from Marx to Trotsky*, London, Harrap, 1976.

Wohlfarth, Irving, 'On the messianic structure of Benjamin's last reflections', *Glyph*, no. 3, 1978.

— 'Der destruktive Charakter–Benjamin zwischen den Fronten', in *Links hatte noch alles sich zu enträtseln . . . Walter Benjamin im Kontext*, ed. B. Lindner, Frankfurt, Syndikat, 1978.

Wolin, Richard, *Walter Benjamin. An Aesthetic of Redemption*, New York, Columbia University Press, 1982.

Woodcock, George, *Anarchism*, London, Penguin Books, 1963.

Yassour, Avraham, 'Al Hitiashvout Shitoufit Va-Tiouss', [Communal Industrialization in the Settlements], *Kibbutz*, no. 2, 1975.

— 'Utopia and anarchism in Buber and Landauer's social thought', in *Buber, Ha-Kibbutz Ve-Harayon Ha-Shitufi* [Buber, the Kibbutz and the Communal Idea], Haifa University, 1979.

Index